D1564730

Music of
the Colonial and
Revolutionary Era

Recent Titles in
American History through Music
David J. Brinkman, Series Editor

Music of the Counterculture Era
James E. Perone

Music of the Civil War Era
Steven H. Cornelius

Music of
the Colonial and
Revolutionary Era

John Ogasapian

American History through Music
David J. Brinkman, Series Editor

GREENWOOD PRESS
Westport, Connecticut • London

Library of Congress Cataloging-in-Publication Data

Ogasapian, John.
   Music of the colonial and revolutionary era / John Ogasapian.
         p.   cm.—(American history through music)
      Includes bibliographical references, discography, and index.
      ISBN 0–313–32435–2 (alk. paper)
      1. Music—Social aspects—United States—History—16th century.   2. Music—Social
   aspects—United States—History—17th century.   3. Music—Social aspects—United
   States—History—18th century.   4. United States—Social life and customs—To 1775.
   5. United States—Social life and customs—1775–1783.   I. Title.   II. Series.
   ML3917.U6O43   2004
   780'.973'0903—dc22   2004048550

British Library Cataloguing in Publication Data is available.

Library of Congress Catalog Card Number: 2004048550
ISBN: 0–313–32435–2

First published in 2004

Greenwood Press, 88 Post Road West, Westport, CT 06881
An imprint of Greenwood Publishing Group, Inc.
www.greenwood.com

Printed in the United States of America

The paper used in this book complies with the
Permanent Paper Standard issued by the National
Information Standards Organization (Z39.48–1984).

10 9 8 7 6 5 4 3 2 1

To my grandson

Nolan James Ellrott

born December 1, 2003

Contents

Series Foreword

The elements of music are well known. They include melody, rhythm, harmony, form, and texture. Music, though, has infinite variety. Exploring this variety in the music of specific time periods, such as the Colonial and Revolutionary Period, the Roaring Twenties, and the Counterculture Era, is the purpose of the "American History through Music" series. The authors of each volume describe the music in terms of its basic elements, but more importantly, focus on how the social, economic, political, technological, and religious influences shaped the music of that particular time. Each volume in the series not only describes the music of a particular era but the ways in which the music reflected societal concerns. For these purposes, music is defined inclusively; this series considers such diverse musical genres as classical, folk, jazz, rock, religious, and theater music, as each of these genres serve as both reflections of society and as illustrations of how music influences society.

Perhaps the most important conclusion that readers will draw from this series is that music does not exist independently of society. Listeners have enjoyed music throughout time for its aesthetic qualities, but music has also been used to convey emotions and ideas. It has been used to enhance patriotic rituals, and to maintain order in social and religious ceremonies. The "American History through Music" series attempts to put these and other uses of music in an historical context. For instance, how did music serve as entertainment during the Great Depression? How did the music of the Civil War contribute to the stability of the Union—and to the Confederacy? Answers to these and other questions show that music is not just a part of society; music *is* society.

The authors of "American History through Music" present essays based in sound scholarship, written for the lay reader. In addition to discussing important genres and approaches to music, each volume profiles the composers and performers whose music defines their era, describes the musical instruments and technological innovations that influenced the musical world, and provides a glossary of important terms and a bibliography of recommended readings. This information will help students and other interested readers understand the colorful and complex mosaics of musical history.

David J. Brinkman
University of Wyoming

Preface

In rural Massachusetts, where I live, the colonial past is very much a presence. Most communities have a designated historic district, and houses dating from before 1800 dot the landscape. White eighteenth-century meetinghouses overlook the green of town commons and cast their shadows on town burial grounds with graves of Revolutionary War veterans, each carefully marked with a small American flag.

There is such a cemetery across the street from my home. Along with a cluster of other patriots, less well known, it holds the grave of Colonel William Prescott, hero of the battle of Bunker Hill (which, in passing, was actually fought on nearby Breed's Hill). I often walk there, usually in the early morning. I normally keep to the paved roadways; however, every so often I leave the road and climb the gentle grade that leads to the old burial ground. I make a point of stopping for a moment to pay my respects to Colonel Prescott; then I wander about for a while, quietly reading some of the centuries-old inscriptions on the weathered black tombstones, here and there straightening a flag that the wind has blown over. Although unromantic objectivity is the coin of good scholarship, I freely admit that on more than one occasion when work on this book seemed to bog down, a walk in that old burial ground with its sense of connection helped me to get going again.

Massachusetts also holds more than its share of superb colonial research collections. It has been my good fortune to live less than an hour away from the incomparable holdings of the American Antiquarian Society in Worcester, as well as the Boston Public Library, and I have made grateful use of both institutions. Deborah Friedman of O'Leary Library at the University of Massachusetts, Lowell, unfailingly located and procured one obscure article after another for me through the blessings of the interlibrary loan system. I am much beholden to her.

I acknowledge my immeasurable debt to all those scholars whose original research over the years has uncovered and illuminated the many elements of musical culture in Colonial and Revolutionary-era America, and whose names and work may be found in the bibliography at the end of this book. My friend and colleague in the field of American music research, Professor Nathaniel Lee Orr of Georgia State University, read and commented on large portions of the text. This book is a good deal better thanks to his sharp eye and incisive criticisms. My students at the University of Massachusetts, Lowell, asked the questions and raised the issues that helped me to see the material from different perspectives as I worked.

Rob Kirkpatrick, my editor at Greenwood Press, read each chapter in draft and made several helpful suggestions and thoughtful criticisms. The series editor, Professor David Brinkman of the University of Wyoming, quietly guided this project with unending reserves of tact and patience. On more than one occasion, he provided me with key material in his own particular area of specialty that I might otherwise not have known of. I'm deeply grateful.

My wife Nancy has helped and encouraged me through several book projects over our years together. As always, it is she who makes the work worthwhile. Our daughter and son-in-law, Lisa and Thomas Ellrott, recently blessed us with our first grandchild. Nolan James Ellrott carefully timed his arrival to coincide with the completion of this book, and it is lovingly dedicated to him, even though he may not get around to reading it for a while.

Introduction

This book is about musical life in the North American colonies and early republic during the period between 1500, when the first Spanish settlements were planted, and 1799, the year of George Washington's death. In other words, it is about the beginnings of America's musical multiculture: our distinctive mix of cultivated music in the "classical" European concert tradition, and a vernacular or "popular" music that constantly changes and grows as it absorbs and incorporates new musics of diverse groups.

In a real sense, the great European musical tradition grew over the years in the sheltered environment of courts and cathedrals. American music, on the other hand, made its own way in the rougher arena of musical entrepreneurship and amateur music making. European music flowered luxuriantly under aristocratic patronage. The varieties of American music—like the men and women who played and sang it, listened and danced to it—contended in the marketplace.

The book's subject is not the music itself, but rather American musical life and culture during the Colonial and Revolutionary era and in the early republic, to about 1800. Accordingly, the text contains no musical examples or analyses, and very little critical commentary on musical forms and styles. Instead, the chapters focus on the place of music in the different and distinctive economic, religious, and social conditions that characterized each region.

Music thrived in colonial homes and had a significant, if sometimes contentious, place in colonial churches. Music played a prominent part in Revolutionary-era political and military life and flourished in the emerging culture of the new nation. Such enterprises as instrument making, music merchandising, and even music printing took root in American cities during the eighteenth century, filling a growing demand for music in the homes and churches, theatres and concert halls. Professional musicians arrived from England and the European continent and cobbled together a living by teaching, organizing concerts, playing in theatre orchestras, selling and repairing musical instruments, and importing or publishing music to meet the needs of an avid amateur market.

This book is organized chronologically and geographically. Its earliest chapters chronicle the musical life among the colonists, from the earliest settlements to the eve of the Revolution. An opening chapter on New Spain is followed by individual chapters on the three regions of British North America that would join to become the United States. Virginia, Maryland, the Carolinas, and Georgia are grouped in a single chapter as the Southern Colonies; New England is treated in another chapter; and the Middle Colonies of New York, New Jersey, and Pennsylvania in yet another.

Succeeding chapters describe musical life during the years of Revolution and the Federal period: the years between the British evacuation in 1783 and the end of the century, when both immigrant professional musicians and native-born amateurs, turned professional or semi-professional, brought about a flowering of musical life, especially in cities. What little information there is on the aural musical traditions of Native Americans and African-American slaves during the years before 1800 is synthesized into its own chapter.

This book begins with a chapter on New Spain, even though the Spanish Catholic colonists and their well-financed cathedral choirs, theatres, and operas, had little in common, musically or culturally, with either the religious commonwealths of New England and Pennsylvania, the merchant enclaves of New York, or the planter aristocracies of Virginia and the Carolinas. Rather, New Spain provides us a glimpse of the brilliant and luxurious continental European musical tradition known as the Baroque, rooted in the Catholic courts and cathedrals, that the Spanish transplanted in their American colonies.

This musical culture might well have prevailed in what is now the United States, had a handful of historical circumstances been slightly different. If the wind in the English Channel on August 8, 1588, had changed direction to favor the Spanish Armada, for instance, Spain might well have defeated England, and North America could have become a Spanish province, like most of Central and South America. As it was, the Spanish attempted unsuccessfully to establish missions as far north as the Chesapeake in the years just before the arrival of the first English colonists.

The chapter also serves to remind us that at least one highly developed native civilization with a complex musical culture of its own, that of the Aztecs, existed on the North American continent in the years before either Spanish or English sails appeared on the eastern horizon. The Spanish destroyed Tenochtitlán, the Aztec capital, and on its ruins built Mexico City. The great plaza where the main temple, with its elaborate ensemble of singers and musicians, had stood became the site of a new cathedral with its own excellent, if rather less elaborate, music establishment. The religion and culture of the Aztecs were suppressed by the Spanish conquerors. The temple singers now sang a new kind of music in the cathedral and churches of a new faith, and their old songs and traditions disappeared from memory.

As it turned out, a Spanish attempt to settle the Chesapeake in 1571 failed, and their supposedly invincible Armada was scattered by the English in 1588. Only a few years later, the English had begun colonizing the east coast of America north of Florida. Over time, they blocked the Spanish adventurers, dispossessed Sweden and the Netherlands of their colonies, and by 1763 had seized French holdings east of the Mississippi.

On the European continent, music had long been fostered by the patronage of the church, royalty, and the hereditary landed aristocracy. In England, circumstances during the sixteenth and seventeenth centuries—primarily the political and religious unrest that culminated in the Civil War of the 1640s—unsettled both the musical traditions of the Church of England and the stability of aristocratic culture in Britain.

If few aristocrats came to the British colonies, apart from the colonial governors temporarily charged with looking after London's interests, it is still important—and worth repeating for emphasis—that the old-world system of great church and court music establishments, patronized and supported by generations of a hereditary aristocracy, had no place in the colonies or early republic. Instead, America evolved its own distinctively populist musical culture, driven by market forces rather than patronage; entrepreneurial rather than elitist, and heavily dependent on amateur music making.

In the course of time, the American colonies developed a prosperous class of wealthy merchants and planters who attended the theatre and concerts and

Some of Thomas Jefferson's most prized belongings on display in the Monticello heirloom exhibit in Washington, D.C. In this group are Jefferson's alabaster clock, a model of H. K. Bush-Brown's statue of Jefferson, and Jefferson's prized violin. Courtesy of the Library of Congress.

even indulged in amateur music making, often at a high level of proficiency. In Virginia, Robert Carter kept a variety of musical instruments for recreation and entertainment both in his plantation home and his town residence at Williamsburg. Among the nation's founders, Thomas Jefferson was an enthusiastic amateur violinist, as was his fellow Virginian, Patrick Henry. Francis Hopkinson of Pennsylvania, like Jefferson a leading statesman and signer of the Declaration of Independence, was also a published composer who played the harpsichord and even trained boys from the local charity school to lead the singing of psalms in Christ Church, Philadelphia.

Probably the single most important cultural factor in the colonies was religion. Even outside the spheres of such intensely pious groups as the Puritans and Quakers, religion dominated aspects of seventeenth-century life to a degree we can scarcely comprehend today. Wealthy, enlightened, and worldly men like William Byrd of Virginia attended church faithfully, collected religious books which they read carefully, and made time each day for prayers.

Even during the era of the Enlightenment in the eighteenth century, when science, politics, and commerce surpassed scripture and salvation as topics of conversation among colonists, ministers lamented their congregations' decline in numbers and fervor, and liberal thinkers like Thomas Jefferson looked to reason rather than miracles and nature rather than scripture, few people doubted the existence of God, at least openly. Most approved of churches and religion as the means of regulating society and encouraging moral behavior. The revivals of the 1740s, known today as the Great Awakening, drew large crowds, and even the rationalist, scientific-minded Benjamin Franklin, by no means a paradigm of piety, published the sermons of the English evangelist George Whitefield.

It is thus not surprising that religion also played a major role in shaping musical culture. In both city and countryside, churches provided the majority of colonists their opportunities for hearing music as well as learning and participating in it. Many churches sponsored singing schools, either periodically or on a continuous basis. By the mid-eighteenth century the singing school movement, begun decades before as a means to improve congregational singing, led to the formation of volunteer choirs. The introduction of these choirs, in turn, strengthened the singing school movement. It remained active well into the nineteenth century, fostering the formation and training both of church choirs singing "church music"—as hymns, anthems, and music for Sunday worship were termed—and singing societies whose members gave periodic concerts of "sacred music"; that is, parts of oratorios by such composers as Handel and Haydn.

Singing schools and church choirs, in turn, led inevitably to the acquisition of organs, the development of a domestic organ-building industry, and a demand for organists. Professional musicians who played those organs supplemented their meager church stipends with teaching, performing, and music merchandising, thereby creating or enhancing a local musical culture.

Natural factors such as geography and climate also had much to do with the shaping of a musical environment. Just as weather and land fertility varied from one North American colony to another, so musical environments varied from region to region. In New England, the land could support little more than subsistence farming, and the large, self-sufficient plantations producing cash crops like tobacco and rice that grew up in Virginia and Carolina were out of the question. Instead, New Englanders turned to the sea, building prosperity through trade. Boston became a wealthy port; however, restrictive Puritan traditions acted as a brake on the natural inclinations of the rising merchant class to make the city culturally cosmopolitan, like Charleston. Theatres and public places of entertainment were severely restricted in Boston. On the other hand, the Puritans had no real objection to private recreational music, and a good bit of musical activity took place in the homes of the wealthy and cultivated among them.

In coastal Pennsylvania, the Quakers who held political control were as inhospitable to music or the arts as the Puritans of New England; indeed, they even frowned on private music making. But the Quakers, unlike the Puritans, placed no religious restrictions on settlers who were non-Quaker. Philadelphia became a thriving seaport and the largest city in the colonies, and a number of non-Quaker English, including Roman Catholics and members of the established Anglican Church, settled there and prospered. As long as the Quakers held political power in the colony, they were able to curb public musical and theatrical events; however, as elsewhere, amateur music thrived in the private homes of the wealthy.

Moreover, although Philadelphia's Quakers disapproved of music even more than Boston's Puritans, their religious tolerance made Pennsylvania a haven for those seeking freedom of conscience, among them communities of German religious dissenters who settled on large tracts of fertile farmland away from the coast. These immigrants brought with them rich musical traditions unencumbered by any religious prohibitions. Many among these Germans were skilled as musicians, able to compose and perform both vocal and instrumental music of high quality. It is thus somewhat ironic that the Quakers, of all British religious dissenters the most averse to music and the arts, came to harbor within the borders of their colony the most diverse and accomplished amateur musical culture in British North America.

In neighboring New York, or more accurately New Netherlands, at least until 1664, the Dutch Calvinist ministers were unsympathetic in their attitudes toward recreation and music, like their Puritan counterparts in New England and the Quakers of Pennsylvania. Their disapproval had little effect on the prosperous merchants and landholding patroons, who certainly enjoyed music in the privacy of their sumptuous homes.

But New Netherlands, unlike New England and Pennsylvania, was neither a theocracy nor a religious haven. Rather, it was in reality a purely commercial enterprise, under the control of a company of merchants in Amsterdam.

The colony's port of New Amsterdam had the finest deepwater harbor in America, and a diverse and polyglot crowd of sailors and merchants, many of them transient, roamed its streets and docks. Fearful lest profitable shipping and trade be lost, the colony's owners back in Amsterdam, faithful adherents to the Dutch Reformed Church, nevertheless restrained their ministers in New Netherlands and especially the efforts of the New Amsterdam clergy and magistrates to curb the port's entertainments.

Britain seized the Dutch colony without a battle in 1664 and renamed it New York. English colonists settled alongside the old Dutch families, and the city became British military and political headquarters. Army officers and expatriate British civilians stationed there produced and staged their own musical and theatrical entertainments. In general however, New York remained primarily a bustling commercial center with little time or inclination for the development of public arts or a distinctive cultural life.

Virginia had also been settled as an economic venture rather than a religious haven, and there were no religious inhibitions to the colonists' free enjoyment of music, either as entertainment or as a leisure activity. Virginia's land was fertile, with navigable rivers reaching far inland. Plantations along the banks had docks for seagoing ships and were thus largely independent and self-sufficient. Williamsburg, the colony's capital, was not a seaport but rather a seat of government. As such, it lacked both the wealth and resident population to be a cultural center like Philadelphia or Charleston. Instead, the planters developed an active amateur musical life under the tutelage of itinerant music masters, who made the rounds of the plantations and Williamsburg townhouses during the periods when the colony's legislative assembly, or burgesses, were in session, teaching and performing.

Farther south, the planter gentry in the Carolinas enjoyed as rich and varied a musical life as their peers back in England, once again due in large part to accidents of climate and geography. Inland Carolina's summer heat and disease caused them to flee their tidewater plantations for sumptuous townhouses in coastal Charleston, leaving their slaves and overseers to work the fields. At the same time, the city's excellent harbor made it the main seaport south of Philadelphia, and a prosperous merchant class grew up there.

This mix of wealthy planters and merchants, living side-by-side in Charleston for much of the year, fostered the richest cultural and musical life of any city in the colonies. Unfettered by Puritan religious scruples, Charleston supported opera, theatre, and the earliest professional orchestra in the British colonies, as well as vibrant amateur musical activity.

Such plantations and urban centers of wealth and culture loom large in our perceptions of musical life in colonial America. It is well to bear in mind, however, that most Americans were not wealthy planters or merchants. Most colonists did not live in the coastal cities, but rather in smaller towns and villages. Thus the majority of Americans had little or no exposure to professional performances or teachers; nor were there music dealers at hand from which to buy instruments or scores. For them, public music was associated with their local churches, with psalm singing during worship, with periodic singing schools to improve congregational singing and after the mid-eighteenth century to train volunteer choirs, and with the semi-amateur singing masters, resident or itinerant, who ran those schools.

If religion and geography played distinctive and important parts in colonial musical life, there are other significant elements to be considered, especially in the years after 1750. Ethnic traditions and identities, political and economic concerns, and the growth of social and cultural institutions apart from churches are reflected in this or that facet of American musical culture. Once the colonists had sought and won their independence, they set about the business of making a new kind of nation out of a diverse group of people and interests, and balancing liberty and equality as best they could to create a new kind of society.

We know less about vernacular or folk music in the colonies, for our understanding depends largely on written documents, and folk traditions are unwritten and transmitted orally. The early colonists brought with them a store of folk lyrics and narrative ballads, which they sang to a body of traditional tunes. Many of those same tunes, played on the violin, accompanied social dancing.

A number of the poorer colonists, English and especially the so-called Scotch-Irish from the border areas and Irish Ulster, moved inland, settling individually or in small groups in the backcountry of Pennsylvania and Virginia, and as far south as the Carolinas and Georgia. Occasional writings of the era make reference to their dancing and fiddling, the singing of their folk songs by Scotch-Irish servants, or the pipers of back-country militia companies; but otherwise, there is little documentary evidence on the music of these Americans during the Colonial, Revolutionary, or Federal periods.

A bit more—though here too, little of substance—can be known of Native American and African-American music during the Colonial era. Explorers and early settlers took note of native music and dancing, and many of the elements they described in their accounts can still be seen in contemporary

Native American music and dancing. Similarly, traits described in accounts of early slave music can be heard in modern sub-Saharan African music as well as some types of distinctively traditional African-American music, like blues and gospel.

Once again, the early data are sketchy. Many native traditions, passed down orally through the generations, were all but destroyed along with the peoples themselves, by a succession of epidemics, wars, acculturations, and forced relocations, long before any thought was given to documenting or preserving them. Similarly, cultural and musical traditions brought from Africa by the slaves were held in contempt by whites, even though blacks were generally considered to have more innate musical aptitude than whites and were often trained to play their masters' favorite tunes on the violin so as to provide music for social dancing by whites.

In one sense life for most people went on as usual during the Revolutionary War. The actual fighting took place at different times and in different areas. New England, for instance, saw no real combat after the British evacuation of Boston in March of 1776. Probably no more than a third of the colonists were strongly in favor of independence, and about the same number were just as strongly against it. For the others, at least those outside an active battle area, the struggle for survival was of primary importance.

Yet American musical culture felt the effects of the Revolution. Both sides issued political propaganda in the form of poems or ballads, printed either in newspapers or on single sheets or broadsides and intended to be sung in taverns, at meetings, and in the streets to well-known melodies. Some of these songs, like William Billings's "Chester," became anthems of independence in their own time, and at least one—"Yankee Doodle"—became a permanent piece of American tradition and lore. Regiments of the British army, as well as those of their Hessian mercenary allies, included not only the regulation fifers and drummers who played for marching and signaling, but also professional bands of wind instruments, paid for by the regimental officers, who played for their entertainment and also took part in public concerts. Following their adversaries' lead, some American units formed similar bands. Probably more important in the long run, a number of professional musicians who arrived in America as players in British and Hessian regimental bands remained after the end of the war, teaching and performing, especially in the cities.

Still more professional musicians emigrated from England and the European continent during the 1780s and 1790s, as a measure of prosperity and peace returned, religious curbs on entertainment were relaxed in places like Boston and Philadelphia, and more theatres were built to entertain a growing urban clientele. Such immigrant musicians made their own opportunities within America's largely amateur and determinedly entrepreneurial musical culture. They played church organs, taught, formed and led musical societies, organized concert series, and established dealerships and publishing businesses.

Although America's professional musicians continued to look to Europe to set the latest fashions in musical taste, few if any longed for the security of an aristocratic patron or the sort of court position they might once have held—or aspired to—in Europe. Indeed, by the end of the century, most of them no longer thought of themselves as European at all, but as American musicians.

New Spain

For over a hundred years before the first English colonists arrived in Virginia and Massachusetts, Spanish soldiers, missionaries, and settlers were carving out an empire including most of South and Central America and stretching north into much of what is now the United States. The conquistadors who won that empire for Spain were cruel and ruthless on one hand and deeply religious on the other. Many considered themselves crusaders. Most were members of the minor nobility, but without money, lands, or title of their own. They aimed to gain both their fortune and benefit for their souls by plundering the peoples they subjected in the name of the cross. Bernal Diaz del Castillo, chronicling Herman Cortés's conquest of Mexico, defined their vision without any sense of irony: "to give light to those who were in darkness, and to grow rich."[1]

The Spanish acculturated the natives, efficiently and systematically, by conquering, converting, and then exploiting them. The type of cultural organization they imposed depended on the level of civilization they found. The island Indians of the Caribbean were enslaved in fields and mines until they were decimated by the combination of Spanish brutality and European diseases. The natives of Central Mexico, on the other hand, were already organized under the domination of the Aztecs, and here the Spanish simply took over the existing civil and social structure. In every case, they were firm and ruthless in imposing their religion; stamping out native rituals and music; and establishing the dark, symbolic, medieval Catholicism they had brought from Spain.

Missionaries from Spain, following in the steps of the conquering adventurers, quickly discovered the effectiveness of music in evangelizing and indoctrinating the natives. The Indians were drawn to the chant of the church and took quickly to the vernacular religious songs the priests invented to teach them doctrine, probably because their old religion had associated the benefits and mysteries of religion with ritual music. The folk-tinged Catholicism of Spain turned out to be surprisingly congenial to the Indians, not only because they responded to its colorful liturgy, music, and ceremony, but also because it enabled the natives to retain many of their old gods by renaming and reimagining them among the numerous saints venerated by the Spanish. Indian communities in cities had their own churches, and agricultural communities in the provinces had their missions, both staffed for the most part by Franciscans.

CARIBBEAN COLONIES

Late in 1493, the first Spanish settlers under the command of Columbus himself landed on the Caribbean island of Hispaniola, occupied today by the nations of Haiti and the Dominican Republic. On January 6, 1494, a mass was sung ashore in the new settlement, the first recorded instance of European music in the Western Hemisphere. By 1512 a cathedral had been chartered for the island's capital city of Santo Domingo, with plans for the sort of full music establishment that was found in Spanish cathedrals, including a choirmaster and organist. Over the next ten years, other cathedrals with similar music establishments were chartered for the cities of Santiago in Cuba and San Juan in Puerto Rico. Santo Domingo's cathedral was completed in 1541, and an account from the early seventeenth century mentions a choir of Indian boys there, singing both vernacular sacred songs and more formal Latin motets. Another witness of the same era reports "extremely lascivious" dancing in the city's streets.

The Spaniards despised the natives' culture and rarely took the trouble to record descriptions of it. As a result, little is known of their music. Bartolomé de las Casas, one of the their pitifully few advocates, described group singing and dancing by Hispaniola's Indians, men with men and women with women, and the playing of such instruments as wooden "bells" and rattles.

But las Casas did not arrive in Santo Domingo until 1502. By then the combination of war, enslavement, and disease had exterminated nine-tenths of the native population, and their culture and music were all but lost.[2]

MEXICO

In August of 1521, Hernán Cortés seized the Aztec capital of Tenochtitlàn after a long and bitter battle in which a number of Spaniards were captured and sacrificed within sight and hearing of their comrades. Fifty years later and safely back in Spain, Bernal Díaz de Castillo, a soldier with Cortés and now eighty-four years of age, blind and deaf, could still recall vividly the musical din as the Spanish captives went to their ritual deaths: the blowing of conch shells and trumpets and the beating of the Aztecs' most sacred ritual instruments, the large, skin-covered drum, the *huehuetl*; and a hollow log drum, the *teponazli*.

> There was a tremendous drum there, and when they beat it the sound was as dismal as an instrument from hell and could be heard more than two leagues away. They said it was covered with the skins of very large snakes. In that small place there were many diabolical things to see, horns, trumpets. . . .
>
> [T]he mournful drum of Uichilobos [the Aztec war god, Huitzilopochtli] sounded again, accompanied by conch shells, horns, and something like a trumpet. All of them together made a terrifying sound, and as we looked at the high *cu* [the ceremonial platform at the top of the temple pyramid] from which it came, we could see our companions who had been captured . . . being forced up the steps to be sacrificed.[3]

Along with their brutal religion of human sacrifice, the Aztecs had developed a highly sophisticated culture. Their music itself is largely lost, but ample evidence of a rich and active musical life still exists. Aztec nobles, like their European counterparts, kept ensembles of household musicians, many of whom were also composers. Most Aztec music was a part of civic and religious ceremonies, with particular pieces for occasions, seasons, and times of day. In the capital city of Tenochtitlán, temple musicians signaled times of prayer through the day and night. Even the smaller, outlying temples had professional singers and instrumentalists.[4]

These professional temple singers, dancers, and players were rigorously re-hearsed, and performance standards were extraordinarily high. Aztec music lacked a notation system, so an excellent memory was required. Temple musicians enjoyed social prestige and an exemption from taxes. On the other hand, any error in performance during a ritual was presumed to have offended the gods, and the unfortunate perpetrator was promptly sacrificed to soothe their anger.[5]

Although the Aztecs used no string instruments, they possessed a variety of winds and percussion: trumpets and conch shells, horns, flutes, whistles, ocarinas, panpipes, gourd rattles and rasps, and above all the two special ritual instruments already mentioned, the *huehuetl* and the *teponaztli*. The *huehuetl* was a cylindrical drum with an open bottom, resting on a three-legged stand. It was played with the hand rather than a stick and could produce two distinct pitches, depending on whether its single head was struck in the center or at the rim. The *teponaztli* was a hollowed section of log with its ends closed. It rested in its side, with an opening underneath and slit on top shaped like a sideways-H. The two resulting tongues were struck with rubber-tipped mallets to produce two distinct tones. Aztec singing favored low women's voices and high thin men's voices. Part-singing was apparently unknown.[6]

SPANISH MUSIC IN THE CONQUISTADOR ERA

The first Franciscan missionaries reached Mexico in late August of 1523. Among them was Pedro de Gante (1480?–1572), musical, educated, and a relative of the Spanish king and Holy Roman emperor Charles V. Like Charles, he had been born in Ghent (Gante = Ghent) in Flanders (now Belgium). Before entering the Franciscan order, he had held a responsible civic position.

Flanders in the time of Charles V and Pedro de Gante was the musical center of Europe. Indeed, during the late fifteenth and early sixteenth centuries, Flemish composers, performers and teachers were in great demand, far and wide. Successive generations including such masters as Josquin des Prez (1440?–1521) and Orlando de Lassus (1530/32–1594), produced exquisite music for court and cathedral. Indeed, the so-called Roman style of polyphonic Catholic church music often attributed in the popular imagination to Palestrina was actually created years earlier by the Flemings. Not surprisingly, Charles V's court employed numerous Flemish musicians, among them the most renowned composer of his generation, Nicolas Gombert (ca. 1495–ca. 1560). Pedro de Gante was certainly familiar with the music of Gombert and other Flemings. Indeed, he probably took part in performances of it.

Gante was also familiar with the indigenous Spanish *villancico* by such composers as Juan del Encina (1468/69–1529) at the court of the Duke of Alba. The villancico was a solo song, usually accompanied by the *vihuela*, a small, plucked string instrument, shaped like a guitar. Its engaging melody and lively rhythm, as well as its clear structure of verses and refrain, made the villancico a handy vehicle for various types of vernacular poetry, including informal religious poems in Spanish.[7]

Music and Missionaries in New Spain

Gante quickly learned the Indians' own language, Nahuatl, and established a school for native boys near the Indian chapel in Texcoco, some fifteen miles east of Mexico City. Its music curriculum consisted of copying chant manuscripts, singing, playing and making instruments, and similar applied skills. The Indians learned music quickly, for it had had a similar significance in their own culture and religion.[8]

In 1527, Gante moved to Mexico City to teach in the native school there. Here too, the Indians took to the new liturgical music quickly, and in October of 1532, he wrote Charles V, "I can tell Your Majesty without exaggeration that there are Indians here who . . . if they were to sing in Your Majesty's Chapel at this moment would do so well that perhaps you would have to see them actually singing in order to believe it possible." By the following year, Fr. Jacobo de Testera could report back to Spain that the newly baptized natives "sang plainsong and played the organ and performed counterpoint, made songbooks and taught others music."[9]

Church and Cathedral Music

Colonies on islands such as Hispaniola and even Cuba were considered settlements by the Spaniards; Mexico, on the other hand, was viewed as a subjected culture with its own social castes and customs. To be sure, the Spaniards ruthlessly suppressed the native religion, destroying its temples and loosing their war dogs on its priests. But otherwise, Spanish rule maintained much of the existing caste structure, and many of the Spaniards married women from the Aztec nobility. Mexico City, built on the ruins of Tenochtitlán, the Aztec capital, quickly became the religious and cultural center of New Spain. In 1526, the Spanish administration was moved there from Santo Domingo, and in 1535, the Viceroy of New Spain established his residence in Mexico City, making the city the official capital as well. It is significant that when the Inquisition, which had come to New Spain as early as 1524, at last became active in the 1570s, only the old Aztec aristocracy was subject to it. Other natives of Central America, like children, were beneath its concern.[10]

Mexico City's cathedral was built on the site of the main Aztec temple complex. In 1528, the Franciscan priest Juan de Zumárraga (1468–1548) became bishop. He promptly set about planning a new cathedral with an elaborate music establishment. Although he supported Gante's teaching the Indians music, Zumárraga's choice for cathedral choirmaster was Juan Xúarez, who arrived from Spain in 1530 to begin a term of twenty-five years' service at the cathedral.

Zumárraga had a head start in his ambition to develop high-quality cathedral music. Aztec ritual had made prominent use of music, and temples—especially the main one in Tenochtitlán, where Zumárraga's temporary cathedral now stood—maintained carefully trained musical establishments whose members were available to the new religion and its hierarchy. Given the Aztec incentives of tax exemption on one hand and sacrificial execution for any mistake in performance on the other, it is not surprising that the musicians had developed a proficiency and standard at least as fine as any in Christian Europe.

Under Zumárraga, the custom of tax exemption for religious musicians was continued. The draconian penalty exacted for mistakes was of course discontinued. Nevertheless, the cathedral's music did not develop as Zumárraga had hoped, and on April 17, 1540, he wrote to Charles V appealing (successfully, as it turned out) for funds to support his singers.

> [S]ince the Indians who are now singing under Canon Xúarez's direction can only devote a small amount of time (for they must do outside work) I appeal to you for stipends for the singers. . . . We are simply singing together simple music . . . since we have such gaps in our choir.

Zumárraga also hired musicians and bought instruments and music copy books in Spain for his cathedral musicians. Zumárraga's dreams of a cathedral edifice and music rivaling Europe were not realized in his lifetime. He laid the foundations for a new cathedral, but the actual building did not begin until 1573, thirty-five years after his death. In the intervening time, the music of the cathedral flourished.[11]

Choirs of natives led by professional Europeans sang Latin plainsong and Flemish polyphony at a level comparable to any in Europe. In addition, Spanish tradition allowed the use of religious songs in a popular folk style with vernacular texts. These sacred villancicos, with their folk character, engaging melodies, and sprightly rhythms, continued to be sung in church to religious texts (especially Christmas texts) through the seventeenth century and into the eighteenth. Fifteen collections of sacred villancico texts by a Jeronymite nun, Sister Juana Inéz de la Cruz, to be sung to popular tunes, were published in Mexico City between 1677 and 1691 and widely used in New Spain. Groups or cycles of them were troped—that is, inserted—into polyphonic Mass movements, especially the Gloria.[12]

In 1575, Pedro de Moya y Contreras, Mexico City's bishop, appointed as cathedral choirmaster the sort of musician Zumárraga could only have dreamed of, Hernando Franco (1532–1585). Franco was born in Spain and trained at Segovia. Although he arrived in New Spain as a young man in 1554, there is no record of his whereabouts before 1573, when he became choirmaster at Guatemala Cathedral. Franco was a talented and prolific composer in the Flemish tradition, fully the equal of his European counterparts. His finely wrought polyphonic pieces and villancicos were in wide use in New Spain and copied out in several manuscripts. Like most of his European colleagues, Franco was also a popular entertainer. Accompanied by a vihuelist or two, he sang in the evenings on the streets of Mexico City, to the delight of passersby. In 1582 the costs of construction forced economies in the other cathedral expenses. The musicians' salaries were cut, and Franco resigned as choirmaster. Funds were quickly restored; however, he became ill by 1584 and although he lived another year, his productive life was over.[13]

Franco's successors included several talented men. Jesus Hernández (1545–1621) established the cathedral's impressive choral library, and his choir of natives sang works by such European masters as Morales, Victoria, Lassus, and Palestrina. The first American-born choirmaster at the cathedral, Francisco Lopez (1608–1674), composed superb masses, motets, and a setting of the Passion text from the Gospel of Matthew. It was during Lopez's tenure that the visiting English priest, Thomas Gage, characterized Mexican church music as "exquisite" to the point of distraction.[14]

The standard of excellence continued into the eighteenth century. Manuel de Sumáya (1678–1755), European-trained and a child prodigy, oversaw the music at Mexico City Cathedral from 1715 to 1739. Sumáya was a gifted composer of both sacred and secular music, and his works for voices and instruments are as finely wrought as those of his better-known European colleagues. Ignacio de Jerusalem (1710–1769) was born in Italy and emigrated from Spain to Mexico City in 1742 as a theatre musician. He replaced Sumáya as cathedral choirmaster in 1749, becoming the first non-Spanish incumbent, and held the post the rest of his life. His melodic, Italian-style music was popular all over New Spain, even in the California missions.[15]

During the late sixteenth and seventeenth centuries, Mexico City Cathedral's music was rivaled by that of Puebla, a city founded by the Spaniards in 1531, near the Indian town of Cholula, between Mexico City and Vera Cruz. Puebla's cathedral was built in 1536–1539, and its bishop collected a distinguished music library at his own expense during the 1540s and 1550s, importing major polyphonic works from Seville.[16]

Choirmasters included the colorful Juan de Victoria of Burgos, who arrived in 1566. In 1570 or 1571 he moved to Mexico City, but in 1574 he was jailed and three years later deported to Spain after the authorities took offense at a play involving his Indian choirboys. Pedro Bermudez, appointed choirmaster at Puebla in 1603, had immigrated to Peru from Grenada around 1599 as choirmaster of the cathedral in Cuzco. His tenure at Puebla was also brief; by late 1603, another had taken over his choir duties, and he disappears from Puebla and history in 1606. Only his fine music remains, in manuscript copies made in 1602 for the library of Guatemala Cathedral.[17]

Juan Gutiérrez de Padilla (1590?–1664) was a native of Malagà and worked at Cadíz before arriving in Puebla in 1622. In 1629, he became choirmaster, and for the next thirty-five years oversaw its generously funded music establishment of singers and instrumentalists. A large amount of his music has survived, including Latin masses and motets as well as sacred vernacular songs.[18]

Native Music and Musicians

Instrumental ensembles were common in Spanish cathedrals before and during the reign of Charles V. Charles's own chapel included some of the finest instrumentalists in Europe. In New Spain, masses were usually sung with instrumental accompaniment. In addition, the instruments doubled voices, alternated with them, and played interludes. Accordingly, there were numerous Indian church bands, even in the smaller rural churches. An estimated 1,000 native choirs and church bands were active in Mexico by 1550. Indian choirmasters often composed masses, polyphony, and villancicos as good as any by Europeans. A Spanish Franciscan reported to his superiors in 1568, "Polyphonic music is the vogue everywhere, and accompaniment of flutes and shawms [an ancestor of the modern oboe] is common. . . . The Indians themselves play all these instruments."[19]

The Indians also continued to use traditional instruments, among them the *teponaztli* that had traditionally been a part of the Aztec ritual of human sacrifice. The Spanish priests quite understandably frowned on native music and musical instruments for their associations with pagan ritual. Even the Inquisition, usually tolerant or dismissive of the natives, condemned Indian music and took steps to suppress it. Traditional dances of the natives were curtailed "to avoid contamination from customs that may contain evil." In 1569, Fr. Alonso de Paraleja of Guadalajara wrote, "We are also careful to see that the Indians know how to sing in their own houses at night suitable Christian hymns."[20]

Native musicians, like their pre-Conquest predecessors, enjoyed prestige in their communities and were often excused from manual labor and exempt from Spanish taxes. Not surprisingly, a surplus of competent native church musicians had developed by the 1550s. In 1555–1556, a provincial council took steps to remedy the situation, and to redirect more of the Indians away from music and back into the fields and mines. The council suppressed the Indian bands in church, directing that parishes "install organs everywhere so that indecorous and improper instruments may be banished from the church." Instrumental bands were restricted to outdoor festivals and special masses. The council also ordered that native choirs be reduced to a select group. "No more Indians than are necessary shall be permitted to continue."[21]

The pronouncements were largely ignored. Ten years later, a second council decreed "further abatement in the excessive number of Indian singers." Indian musicians would no longer have the tax exemption they had enjoyed since Aztec times; but implementation of the ruling was apparently uneven. As late as 1576, no less a personage than the Viceroy of New Spain himself found it necessary to inform a group of native church musicians that their traditional tax exemption was at an end.[22]

Instrument Making and Music Publishing

Although the first instruments used in the churches of New Spain were generally imported, native craftsmen soon began making excellent copies. Flutes were known to the Indians before the Conquest; and native makers had little difficulty in copying European recorders and other wind instruments. They also made percussion instruments, with which they were familiar. In due course, the natives mastered the art of building string and keyboard instruments as well. In 1723, Juan de Torquemada reported, "[I]nstruments which serve for solace or delight on secular occasions are all made here by the Indians who also play them."[23]

Mexico City Cathedral had imported a small organ from Seville by 1530, and tradition holds that an organ now in the Church of Santo Domingo in Zacatecas, dating from about the same period, is that very instrument. Cathedrals, wealthier churches, and monasteries imported European organs; but there was also a small domestic organ-building industry. Generally, the work was supervised by European craftsmen who employed skilled native labor.[24]

The church council's 1555 pronouncement endorsing the organ as the only proper church instrument energized the organ-building industry. Augustín de Santiago built organs in Puebla around 1582. A century later, organs were to be found in most churches in New Spain. As Juan de Torquemada wrote in 1723,

> Organs have also been installed here in nearly all the churches which are administered by the orders. However, with these, not the Indians but rather Spanish builders have taken charge of construction, since the Indians do not have capital for such larger enterprises. The Indians make the organs under supervision, and they play the organs in our monasteries and convents.[25]

Mexico City's first printing press was set up around 1535. By the end of the century, the city's publishing activity equaled Toledo's and exceeded Seville's and Salamanca's. The first printed music, a liturgical *Ordinarium* containing chants, was printed in 1556. Over the next century, a total of thirteen liturgical books with music were published in Mexico City, including Juan de Navarro's *Quattuor Passions* of 1604, the first printed music composed in America.[26]

Secular Music

Evidently, there was relatively little serious amateur musical activity among the upper classes in New Spain, apart from social dancing, right up through the eighteenth century. In New Spain, as in Spain, gentlemen avoided manual labor and perceived it as undignified, and the playing of instruments was regarded as manual labor. Music for entertainment and social dancing was provided by African slaves, native musicians, and immigrant professionals. A few collections of dance music dating from the seventeenth and eighteenth centuries exist in Mexican libraries.[27]

At least one Spanish musician had come to the Caribbean with the first conquistadors. Alonso Ortiz, a musician and soldier in Cortés's expedition of conquest, opened a dancing school in Mexico City as early as 1526. Later, immigrant musicians found employment in cathedrals and large churches, and their activity in sacred music is easier to trace because of the careful records kept by church authorities. From time to time they entertained at gatherings in private homes of the wealthy and for the general public. With the increasing cosmopolitan character of Mexico City in the seventeenth and eighteenth centuries, theatres began offering steady employment, and musicians came from Italy and other European nations. For example, as mentioned earlier, Ignacio de Jerusalem, who composed and directed music in Mexico City Cathedral with distinction during his mature years, was an Italian who began his career in New Spain as a theatre musician.

Florida

Spanish explorers from Mexico penetrated far into what is now the United States. Except for a brief and unsuccessful attempt by Jesuits on Chesapeake Bay in 1571, colonies and missions were mainly located in Florida and the Southwest. Not until the last half of the eighteenth century did the Spanish settle what is now California, and then only in response to a perceived threat from Russian adventurers.

Florida attracted a few explorers in the years after Ponce de León's visit in 1512. Alvar Nuñez Cabéza de Vaca (1490–1557) described the dancing of Florida's Indians to the music of cane flutes, gourd rattles, and hand-clapping, as well as their belief, like most other natives, in the connection between music and the supernatural. Dominicans tried to establish missions in Florida from 1520 on with no success.

The sea route taken by Spanish treasure ships bound for Europe passed between Florida and the Bahamas, an area prone to storms and plagued by pirates, especially French privateers. In the spring of 1564, French Protestants—Huguenots, as they were called—planted a colony named Fort Caroline near what is now Jacksonville, an ideal location for harassing Spanish treasure ships. In August of 1565, a Spanish expedition under the newly appointed governor of Florida, Pedro Menéndez, landed nearby and took over a native village renaming it San Augustín, or Saint Augustine. The next month Menéndez and his men overran Fort Caroline and killed most of its defenders. Among those spared were the musicians, who were taken back to Saint Augustine. In addition to the usual military band of fifes, drums, and trumpets, Menéndez had a personal retinue of singers as well as a harpist and a vihuelist for his own entertainment. The Fort Caroline victory not only augmented his military band, but also added a horn player, a violinist, and a keyboard player to his personal ensemble.[28]

The Spaniards occupied Fort Caroline, renaming it San Mateo. In 1568, a French expedition under Dominique de Gargues, joined by local Indians, seized San Mateo and killed its defenders in retaliation. The French quickly departed, and the Spanish rebuilt San Mateo. Using African slaves, they also enlarged the military outpost of Saint Augustine into a typical colonial town, with a central square, churches, governor's palace, and monastery. Eighteen years later, Saint Augustine reaped the final fruits of Menéndez's campaign against Fort Caroline. One of the captured French musicians betrayed the city to the English marauder, Sir Francis Drake, enabling him to pillage and burn it in May of 1586.[29]

From this brief but bloody conflict between the French and Spanish in Florida there survives an incidental vignette relating to the Huguenots' singing, for worship and recreation, of psalm texts translated into French rhymes and set to engaging melodies. The Huguenots of Fort Caroline, like their French compatriots but unlike the greedy and cruel Spanish adventurers, had enjoyed generally good relations with the natives. Local Indians had learned some of the psalm tunes by rote and for years after the fall of Fort Caroline, they used those melodies as a means of recognition, to ascertain whether whites they encountered were French or the more dangerous Spanish.[30]

As usual, the Franciscan missionaries employed music to convert and teach the natives of Florida. A 1597 poem by the Florida Franciscan missionary Fr. Alonzo Escobedo describes native choirs trained by Fr. Fernando Chozar singing polyphony. By 1675, the Franciscans had made some 20,000 Florida Indian converts and built thirty-six churches over territory stretching into present-day Georgia.[31]

New Mexico

During the 1580s, the Spanish attempted unsuccessfully to colonize the northern frontier lands that now make up Arizona, Texas, and New Mexico. Finally, in early 1598, a company under the command of Juan de Oñate crossed the Rio Grande at what is now El Paso and established the town of San Gabriel on the site of a native pueblo.

In New Mexico too, the Spanish found that music was an effective tool in the conversion and instruction of the Indians. Cristóbal Quiñones, a priest in Oñate's expedition, taught the natives chant, villancicos, and vernacular songs between 1598 and 1604 at his San Felipe mission. San Felipe may even have had an organ before 1604, although the first firm evidence of the instrument dates from 1630. Ten years later, over a dozen organs were in use in missions.[32]

The Franciscans taught the natives to sing and play; and as usual the Indians proved to be fast and eager learners. Native bands and choirs of boys flourished to such a degree that by 1630, Alonzo Benevides, Franciscan Custodian of New Mexico between 1626 and 1630, reported back to Philip IV in Spain how elated he was "to see in such a short time so many choirs with polyphonic music."[33]

Benevides's enthusiasm notwithstanding, it is doubtful that mission choirs sang much if any complex European polyphony. There were no urban centers nearby apart from Santa Fe, which in 1630 numbered only 750 inhabitants, more or less, and therefore no cathedral choirs against which mission choirs and their repertoires could be measured by Benevides and others. In all likelihood, the mission choirs' repertoires consisted mainly of chant and vernacular songs and possibly some simple part music. In any case, archives and libraries that might provide information were destroyed in the sudden tumult of the 1680s.

As usual, the Spaniards seized what they needed from the natives. The colonists were frequently in conflict with the missionaries, who had energetically gathered the Indians into mission compounds to protect them from that exploitation. Yet at the same time, the Franciscans looked down on the natives and their culture, treating them as errant children; regulating their customs, dress and behavior; and exercising iron control, often by imposing corporal punishment. Poor harvests in the 1660s and 1670s and Spanish refusal to moderate their demands reduced the natives to starvation and desperation.

In August of 1680, a coordinated rebellion drove out the Spanish. The Indians destroyed missions and their archives and libraries, as well as the Spanish settlements and churches. Among the 400 Spaniards killed were at least half the Franciscan missionaries. Some 2,000 surviving colonists fled back to Mexico. Twelve years later the Spaniards returned to recapture the territory; but the missionaries had learned their lesson, and henceforth treated the natives with somewhat more respect, tolerating the customs and rituals and indeed, incorporating a number of them into Catholic rites.

California

In the twilight of its imperial grandeur, Spain made one final advance into what would become U.S. territory. Juan Rodriguez Cabillo had visited the coast of southern California in 1542, and in 1602 another Spaniard, Sebastién Vizcaino, explored the same area, naming it San Diego. Antonio de la Ascension, a Carmelite priest with Vizcaino's expedition, noted in his diary, later published as *A Brief Discovery in the South Sea*, "It would be well to bring from New Spain Indian minstrels, with their instruments . . . and to teach the Indians of the land to sing . . . selecting among the young men and boys the most docile, talented and capable."[34]

Meanwhile, during the summer of 1579 and far up the coast just north of San Francisco Bay, Sir Francis Drake, the Spaniards' bitter enemy, had beached his vessel, the *Golden Hinde*, for repairs. Drake's chaplain, Francis Fletcher, marveled at the Indians' response to his company's singing of metrical psalms: "In the time . . . of singing of psalms . . . they sate very attentively . . . greatly rejoicing in our exercises. Yea, they took such pleasure in our singing of psalmes, that whensoever they resorted to us . . . they entreated that we should sing."[35]

Fearing Russian incursion, the Spanish finally organized an expedition in 1768. The next year a mission was established in San Diego by the Franciscan Junípero Serra (1713–1784). By 1823, twenty more had been built, each a day's walk beyond the last, as far north as Sonoma. Four military outposts or *presidios* were planted along the route, around which towns grew. As usual, the natives provided necessary labor, and the Spanish settlers enjoyed a gracious and easy lifestyle. Music for their recreation and entertainment was provided by natives playing popular Spanish and Mexican songs on guitars and violins.

Here too, mission Indians showed musical interest and aptitude. They quickly learned to sing liturgical music and to play instruments. Serra himself had musical training, as did the other Franciscans. Indeed, some were quite proficient; Florencio Ibañez, for instance, had been choirmaster at Zaragosa before emigrating and had worked in Mexico City. Narciso Durán (1776–1846), an amateur musician who began his work in California in 1806, established a school at Mission San José, where he taught the natives to copy music for other missions and compiled a book of mission music in 1813. Durán also composed music and developed a highly effective teaching system.[36]

The California Indians were taught chant along with some hymns and vernacular religious poems adapted to popular melodies. And as elsewhere, the missions soon had proficient choirs of native men and boys. Select groups of ten to forty voices led congregations in unison hymns and chants and sang simple part music, accompanied by an instrumental ensemble. Much of the music used in the California missions survives in manuscripts from the period.[37]

Instrumental groups varied in size, from a forty-three-piece orchestra at Mission Santa Barbara to such modest ensembles as Mission San Francisco's viola, cello, and two flutes. Small organs appear in the California mission records. Mission Santa Barbara had two organs in the 1840s. Many of these instruments were barrel organs, instruments requiring no skill but were played by turning a crank which pumped wind and at the same time rotated a barrel with pins that depressed the playing mechanism for the various notes. The missions at San Juan Capistrano, San Carlos, and San José had barrel organs, and one of English manufacture still exists in the museum at San Juan Batista.

One effect of the barrel organs was to broaden the native ensembles' repertoire in a surprising manner. A French visitor at Mission Santa Clara in 1829 was bemused by the Indian orchestra's rendition of the *Marseillaise* and some popular marches and dances during Mass. The leader had evidently transcribed the melodies from a barrel organ.[38]

The missionaries did their best to suppress the indigenous culture and to impose the Spanish language, music, and customs, but they had only limited success. As late as 1814, Father Felipe Arroyo de la Cuesta, at Mission San Juan Batista, described the natives' music for war, hunting, and storytelling, and their dancing to the sound of rattles: "[The Indians] are fond of music and song," he remarked ruefully, "but their instruments also remember the pagan tunes."[39]

The Spanish had moved to colonize California only after they had lost the military and political power to hold the territory and prevent settlement by other groups. Colonists flouted Spanish law and traded freely with merchants from other nations, and Russian fur traders established outposts in northern California with impunity. Even as the last missions were being established in 1823, Spain had yielded independence to Mexico and a republic had been established. By 1825, California was a Mexican territory; and in 1833, the government in Mexico City dismantled the mission-controlled Indian communities and freed their vast landholdings for ranching and other uses. The Franciscans returned to Spain, and the era of California mission music and culture was over.

CONCLUSION

Musical activity in New Spain unquestionably centered on the church. As such, it reflected the close ties between church and state that characterized Spanish culture of the era. Cathedrals and urban churches drew trained professionals from Europe, and missionaries placed the highest priority on teaching music in their native schools.

Spanish colonial society had little serious interest in the arts. There were few if any amateur ensembles. Professional musicians were available for entertainment, civic and social occasions, and eventually even the theatre, only because the church assured them of a steady living. Similarly, native ensembles were available only because the church trained them through the agency of missionaries, primarily the Franciscans.

But for all the Spanish success at adapting and creating native musical organizations, there were clear purposes that had nothing to do with art. At one level, those purposes were clearly honorable. In a time when death came easily and often, hell was literal and immanent, and heaven was attainable solely through the ministrations of Catholicism. Conversion of the natives was a primary concern, not only to the missionaries themselves, but also to the rulers of Spain who sponsored them. Literally from first contact, the natives had responded strongly to the music of Catholic ritual, and the missionaries soon realized that they had both an interest in and an aptitude for all aspects of the art. Music was a valuable tool not only for attracting the natives, but also for holding and teaching them.

However hard the Spaniards may have labored to assure the salvation of the natives by making them good Catholics, they were far more intent on the less admirable objective of exploiting the Indians by imposing customs and culture dominated by the Spanish state and church. To that end, it was clearly necessary that the Spanish suppress the natives' own culture, customs, traditions, and religion. Here also, music provided a ready means; for native belief held that music had mystical properties and each civil or religious rite had its own integral music. New music represented new ritual to the Indians, and with it came the new culture and new customs of their conquerors.

New England

New England was settled in the early seventeenth century by English Puritans, so called by their adversaries because they sought to purify the English church by ridding it of bishops, ritual, and elaborate music. They left England because of the religious demands and restrictions imposed during the reign of Charles I by his Archbishop of Canterbury, William Laud. They had no intention of establishing a haven for religious liberty, but rather a place where they might impose their own set of religious demands and restrictions.

Unlike the Spanish colonists, they sought no personal wealth. Yet many attained it, for the Puritans worked hard, believing that diligence pleased God and success was a sign of His favor. Few had any real interest in converting the natives or incorporating them into a neo-English commonwealth. In fact, alert to signs of divine approval or anger, the Puritans interpreted the European diseases that had decimated the native population and left cleared fields and empty villages as signs of God's intervention and blessing. By century's end, their colonies had spread up and down the coast, inland, and north and south to Maine, New Hampshire, Rhode Island, and Connecticut.

PURITANS AND MUSIC

The Puritans in both England and New England had mixed feelings about music. All agreed that neither instruments nor any other sort of music apart from unaccompanied congregational singing of psalms in unison had any place in public worship that centered on plain-spoken sermons designed for forthright clarity rather than artful rhetoric. The Puritans had no objection to music and instruments in civil or military ceremonies. Beyond this, however, opinions varied. Some thoughtful Puritans feared what they perceived as music's ability to influence thought and behavior. Many were wary that music, like any other diversion, engaged time that might more profitably be spent in study or industry.

On the other hand, the first generation of Puritans came to maturity during a rich musical period in England, and the great Elizabethan composers William Byrd and John Dowland (ironically, both of them Catholic) were still active in the early seventeenth century. Music was an integral part of British culture, and if some among the Puritans were suspicious of music's ability to seduce the emotions or to engender idleness, many others enjoyed singing, playing, and listening to instruments, and even dancing. So visible a Puritan as Oliver Cromwell, Lord Protector of England during the Commonwealth period, had an organ installed in his residence and engaged an instrumental ensemble to accompany dancing at his daughter's wedding.[1]

A number of Puritans in New England were likewise fond of music and owned instruments for private use and recreation. In general though, the early colonists were probably somewhat more restrictive in their attitudes toward public music and entertainment than were their counterparts in England. One can scarcely imagine a prominent New England Puritan—even one partial to music, like Samuel Sewall, for instance—hiring musicians for dancing. Many colonial Puritans tended to be more circumspect about musical activity for a number of reasons. First, they were engaged in wresting a living from a wilderness. From the perspective of most, what little leisure time they might steal from the struggle for survival was far better spent in study, prayer, and meditation than in idle music making. Second, they were the most zealous among the English Puritans, who had risked all to cross the Atlantic and build a pious community far from what they saw as the worldliness that corrupted the church in England. Having planted their "city upon a hill," in John Winthrop's famous words, they were attentive to the godly character of their community, restricting voice and vote in civic affairs to church members alone. Consequently, for at least its first fifty years, New England's culture lacked the kind of moderating balance old England's considerable non-Puritan population afforded.

Metrical Psalmody

The music of Puritan worship was metrical psalmody; that is, the texts of the psalms set in simple verse and sung by all to simple tunes. Cultured Puritans might play or sing the music of psalmody in parts for recreation in the privacy of their homes. For public worship, however, the whole congregation sang the melody of the psalms without instrumental accompaniment or harmony.

It is an irony of sorts that a short-lived musical diversion in the idle Catholic courts of Europe survived and flourished as music for Protestant worship. As early as 1533, sprightly metrical translations of selected psalms by Clement Marot (1497?–1544), a courtier to the French king Francis I, began circulating among the French nobility who playfully sang them to popular tunes of the day. There was even some interest in the fashion among the members of the solidly Catholic court of the Holy Roman emperor and Spanish king Charles V.

Marot may or may not have had genuine Protestant sympathies, but his metrical psalms were ideally suited to the needs of Reformed Protestants, who dispensed with choirs and instruments in favor of plain congregational singing. The earliest collection of versified psalms for Protestant worship was printed in 1539 in Strasbourg. But it was the 1562 Genevan Psalter, with metrical psalm texts by Marot and others, and tunes from numerous sources, that was eventually adopted by most Reformed congregations on the European continent and subsequently translated from its original French into some twenty languages.

England and Henry VIII broke with Rome in 1534. The ceremonial of the Church of England remained Catholic under Henry, but after the accession of the nine-year-old Edward VI in 1547, Protestant reformers gained ascendancy at Court, among them several with distinctly Puritan leanings. Edward VI was followed by Mary, who attempted to return England to Catholicism; however, with Elizabeth's ascent to the throne in 1558, Protestantism was firmly established in England.

Shortly after Henry's death, one of his courtiers, Thomas Sternhold (1500?–1549) published a set of nineteen psalm translations set to verse in the style of popular ballads. Around 1549, these translations were reissued, along with eighteen more versified psalms by Sternhold and an additional seven by John Hopkins. The collection was adopted by the English reformers and went through numerous editions. Psalm translations by others were added over the years; however, the psalter would continue to be known as Sternhold and Hopkins, or more frequently, the "Old Version."

The stanzas of most Old Version psalms were in regular four-line patterns, and they could be sung to a number of well-known song melodies. Indeed, their instant popularity doubtless sprang from their being sung to popular airs—"roguish tunes" and "prophane jiggs," as one writer put it—although a body of tunes especially for the singing of metrical psalms had emerged well before the end of the sixteenth century. The majority of metrical psalm texts were in common meter: four-line stanzas alternating eight and six syllables, four of them accented in the first and third lines, and three in the second and fourth. Common meter, as the name implies, was the meter in which most of the popular ballad texts were cast:

> A-WAKE all MEN, I SAY a-GAIN,
> Be MER-ry AS you MAY,
> For HAR-ry our KING has GONE hunt-ING
> To BRING the DEER to BAY.

This same common meter can be seen, as one example among many, in Psalm 23. It is probably most familiar in its King James wording: "The Lord is my shepherd, I shall not want. He maketh me to lie down in green pastures; He leadeth me beside still waters." The Old Version as printed by John Day's *The Whole Booke of Psalmes* (London, 1562) has two translations of Psalm 23, both in common meter. The first stanza of Thomas Sternhold's rendition is as follows:

> The Lord is only my support
> And he that doth me feed.
> How can I then lack anything
> Whereof I stand in need.

Bishop William Whittingham's alternate text is somewhat more polished, but in the same metrical pattern:

> My Shepherd is the living Lord
> Nothing therefore I need.
> In pastures fair near pleasant streams
> He setteth me to feed.

Long meter was also a familiar ballad scheme. Long meter stanzas had four eight-syllable lines, with four accents in each line. Probably the best known of the Old Version long meter psalms is Thomas Kethe's versifying of Psalm 100, in the King James Version: "O be joyful in the Lord all ye lands; Serve the Lord with gladness and come before his presence with a song":

> All people that on earth do dwell,
> Sing to the Lord with cheerful voyce.
> Him serve with fear, His praise forth tell,
> Come ye before Him and rejoice.

Short meter is rare in ballad texts, and less frequently encountered in metrical psalms. Its four-line stanzas are in the pattern of two six-syllable, three-accent lines; an eight-syllable, four-accent line; and another six-syllable, three-accent line. Psalm 25—in the King James Version, "Unto thee, O lord, do I lift up my soul. O my God, I trust in thee; let me not be ashamed," is rendered in short meter by Sternhold:

> I lift my heart to Thee,
> My God and guide most just.
> Now suffer me to take no shame,
> For in Thee do I trust.

The complete Old Version Psalter, as published in London by John Day in 1562, became the standard for public worship. Day's psalter also contained forty-six psalm tunes. In general, however, most congregations probably used only a handful of tunes for singing all the psalms, one each for short and long meter texts and two or three for common meter psalms.[2]

Although Elizabeth was herself firmly Protestant, she loved liturgical ceremony. Her Chapels Royal, Westminster Abbey (which was under Crown control), and most of the cathedrals reinstituted their elaborate music establishments. Parish churches, on the other hand, adopted metrical psalms, with their verses in simple English that all could understand and familiar melodies that all could join in singing, worship music both accessible to all and specifically endorsed in Scripture. Even Parliament began its sessions singing a psalm, much to Elizabeth's disgust. She frankly loathed metrical psalms, referring to them with contempt as "Geneva jigs." Nevertheless, as the sixteenth century drew to a close, Elizabeth's reign gave way to that of James I, and as the first English colonists set foot in North America, English church music was firmly channeled in two distinct streams. The cathedrals, collegiate churches, and chapels royal maintained choirs and a choral tradition. The majority of parish churches adopted congregational psalmody. It was, of course, this latter practice of metrical psalmody that the first colonists, both Puritans in New England and Anglicans in Virginia, brought with them.

THE PLYMOUTH COLONY

In 1607, the year of England's first permanent American settlement in Jamestown, Virginia, a small group of separatist Puritans from Nottinghamshire, desirous of breaking altogether with the established Church of England but under official pressure to conform, chose instead to move to the relatively tolerant religious atmosphere of Amsterdam. There they encountered other English exiles, among them the Reverend Henry Ainsworth (1570/71–1622/23).[3]

Ainsworth published his own careful translation of the psalms in 1612 for the use of the English exiles in the Netherlands. Ainsworth's psalter made use of a variety of regular and irregular rhythms, rather than the usual ballad schemes. His setting of Psalm 23, for instance, did not fit into common meter, like Sternhold's and Whittingham's in the Old Version:

> Jehovah feedeth me, I shal not lack.
> In grassy fold He dooth make me lye;
> He gently leads me quiet waters by.

A prose translation was printed alongside each verse psalm, and a brief commentary appeared at the bottom of the page. Ainsworth provided forty-eight tunes taken from English and continental psalters, though he wrote in his preface: "Tunes for the Psalmes, I find none set of God: so that e[a]ch people is to use the most grave, decent, and comfortable manner of singing that they know." The newly arrived separatists adopted Ainsworth's psalter for their common worship. Its variety of meters and the rhythms suggests that they had some musical skill. Indeed, one of their number, Edward Winslow, termed "many of the Congregation very expert in musick."[4]

Eleven years later, the group decided to move once more. Part of the congregation departed for England and, late in the summer of 1620, sailed from there for America. They settled at what is now Plymouth, and entered popular history as the Pilgrims. Simple artisans and tradesmen for the most part, they sought only to worship unhindered. Their agreement, the *Mayflower Compact*, aimed only to regulate society and maintain order. They had no lofty aspirations to "be as a city upon a hill," like the Bay colonists who followed

some ten years later. They had no minister; elder William Brewster led their
worship. Although they surely shared in the rich folk ballad tradition that
flowered in Elizabethan England, there is no evidence that they owned any
musical instruments, apart from the usual drums and trumpets used for signaling. Yet for two generations, until 1682, they continued to sing their
psalms in Ainsworth's complex meters and tunes in their worship, rather
than the simple Old Version psalms (see Appendix 4, Example 1).[5]

The Bay Colony

In 1628, a small company of Puritans settled at Salem. Like the Plymouth
group to the south of them, they used Ainsworth's psalter in their worship;
however, they were not separatists, and their colony was established for commercial rather than religious reasons. They were the vanguard of what became known as the Great Migration. Two years later, in the spring of 1630,
the *Arbella* sailed into Massachusetts Bay with the first contingent of English
Puritans who would arrive over the next decade, intent on building their
Godly Commonwealth in and around Boston. Most were middle class and literate, among them a number of ministers, university-trained and in many
cases related to one another by marriage.[6]

The Bay Puritans, unlike the Plymouth separatists, considered themselves
within the Church of England, even though they disdained its ritual. On the
other hand, their worship was the same as that of the Plymouth colonists, except that they sang psalms from the Old Version rather than Ainsworth. Indeed, once settled, they too separated themselves from Anglicanism in polity
as well as worship practice, rejecting the authority of bishops.

Many of the Ainsworth tunes, as used by the Plymouth and Salem
churches, had about them a grace and melodiousness characteristic of their
continental origin. The Bay Colony's Sternhold and Hopkins tunes were
plainer and less gracious. Overall, however, the attitude both of the Bay and
the Plymouth colonists toward worship music reflected their view of the service as a teaching occasion with the sermon as its centerpiece. Any ritual not
specifically justifiable from Scripture was to be shunned as a theatrical distraction. Indeed, of the very building in which the congregation gathered, Cotton Mather later wrote, "A MEETING HOUSE is the term that is most
commonly used . . . [there being] no just ground in Scripture to apply such a
trope as *church* to a place for assembly."[7] The sermon, lasting about two hours,

offered not only religious instruction but also advice on everyday matters, intellectual stimulation, and even entertainment, in a manner of speaking.[8]

Like the early church fathers with whose writings they were familiar, Puritan ministers were suspicious of music's affective ability to lull the listener and to arouse unworthy emotions. They considered it extraneous to the substance of worship except as a tool for reaching the intellectually dull.[9] Doubtless, some of them would have been happy to suppress music in worship altogether. Nevertheless, as in all things Scripture was their guide and rule. The singing of psalms was clearly directed by example in the New Testament; so they permitted and even encouraged it, but only within clearly drawn limitations.

Above all, the music had to be such that the congregation as a whole could sing it, the uncultured as well as the educated and well-to-do, so that each might render his or her own praise. Choirs were proscribed as a corruption of the unreformed church. The melodies were sung unadorned, neither in parts nor with instruments, lest they detract from the serious intellectual business of the sermon, or cause the listener to "mistake the natural Effects of *Musick*, for the Comforts of the Holy Spirit."[10] In short, the place of metrical psalmody in worship was purely didactic, and certainly not to enhance the aesthetic character of the service.

Psalters with the tunes harmonized in parts could be found in the colonists' homes (with the probable exception of Plymouth), and the Puritans sang from them for recreation or private devotions, often with instrumental accompaniment. Day's 1563 collection with tunes "in foure parts which may be song to al musicall instruments" had given way to other collections, mainly Thomas Ravenscroft's *The Whole Booke of Psalmes* of 1621. Ravenscroft's collection contained ninety-seven tunes, harmonized by prominent composers, among them the Catholics John Dowland (1563–1626) and Thomas Morley (1558–1602). For worship, however, the whole congregation sang the tune with neither harmony nor instrumental accompaniment.[11]

The Bay Psalm Book

The Bay colony was barely established when its ministers set about preparing their own metrical psalter. Educated clergymen like John Cotton (1584–1652) of Boston's First Church considered the Old Version translations inaccurate. The new translation was prepared by thirty "pious and learned

Ministers," and printed in Cambridge by Stephen Daye on a press at Harvard College in 1640, the first book published in the colonies. Entitled *The Whole Booke of Psalmes Faithfully Translated into English Metre*, it is more commonly known as the "Bay Psalm Book." Its preface, possibly by John Cotton, made the historical and scriptural case for congregational psalmody, and defended translations into metrical verse on the grounds that the psalms were poetry in their original language. As to the new translations,

> If therefore the verses are not always so smooth and elegant as some may desire or expect; let them consider that Gods Altar needs not our pollishings . . . for wee have respected rather a plaine translation, then to smooth our verses with a sweetnes of any paraphrase, and so have attended Conscience rather than Elegance, fidelity rather than poetry, in translating the hebrew words into english language, and Davids poetry into english meetre, that so we may sing in Sion the Lords songs of prayse according to his owne will.[12]

For all their linguistic accuracy, the translations were indeed inelegant, compared to the Old Version. The Bay Psalm Book's Twenty-Third Psalm, for instance, retains the common meter of the Old Version, but the lines are awkwardly structured.

> The Lord to me a shepherd is,
> want therefore shall not I:
> He in the folds of tender grass
> doth make me down to lie:

As with the Old Version, the great majority of psalms were in common meter. In 1651, Henry Dunster smoothed some of the awkward though literal translations with "a little more of Art," as he put it, and added alternate texts and some scriptural hymns. The version with his emendations formed the basis of over fifty subsequent editions.

Although the preface also mentions "the difficulty of *Ainsworths* tunes" as sung in the Salem and Plymouth churches, early editions of the Bay Psalm Book contained no tunes. Instead, readers were referred to Ravenscroft and other of "our english psalme books." The first Bay Psalm Book with melodies was the ninth edition, of 1698. The thirteen tunes, nine of them in common meter, appeared, strangely enough in two parts, reprinted exactly from Playford's *Brief Introduction to the Skill of Musicke* (London, 1674 and 1679), in two-voice settings, melody over bass. Playford had clearly intended the two-part settings for private use, since congregations in England, as in New England, sang only the melody and without instrumental support (see Appendix 4, Example 2).[13]

Lined-Out Psalmody

By mid-century, the general level of proficiency and interest in congregational psalm singing had declined, as had the number of tunes used by congregations. Moreover, the substitution of the new Bay Psalm Book texts in place of the familiar Old Version psalms that congregations had long associated with the same tunes surely have bred confusion. By the time John Cotton published his treatise, *Singing of Psalmes a Gospel-Ordinance* (Boston, 1647), congregations had begun to rely on the practice, evidently Scottish in origin, of lining out by minister or deacon. Cotton wrote:

> It will be a necessary helpe, that the wordes of the *Psalme* be openly
> read before hand, line after line, or two lines together, that so they
> who want either books or skill to reade, may know what is to be
> sung, and joyne with the rest in the dutie of singing.

He did not endorse lining out as any more than a temporary expedient.

> We for our parts easily grant, that where all have books and can
> read, or else can say the *Psalme* by heart, it were needlesse there
> to read each line of the *Psalme* before hand in order to sing.[14]

In practice, the method varied. In some churches, the deacon or minister read the psalm line by line and the congregation responded with the customary melody, led by a lusty-voiced "precentor" who set or "raised" the tune. In other churches, the deacon set the tune as well, singing the psalm line by line, the congregation repeating each line after him.[15]

However temporary an expedient Cotton may have considered lining out, the practice quickly became widespread if not general. Only a few urban churches with educated and literate congregations managed to dispense with it. The practice of lining out, at least among New England congregations, seems to have been closely tied to the adoption of the Bay Psalm Book.

Boston's Brattle Square Church, founded in 1698/99, chose the New Version of Tate and Brady instead and never adopted the custom of lining out.[16]

The church in Plymouth continued to sing Ainsworth's psalms without lining out until the 1680s. But on June 19, 1692, a year after Plymouth was merged into the Bay Colony by royal decree, the congregation voted to abandon its old psalm book, because it had "such difficult tunes as none in the church could sett"; and on August 7, "that when the Tunes were difficult in our Translation, wee should sing the Psalmes now in use in the neighbour-churches in the Bay." The Salem church had changed from the Ainsworth to the Bay Psalm Book in 1667, because of "the difficulty of the tunes and because we could not singe them so well as formerly."[17]

The New Version

Outside of the Puritan churches, the Old Version remained in use; but as the century passed, it had begun to wear thin with many congregations. In 1696, Nahum Tate and Nicholas Brady's *New Version of the Psalms of David, Fitted to the tunes used in churches*, was published in London, and promptly dubbed the "New Version" to distinguish it from the Sternhold and Hopkins Old Version. The New England ministers viewed this New Version as a paraphrase; nevertheless, its verses possessed far more grace than their own Bay Psalm Book translations. The New Version's Psalm 23 provides a good example.

> The Lord himself, the mighty Lord
> vouchsafes to be my guide;
> The shepherd by whose constant care
> my wants are all supplied.

Within the next ten years, a number of Anglican congregations in America had adopted the New Version, among them Trinity Church in New York in 1707 and King's Chapel in Boston in 1713. A few non-Anglican congregations also adopted the New Version, among them Boston's Brattle Square Church. The New Version remained in use alongside the Old Version in England, but more or less supplanted it in America, except in the majority of Puritan churches of New England, where the Bay Psalm Book held sway. Collections of musical tunes for the New Version texts were published from 1700 on. Many of those tunes gained a permanent place in Protestant hymnody; for instance, William Croft's well-known "St. Anne," sung to the later paraphrase of Psalm 90 by Isaac Watts, "O God, Our Help in Ages Past."[18]

Usual Singing, Regular Singing

As the seventeenth century turned to the eighteenth, most congregations in Massachusetts knew but a handful of tunes, to which they sang all the psalms, line by line, as the deacon gave out the text. The quality of psalm singing in New England and in the English-speaking colonies had declined along with the number of tunes so that individual singers in the congregation moved at different tempi, coming together only at the beginning and end of lines. The general pace of singing was painfully slow, and some singers improvised their own turns and ornaments in the melodic line as they waited for other members of the congregation to catch up. The sorry condition did not go unnoticed.

> [M]ost [notes are] too *long*, and many *Turnings of*, or *Flourishes with the Voice*, (as they call them) are made where they should not be, and some are wanting where they should have been.[19]

> [S]ome affect a quavering flourish on one note, and others upon another which . . . they account a grace to the tune; and while some affect a quicker motion, others affect a slower and drawl out their notes beyond all reason.
>   . . . Tunes that are already in use in our Churches; which, when they first came out of the Hands of the Composers of them, were sung according to the Rules of the *Scale of Musick* . . . are now miserably tortured, and twisted, and quavered, in some Churches, into an horrid medley of confused and disordered Noises. . . . Yea, I have my self heard (for Instance) *Oxford* Tune sung in three Churches . . . with as much difference as there can possibly be between *York* and *Oxford*, or any two other different Tunes.[20]

In a sense, such singing was legitimate and even preferable, when one considers that Puritan thought valued individual praise over coordinated congregational singing that might well bring to mind unreformed ritualism. Indeed, this free singing style—"usual style," as it was termed—was in a sense a genuine folk practice. To most—though by no means all—of the educated clergy of the time, however, it was one more sign of a general religious laxness they had come to deplore in their sermons. As one of them put it, "[O]ur *Psalmody* has suffered the like Inconveniences which our *Faith* has laboured under, in case it had been committed and trusted to the uncertain and doubtful Conveyance of *Oral Tradition.*"[21]

In 1720, Thomas Symmes (1678–1725), Harvard graduate and minister of the church in the northern town of Bradford, published a pamphlet, *The Reasonableness of Regular Singing, or Singing by Note*. Symmes had been acting both as preacher and precentor in his church, and knew whereof he wrote. He reminded readers that psalm singing was an obligation, and that the rules of music had been studied at Harvard from its founding in 1636. Yet psalmody was now neglected. His solution was the adoption of singing schools to train singers from the congregation in the "rules" of and reading of music, so that they in turn could lead the body in psalmody. "Regular" singing, that is, by "rule," meant singing together from the notes, as opposed to the "usual" way of singing by rote and recollection, each individual choosing a pitch level and tempo independent of the rest of the congregation, changing and adding notes at whim.

> People that want *Skill* in *Singing*, would procure a *Skillful Person* to *Instruct* them, and meet *Two* or *Three* Evenings in the Week, from *five* or *six* a Clock, to *Eight*, and spend the Time in Learning to Sing. Would not this be an innocent and profitable *Recreation?*[22]

Cotton Mather (1663–1728), John Cotton's grandson and Boston's leading minister, agreed. As early as 1717, his own family had become "so indifferent at singing" that in their private devotions he was often forced to dispense with singing, even though he considered psalmody a form of prayer. During the spring of 1721, he worried about the state of singing in his Second Church, the largest congregation in Boston. On March 13, he wrote in his diary: "Should not something be done towards mending the *Singing* in our Congregation?" And on June 5, "I must of Necessity do something that the Exercise of *Singing* in the sacred *Psalms* in the flock may be made more beautiful." That year he published his pamphlet, *The Accomplished Singer*, advocating the improvement of congregational singing through training in the "rules" of music, characterizing such "regular singing" as all-but-divinely ordained. Mather wrote, "*Regular Singing* must needs be *Better* than the confused Noise of a wilderness."[23]

There is evidence that a singing school was operating in Boston as early as 1714, and Mather would surely have known of it. In 1722 there was a Society for Promoting Regular Singing in Boston. And by October 1, 1723, Reverend Joseph Green wrote to a friend, describing with evident approval, "ye delightful exercise of singing performed at the New Brick Church [in Boston's North End] ... only by ye masters of it, viz., men and women, seated in the front Gallery on purpose for it."[24]

But not all ministers agreed, and the resistance against the imposition of regular singing was spirited. As one correspondent wrote, in the *New England Chronicle* in 1723, "Truly I have a great jealousy that if we once begin to sing by rule, the next thing will be to pray by rule, and preach by rule; and then comes popery." Elsewhere, objections were made on the grounds of custom. Churches and ministers favoring the retention of singing in the usual manner tended to be rural; those arguing for regular singing were for the most part urban and centered in Boston. At least one church, the Glastonbury, Connecticut, parish, briefly attempted to compromise by singing in the usual manner half the year and in the regular manner the remaining half.[25]

Feelings ran high. In the Reverend Samuel Niles's South Braintree congregation, *The New England Courant* reported, on February 10, 1724, twenty "opposers of Regular Singing ... publicly declared for the Church of England." Nor was the conflict eased by Symmes's pamphlet, *Utili Dulci*, published in 1723. Among other things Symmes ridiculed the advocates of usual singing as Anti-Regular Singers, abbreviated to "ARSes."[26]

Singing schools were held with increasing frequency after 1720, and were extremely popular, especially among the young people, as an opportunity for mixed socializing in a church-sanctioned situation that was above reproach. Until mid-century, most singing schools relied for instruction on two manuals printed by Bartholomew Green and sold at the bookstore of Samuel Gerrish. The first of these was advertised by Gerrish in the *Boston News-Letter* for January 2 and 9 of 1721:

> A Small Book containing 20 Psalm Tunes with Directions how to
> Sing them, contrived in the most easy Method ever yet Invented ...
> [and] may serve as an Introduction to a more Compleat Treatise for
> Singing which will Speedily be published.

No copies of this first edition of *AN INTRODUCTION To the Singing of Psalm-Tunes, In a plain & easy Method* ... by John Tufts (1698–1750), first cousin of

Cotton Mather and minister of the church in Newburyport, appear to have survived; however, several copies of the fifth edition are extant.[27]

Tufts began with an explanation of the rudiments of singing, musical notation, intervals, scales, and time. The three-part tunes that followed were largely from John Playford's *Whole Book of Psalms* of 1677.[28] The "most easy Method," as touted in Gerrish's notice, consisted of Playford's syllable as reprinted with Playford's tunes in the 1698 edition of the Bay Psalm Book. Tufts, however, placed them directly on staves of the tunes, and used dots to indicate the duration of each note. The *Introduction* measured some three by five inches, small enough to fit in a pocket and often bound with copies of the Bay Psalm Book. Although it was limited, even for its purpose, it went through eleven editions, the last of them in 1744.

The second and larger book promised by Gerrish appeared in July of 1721, Thomas Walter's (1696–1725) *The Ground and Rules of Musick Explained: Or An Introduction to the Art of Singing*. Like Tufts and Symmes, Walter was a minister, assistant to his father who was pastor of the church in nearby Roxbury. His mother was a sister of Cotton Mather, and his grandfather Increase Mather was one of fourteen Boston ministers to sign "A Recommendatory Preface" to *The Ground and Rules*. Walter's book was oblong, like most of the collections that followed it over the next century and a half. Its sixteen pages of tunes were printed on three staves, with the melody in the middle voice, a bass part below, and a countermelody above. Since congregations sang only the melody, the tunes as printed were clearly intended for private use. Although Walter died of tuberculosis at age twenty-nine, his book remained in print for some forty years as a basic resource for singing schools in New England.

THE GREAT AWAKENING

The regular singing movement had quick success in some places; but elsewhere, change came slowly as churches only reluctantly gave up the usual singing to which they were accustomed. The singing school movement had begun, but it would not triumph until the second half of the eighteenth century. At the same time, the exclusive use of psalm texts for congregational singing was challenged. A series of religious revivals swept through England and the colonies, stressing an emotional response of faith as against the communal covenant and intellectual rigor of pure Calvinism, as well as the newly fashionable rationalism of the Enlightenment. In America, the movement reached its height with the Great Awakening of the 1740s. Music played a major role in the revivals, arousing the emotions of congregations and making them more receptive to the preachers' words. Psalmody suited the tightly reasoned scriptural expositions of the old Puritan ministers, but it proved inadequate to the expression of personal faith as preached by the new revivalists.[29]

The first great revivalist in America, George Whitefield (1714–1770), brought with him from England new texts by Isaac Watts (1674–1748), a London minister, set in the usual meters and therefore usable with the very tunes to which congregations were accustomed. The first of these, *Hymns and Spiritual Songs* (London, 1707) contained twenty-two texts. Cotton Mather himself approved of them in private devotions, as he wrote Watts, and *Hymns and Spiritual Songs* was reprinted in Boston in 1720, an indication of its popularity.[30]

Mather was far less pleased with the set of texts Watts sent him from London in March of 1717/18, along with a letter of explanation.

> Tis not a translation of David I pretend; but an imitation of him
> so nearly in Christian hymns . . . If I may be so happy as to have
> your free censure and judgment of 'em it will help me in correct-
> ing others by them. I entreat you, Sir, that none of them may steal
> out into public.

Watts published his *Psalms of David Imitated in the Language of the New Testament* in 1719. The texts, intended for public worship, paraphrased the psalms into a Christian context. Mather, far more rigid than Watts, condemned the collection as lacking "any Air of the Old Testament."[31]

Watts's texts were indeed paraphrases, but they were graceful, deeply personal poetry. No wonder that his texts are still a cornerstone of modern hymn collections. Watts's rendering of Psalm 23 retains the common meter of the Old and New Versions and the Bay Psalm Book, but with a fresh, engaging choice of words.

> My Shepherd will supply my need,
> Jehovah is His name.
> In pastures fresh He makes me feed
> Beside the living stream.

In 1718, doubtless by way of response to the texts Watts had sent him, Mather published his own 464-page *Psalterium Americanum* containing a set of faithful translations in blank verse, "fitted to the *Tunes* commonly used in the Assemblies of our *Zion*." Mather's psalter never attracted a following, whereas Watts's texts gained favor with many congregations, and several editions were published. In 1741, Jonathan Edwards (1703–1758) had an edition of Watts's *Psalms of David Imitated* printed in Boston for use in his Northampton church as a supplement to the Bay Psalm Book. So popular did the new texts become that on his return from a journey the next year, Edwards was dismayed to learn that his congregation was now using only Watts texts.

Other churches added Watts texts to their psalmody. Brattle Square Church in Boston, urbane and anti-revival, had an *Appendix, Containing a Number of Hymns, taken chiefly from Dr. Watts's Scriptural Collection* printed for use with their New Version psalter. Old South Church continued to use the Bay Psalm Book, but allowed its pastor, Thomas Prince, to revise and supplement the collection. The resulting *The Psalms, Hymns, and Spiritual Songs*, printed in Boston in 1758, contained forty-two texts by Watts.[32]

POPULAR MUSIC AND DANCE

Secular music in Puritan New England is more difficult to chronicle than psalmody, if for no other reason than that the most literate Puritans, who produced the diaries and pamphlets, were ministers. Naturally, they focused on psalmody; however, the issue of recreational music occupied their attention from time to time.

In his *Remarkable Providences* of 1684, Cotton Mather opined that music was "of great efficacy against melancholy discomforture." But there were firm limits to his tolerance, and popular ballads tested those limits. As early as 1664, Mather's grandfather John Cotton had chastized young men for "meeting together in places of publick entertainment [taverns] to corrupt one another . . . by rudely singing & making a noyse." On the other hand, Cotton's son and Mather's uncle, Seaborn, made copies of such ballads for himself during his years as a Harvard student. In a diary entry dated September 27, 1713, Cotton Mather complained of the "Minds and Manners of many People [being] corrupted by foolish songs and Ballads," rather than more edifying "Composures full of Piety," such as Watts's hymns. Accordingly, as Thomas Symmes wrote, singing schools for psalmody would give young people a musical alternative to *"Idle, Foolish,* yea *Pernicious* Songs and Ballads and banish all such *Trash* from their minds."[33]

Such popular songs were the heritage of all Englishmen of the era. Most, including the Puritans of New England, knew well such songs as the "The Carman's Whistle."

> As I abroad was walking,
> By the breaking of the day,
> Into a pleasant meadow
> A young man took his way.
>
> And looking round about him
> To mark what he could see,
> At length he spied a fair maid
> Under a maple tree.

These popular songs provided much of the social music in common English culture. Ballad melodies were danced to, as well as sung, and many were used over again as vehicles for new texts, cheaply printed in pamphlets called "chapbooks," or on single sheets, or broadsides. Broadside ballads might be amorous, political, or historical. Sometimes they were satirical and focused on current events and public individuals. Ballads were popular but in most cases short-lived. Written quickly and printed in large quantities, the broadsides were sold cheaply in shops and by itinerant peddlers, sung enthusiastically, and then discarded for newer ones.[34]

Upper-class English Puritans generally agreed with other English gentry that dancing was an appropriate and necessary social grace. The London publisher John Playford issued the first edition of his highly popular *The English Dancing Master* in 1651, during the rule of the Puritan Commonwealth. Each of Playford's tunes was accompanied with directions for executing steps and movements that went with it.[35]

Colonial Puritans, even a number of the ministers, took a somewhat warier but still relatively tolerant view of dancing, provided that it was kept within strict limits. Country dances, as found in Playford's book, were most popular. Such dances involved any number of couples arranged in lines, men facing women, and executing a series of simple steps. As early as 1625, John Cotton gave a measure of approval to such "mixt dancing" by couples, so long as they avoided "lascivious dancing to wanton ditties . . . amorous gestures

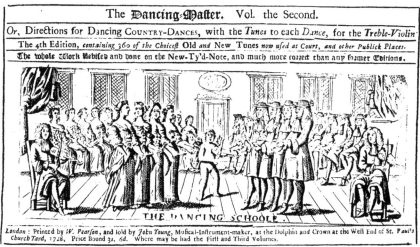

The Dancing-Master. Vol. the Second.

Or, Directions for Dancing COUNTRY-DANCES, with the *Tunes* to each *Dance*, for the *Treble-Violin*

The 4th Edition, *containing 360 of the Choicest* Old *and* New *Tunes now used at Court, and other Publick Places.*

The whole Work Revised and Done on the New-Ty'd-Note, and much more correct than any former Editions.

THE DANCING SCHOOLE.

London : Printed by *W. Pearson*, and sold by *John Young*, Musical-Instrument-maker, at the Dolphin and Crown at the West End of St. *Paul's* Church Yard, 1728, Price Bound 3s, 6d. Where may be had the First and Third Volumes.

⁎⁎ *Note*, Here is also to be had, the Basses to all the Dances contain'd in the First Volume. Price Stitch'd 1 s. 6d.

Originally published in 1650 under the title of *The English Dancing Master*, this work went through numerous editions from 1652 to 1728, first by John Playford (1623–1686?), then by Henry Playford, and, after 1706, by the publisher John Young. Courtesy of the Library of Congress.

and wanton dalliances." It was probably Cotton's equally eminent son-in-law, Increase Mather (1639–1723), who wrote, "Not that Dancing, or Musick, or Singing are in Themselves sinful: but if the Dancing Master wished they are commonly abused to lasciviousness, and that makes them to become abominable." Mather and the other community leaders in Boston were scrupulously careful in the matter of dancing masters. In 1672 and 1681, they prevented any from settling in the city; and in 1685 a group of ministers lodged a formal complaint against the dancing master Francis Stepney, who had gone out of his way to speak disparagingly of them.[36]

A year before the Stepney protest, however, the colonies of New England had been combined into a Royal Province, and the authority of the resident magistrates and ministers curtailed. The latter were forced to accept the presence among them of a Church of England minister in 1686, and the erection of an Anglican church, King's Chapel, in 1689. Boston became the provincial capital and the Puritan ministers lost much of their social and cultural influence in the community. Whether the ministers liked it or not, the Royal Governor's residence was the scene of regular social events. Prominent Puritans attended the gatherings and danced the same gavottes and minuets that were fashionable in European courts. George Brownell (1703?–1750?)

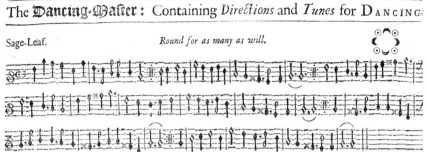

A page from the treatise *The English Dancing Master*, originally published in 1650. Courtesy of the Library of Congress.

opened the first dancing school in Boston in 1713. Edward Enstone, who had arrived from London to become organist of King's Chapel in December of 1714, set up in February of 1715 as a dealer in music, selling and repairing musical instruments and offering to teach "Musick & Dancing."[37]

INSTRUMENTS

Judge Samuel Sewall (1652–1730), Puritan stalwart and pillar of Boston's South Church, noted in his diary for December 1, 1699, "Was at Mr. Hillers to enquire for my wives [sic] virginals." In other words, Sewall's wife owned a small harpsichord. Moreover, Sewall himself enjoyed instrumental music. Ten years earlier, he had visited England with his friend and fellow music lover Thomas Brattle. On February 11, 1688/89, as Sewall recorded in his diary, he and Brattle "went to Covent Garden for Consort Musick." Two weeks later, on February 27, the pair visited Salisbury Cathedral where Sewall persuaded the organist to "give us some musick."[38]

Nor were Sewall and Brattle exceptional, even by Boston standards. Probate inventories and other records list nearly 200 instruments belonging to prominent New England Puritans in the seventeenth and early eighteenth centuries, including keyboard instruments, plucked and bowed string in-

struments, and winds. Surprisingly enough, ministers seem to have been especially active as amateur musicians. Reverend Peter Bulkeley (1583–1659),
considered "very pious" by Cotton Mather, owned two lutes. At his death in
1678, Edmond Browne, minister in the town of Sudbury, west of Boston, left
a "bass voyall" along with books of music. Charles Morton, minister of the
church in Charlestown and a friend of Sewall's, left at his death "2 Base Vi-
olls . . . and 3 old Violl Inns."[39]

The three violins are especially noteworthy in the estate of a Puritan minister, since the violin was especially associated with dancing. Dancing masters carried small violins, called "kits," with which they accompanied the
dancers. Viols were somewhat different in use and association. A consort of
viols—treble, tenor, and bass—normally played cultivated "consort" music,
and owning one or more indicated a relatively high level of musical sophistication and skill. Viols might play music expressly written for them or tran-
scriptions of vocal music by leading composers, collections of which were
printed with the advisory note, "Apt for Voices and Viols." In any case, the
music had to be imported from England. Viols might also play psalm tunes
in parts, either alone or with singers, for private devotions or for musical
recreation at home or in small gatherings.

There was also a considerable body of solo music for keyboard instrument,
composed by such masters as William Byrd, Orlando Gibbons, and John Bull,
and printed in London. Music for the lute and its sturdier relative the cittern,
by John Dowland and his contemporaries could easily be imported from England. And there can be no doubt that both keyboard and plucked-string instruments were also used for pleasure and to accompany private psalmody.

Probably the most famous instrument from Puritan New England is the
so-called Brattle organ, still playable and now located in a side gallery of St.
John's Episcopal Church in Portsmouth, New Hampshire. Thomas Brattle,
treasurer of Harvard and prominent Bostonian, acquired the instrument late
in the seventeenth century. His friend Samuel Sewall mentions the small
chamber organ in his diary entry of September 3, 1708, in regard to a funeral
he had attended that day: "I used to go to the same room for the sound of
Mr. Brattle's organs." Three years later, the Reverend Joseph Green recorded
in his diary May 29, 1711, that he "was at Mr. Brattle's, heard ye Organs and
saw strange things in a Microscope."[40]

Brattle died in 1713, and his will directed that the organ go to Brattle Square
Church, where he had been a member. Liberal though it was for a Puritan
congregation, the church declined Brattle's bequest, whereupon the instru-

ment was offered to King's Chapel, the city's first Anglican parish, which had been established in 1686. That congregation readily accepted it and brought Edward Enstone from London to be organist. Not until 1736 and 1744, respectively, did Boston's other Anglican parishes, Christ Church and Trinity Church, install organs. Puritan congregations in Boston and elsewhere resisted organs until the end of the century.[41]

CONCERTS, MUSIC MASTERS, AND AMATEURS

By 1725, the Puritans' hold on New England's culture had all but ended along with their control of its government and religion. Cotton Mather, one of the last symbols of the old regime, died in February of 1728. Ironically, close to the anniversary of his death, the *Boston Gazette* carried a notice in its February 3 and February 10, 1729, issues of the city's first public concert: "Musick performed on sundry Instruments, at the Dancing School in King-Street on Tuesday the 18th at Six o Clock in the Evening; and the Tickets for the same will be delivered out at Seven Shillings and six pence each."[42]

Meanwhile, William Burnet (1687–1729) had arrived in Boston in July of 1728 as Colonial Governor of New England. He had been governor in New York since 1720. Burnet was the son of Bishop Gilbert Burnet of Salisbury and godson of the late King William III. Born and raised in The Hague, he had enjoyed a warm relationship with the Dutch residents in New York and had taken as his second wife the daughter of one of its prominent families. She died in 1727, and Burnet subsequently presented the Dutch church in New York with an organ, possibly in her memory and probably a small instrument he himself owned. He took his other instruments to Boston, including a harpsichord and a clavichord, wind instruments, two violins, a viola and a cello (or possibly a consort of viols: two trebles a tenor and a bass; the list in the 1729 probate inventory of his estate is not clear).[43]

Burnet's friend Stephen Deblois (1699–1778), who had traveled with him from England to New York, joined him in Boston. Burnet died only a year later; but Deblois remained in the forefront of Boston musical activity for nearly a half century. During the 1730s and 1740s, he was organist first of King's Chapel, then of Christ Church, then again of King's Chapel. During those years he organized and performed in a number of paid-admission concerts of instrumental and vocal music at his home. No lists of the music played in those concerts has come down; however, it would probably have been a varied mix of songs, marches, Italian arias, and similarly accessible pieces calculated to attract and please a paying audience. With the completion of Faneuil Hall in 1742, Deblois shifted his activities there; and finally, in 1754, he opened Boston's first concert hall on the second floor over his two sons' highly successful music and dry goods business.

Indeed, in the years after 1730 it was the prosperity of Boston's growing merchant class, including Deblois's sons Lewis and Gilbert, that supported an ever more active urban cultural life. Many of those merchants were talented amateurs, and men like Deblois and Peter Pelham (1697–1751) organized and performed in concerts in which gentlemen played alongside professors, as amateurs and professional musicians, respectively, were termed.

Pelham was another concert impresario. Born in England and trained as printer, engraver, and artist, he organized concerts from 1731 on. His son, also named Peter (1721–1805), became a composer and performer of some renown. The younger Pelham studied with Charles Theodore Pachelbel (1690–1750), son of the German master Johann Pachelbel, who had come to Boston around 1732. Young Pelham followed his teacher to Newport, Rhode Island, in 1733 when the vestry of Trinity Church in that city summoned Pachelbel to erect and play the new Richard Bridge organ given them by Bishop Berkeley.

Pelham's musical apprenticeship with Pachelbel continued when the latter left Newport for New York in 1735 and then moved again to Charleston, South Carolina, in 1737 to become organist of St. Philip's Church. Shortly after, in 1743, Pelham returned to Boston and the next year became organist of Trinity Church, which had just installed an organ built in London by Abraham Jordan. In 1750, Pelham moved to Virginia and shortly thereafter became organist of Bruton Parish Church in Williamsburg, where he spent the rest of his life.[44]

CONCLUSION

The Puritan culture of New England's early colonial era gradually gave way to the commercial and political culture that led, among other things, to the Revolution. As might be expected, metrical psalmody dominated the music for much of the period. Recreational music, however much the ministers and magistrates might have tolerated it, was generally restricted to homes and private gatherings. The public dissemination and singing of ballads was viewed with disapproval, and dancing was acceptable only within clear lines of propriety. By the 1730s, the coming of commerce, enlightened English liberalism, and the Anglican Church had changed forever the original Puritan vision of a "city upon a hill." The first and second generations—Cotton, the Mathers, Sewall—were gone; and their descendants left Harvard to become merchants and lawyers, rather than ministers. But the Puritan way was deep rooted; significant concert activity, theatre and opera, and the breakdown of prejudice against organs and choirs in churches would come only in the years after Independence.

4

The Southern Colonies

During the seventeenth century, England planted colonies along the Atlantic coast. Differing religious views and purposes for emigration distinguished these colonies, one from another; but geography and economics also played a significant role in their differing social, cultural, and musical development. On the other hand, the fact that most colonists were English meant that all colonies shared a common store of British traditional melodies, well known to all for generations, to which they both danced and sang various ballad texts, old and new. Other tunes served for the singing of metrical psalms—psalm texts translated into simple, ballad-like poems—and in the eighteenth century for newer hymn texts by Watts and others. Even in later years, when tastes among colonial gentry in America became more elevated in response to London fashions, the older music retained its popularity among the majority of common folk.

The strict Puritanism of New England never gained a foothold in the South, although there were English Puritans among the settlers in Virginia, Maryland, and the Carolinas. Maryland's capital, Annapolis, was settled by Puritans fleeing Virginia governor William Berkeley's repressive measures, and Puritans from New England made an unsuccessful attempt to settle the Cape Fear area of North Carolina.

Southern geography worked against the sort of close-knit communities that held Puritan New England together. Wide tracts of fertile land throughout the southern colonies resulted in separate, self-contained plantations growing crops for export, rather than New England's small subsistence farms within easy distance of town and meetinghouse and easy oversight of minister and magistrate. As a result, southern Puritans and Cavaliers quietly compromised on an expansive version of official piety that was flexible in the matter of daily life and its pleasures. Throughout the South, dancing masters could come and go without official hindrance, and no bitter pamphlet battles attended either the introduction of the new Tate and Brady psalms or of regular singing, largely because church music was unimportant to the colonists. Indeed, one was more likely to find churches with no music at all in the southern colonies than in the north. In some rural churches, itinerant Anglican ministers read service, psalms, and sermon from authorized books only one or two Sundays a month to sparse congregations.

Visitors from New England viewed the southerners as religiously and intellectually soft, and interested only in pleasure. If there was a grain of truth in their assessment here and there, they largely misunderstood the planter culture. The southern gentry looked to British schools and universities to educate their sons, even after the College of William & Mary was established in 1693. William & Mary's classical curriculum was patterned on Oxford and Cambridge and aimed to educate gentlemen, whereas Harvard's curriculum focused primarily on the training of Puritan ministers. As it turned out, the planters and their sons were better and more broadly educated than the New Englanders. If Cotton Mather of Boston could read the Bible in its original Hebrew and Greek, so could his earthy Virginia contemporary and fellow diarist, William Byrd II of Westover. And Byrd, educated in the Netherlands and England, could also manage his plantation, discuss civil law and agriculture, appreciate music and literature, survey large tracts of land, and dance or attend the theatre without the slightest pang of conscience. The southern colonies were an outpost of English society and culture, with men like Byrd a landed gentry class.

EARLY COLONISTS

As early as 1517, two years before Cortés landed in Mexico, plans for an American colony were afoot in London. But nothing came of them, for despite earnest efforts, English entrepreneurs failed to establish a profitable trade with the natives. During the 1580s, a group of promoters advocated the resettling of urban poor in colonies that would produce goods for the English market. General James Oglethorpe would attempt a similar scheme in settling Georgia a century and a half later.[1]

In the spring of 1585, a group of colonists, all men, departed England under the leadership of Sir Richard Grenville. Tough and arrogant, Grenville kept a private ensemble of shawms and trumpets and usually took his meals aboard ship to their loud wailing. In June he brazenly landed at Spanish Santo Domingo with a show of arms to reprovision his ships. Luckily for the English, the commander of the Spanish garrison was that rare conquistador who preferred good food and company to battle. A banquet was spread, and Spanish and English feasted together to the accompaniment of Grenville's noisy wind band: "the sound of trumpets, and consort of musicke wherewith the Spaniards were more then [sic] delighted." The official Spanish account of the incident, dated June of 1585, noted only that the English had brought with them "many musical instruments . . . because they said, the Indians like music."[2]

The freshly provisioned colonists continued on to Roanoke Island in Chesapeake Bay, off what is now the North Carolina coast. But here their luck ran out. The soil was poor, and they made enemies of the natives. By 1586 the colonists had given up, and when Sir Francis Drake called on his way home after sacking St. Augustine in Spanish Florida, they abandoned their settlement and sailed back to England with him. In 1587, another settlement was planted on Roanoke Island, this time including women and children. Once again, hardship and hostile natives doomed the settlers. War with Spain delayed help from England, and by the time a relief expedition arrived in 1590, all that could be found of this "lost colony" was the word "croatoan" carved in a tree trunk.

JAMESTOWN

In December of 1606, 105 persons, among them thirty-five "gentlemen," set sail for America. Some of the latter had lost their fortunes and were hoping for a fresh start. Others, like George Percy, younger son of the Earl of Northumberland, had been forced to seek fortunes on their own by the English custom of entail, the system whereby land and title passed unbroken to the eldest son. None of them were accustomed to manual labor, which they doubtless assumed would be done in the colony by the seventy tradesmen, farmers, and indentured servants on board.

In April of 1607, they planted Jamestown in Virginia, beside the wide and navigable James River (named, like the town, in honor of the English king), sixty miles upstream to seclude it from Spanish raiding parties. Once again, conditions were harsh. During the following months most of the original settlers died; and though subsequent arrivals increased the total number of immigrants to 500, only sixty survived the "starving time" winter of 1609/10. Only the timely arrival that spring of English ships carrying more settlers and provisions kept Jamestown from being abandoned.

Sixteenth-century England had a vibrant musical culture at all levels of society, so most if not all of the Jamestown colonists, whatever their social class, would have enjoyed music and dancing. Those of the so-called Better Sort, from families of gentry and aristocrats, were accustomed to the best, for both royal court and aristocratic households maintained excellent musical establishments. In all probability a number of these particular colonists were themselves skilled amateurs. Settlers of more humble background would have delighted in dancing to the music of itinerant players, almost always fiddlers, who roamed the English countryside with neither the social status nor the economic security of court and household musicians. All the colonists shared in the rich heritage of English ballads and folk melody, as well as freshly written lyrics on current events and popular topics, cheaply printed on single sheets (hence the name "broadside ballad") and sold in the streets and taverns for a pittance, to be sung to popular airs.

The struggle for survival in Jamestown left little leisure time, so it is not surprising that scant evidence of musical activity remains. Captain John Smith remarked on the interest the natives showed in the colonists' psalmody: "Our order was, dayly, to have praier with a psalm at which solemnitie the poore Salvages much wondered." Smith also described the Indians' playing of "Rattels made of small gourds" at various pitches and flutes made from cane. Another settler, George Percy, wrote of the natives' reed flutes. Excavations on the site of the Jamestown settlement have yielded only a scattering of brass and iron Jew's harps, probably intended for trade with the natives.[3]

There is no record of music by early African slaves, the first twenty of whom arrived in Jamestown on a Dutch vessel in August of 1619. Before strict slave codes were enacted late in the seventeenth century, Africans in the southern colonies were often allowed to maintain some of their culture and their own music. In 1623, the British slave trader Richard Jobson wrote, "no people on earth [are] more naturally affected to the sound of musicke." Nearly two centuries later, the former slave Olaudah Equiano mused of his forbears, "We are almost a nation of dancers, musicians and poets."[4]

Slaves with musical aptitude took up European instruments favored by their masters, especially the violin, probably because white musicians were in such short supply during the early years of the colony. In 1620, there had arrived in Jamestown one John Utie, who had entertained the other colonists aboard ship by playing the "violl." Once ashore, however, he promptly abandoned music altogether for farming. Before the decade was out, he was growing tobacco, cultivating ever-larger tracts of land with the labor of indentured servants and slaves. Utie became a prosperous planter and in due course was elected to the House of Burgesses. Indeed, when in 1625 a political opponent publicly recalled his past life by calling him a "fiddlinge Rogue and Rascall," Utie indignantly resorted to court action.[5]

Amateur Music in Virginia

As planters like Utie prospered, society and culture came to be centered in their great plantation houses along the rivers rather than in towns. These planters, and especially their eighteenth-century sons and grandsons, became the colonial equivalent of British country squires, ruling over small, self-contained communities, each with its processing facilities and wharf from which cured tobacco could be shipped directly to England. Like his English counterpart, the planter saw to the health of his family and slaves, acted as a justice of the peace for his tenants, and represented their interests and his own during the spring and fall court sessions in Williamsburg, where the capital had been moved from Jamestown in 1699.

The usual planter's library contained books on law and medicine, as well as science, literature, and the arts, all ordered from London. His son and heir would be educated in England, at Oxford or Cambridge, or as a lawyer at one of London's Inns of Court. In the process, the young man would also acquire the manners and interests of the English gentry, including a taste for music. The planter's daughters would acquire a smattering of music along with other social graces: singing, as well as a bit of skill at the keyboard or violin. Keyboard instruments certainly appeared in Virginia well before the 1685 estate inventory of Thomas Jordan, which listed "very old virginals." Individual keyboard instruments were commonly styled in the plural, as a "pair of virginals" or "pair of organs." Flutes and oboes (or hautboy, as it was then known) also appear on estate inventories from the late seventeenth century; however, wind instruments were generally considered inappropriate for ladies to play.[6]

Itinerant music "professors" made a circuit of the plantations, giving lessons in music as well as drawing, dancing, needlework, and fencing, and playing for special occasions. In 1722, Robert "King" Carter engaged two violinists, Charles Stagg and John Langford, to accompany dancing at his daughter's wedding. But Virginia's musical culture was primarily and enthusiastically amateur rather than professional. During the 1730s, Carter, by now in his sixties, ran his 2,500-acre plantation with its 1,000 slaves and still found time to study law, literature, and music. His house contained a harpsichord, a piano, a guitar, and a glass harmonica, as well as violins and flutes. His teenaged daughters played keyboard instruments and the guitar, and his family and their guests often spent evenings rehearsing and playing chamber music. Carter even imported a pipe organ from England for his residence in Williamsburg, which he occupied only during the fall and spring court sessions.[7]

Wealthy musical amateurs regularly ordered sheet music as well as books from England. Many of them also subscribed to *Gentleman's Magazine*, published monthly in London from 1745 to 1755. Each issue contained one or more songs or instrumental dances by fashionable composers like Handel, William Boyce, Thomas Arne, and John Stanley. Dancing masters imported instruction books with both tunes and directions for the dancers' steps and movements.

In the 1740s, Henry Lee of Westmoreland had a number of servants as well as two daughters who played various instruments. The servants and daughter of John Tayloe II of Mount Airy regularly played chamber music. At one point in his life, a youthful Thomas Jefferson practiced his violin three hours a day. He and his law teacher George Wythe played chamber music with John Tyler (father of the future president) as cellist. In 1751, John Blair made note of a visit from John Randolph who played the violin for him. In Williamsburg for court season, Langdon Carter remarked tartly on the "constant tuting" emanating from houses along Duke of Gloucester Street.[8]

Social Dancing in Virginia

Dancing was a virtual requirement for gentry of the southern colonies, as evidenced in a resolution adopted by the College of William & Mary's Board of Visitors in 1716, allowing a dancing master the use of a room at the college until his own establishment in Williamsburg was ready. The college considered dancing, like fencing, an indispensable part of any gentleman's education. The Presbyterian minister Philip Fithian, a guest at the Carter plantation, described the visit of an itinerant dancing master during Christmas season of 1773, and noted with approval the "young persons . . . moving perfectly to well-performed music" as they changed from a formal minuet to country dancing. Planters gave one or two balls a year, lasting two or three days each, with card tables for those who preferred to gamble, and plenty of food and drink. Guests attended from other plantations. Those from nearby went home to sleep; those from farther away stayed at their host's.[9]

Men and women alike took their dancing skills seriously. William Byrd II of Westover (1674–1744) practiced dancing regularly as part of his morning routine. His diary, enumerating the most mundane details of his daily life: the food at his meals, his reading, and even his marital relations with his wife, contains the brief notation, "Danced my dance" numerous times. Elsewhere, Byrd makes several references to dancing, and to the fiddlers who played for it.[10]

Although professional musicians were sometimes hired to provide dance music for such special occasions as the governor's annual ball on the king's birthday and the wedding festivities for Robert Carter's daughter, and dancing masters almost always carried violins with which to accompany their students, most plantation balls relied on slave musicians. The *Virginia Gazette* regularly carried advertisements for slaves whose talents included proficiency on a musical instrument, usually the violin, as well as notices of runaway slave fiddlers. Slave records contain many such references as "accomplished black fiddler," and one notice, published in the *Virginia Gazette* of August 18, 1768, noted of a runaway, "He makes fiddles and can play upon the fiddle and work at the carpenter's trade." Carter himself owned a slave, "John the Waiting Man," who played the violin for dancing.[11]

Professional Musicians in Virginia

Although the musical culture of Virginia was overwhelmingly amateur and rural, it had at its core the professional musicians or "professors," already mentioned. They made the rounds of plantation houses teaching singing, various instruments, and sometimes dancing and such nonmusical skills as drawing, fencing, sewing, and needlework. These musicians could also be hired to play for dancing and other events, although that task usually fell to a slave. The circuit-riding music master was a welcome guest for his periodic three- or four-day visit, dining and socializing as an equal with the planter's family during his stay. Still, he was regarded as a tradesman by a class-conscious culture in which the planters considered themselves the equivalent of English squires in deriving their income from the land worked by their slaves, indentured servants, and tenant farmers. Like the English squires, the planters looked down on tradesmen and even merchants.

Williamsburg was the political capital of Virginia, yet even in court season, the population of this inland town did not approach that of coastal Charleston, the cultural, social, and economic capital of South Carolina. Virginia's planters spent most of the year on their estates where their cultural life centered. And in any case, Virginia's commercial hub was its seaport, Norfolk. As a result, Williamsburg lacked the critical level of population to support a core of music professors, let alone an orchestra. Even though there was a theatre as early as 1716, a performance in the 1750s of John Gay's popular *The Beggar's Opera* by a touring company had to be done with harpsichord accompaniment because no other instruments were available. By that time Charleston, with its St. Cecilia Society, or even Annapolis with its Tuesday Club, could easily have assembled a suitable ensemble of gentlemen amateurs and professors.

It is worth repeating that although Anglican churches in the South had none of the New England Puritans' restrictions on worship music, there was in fact rather little of it in Virginia's primarily rural churches. The three with organs and organists prior to 1750—Hungar's Church in Northampton County, Petsworth Church in Gloucester County, and Bruton Parish Church in Williamsburg—were atypical. Many if not most parishes made less use of music than the Puritans, in some cases even dispensing with simple psalmody. Instead a clerk or itinerant minister read a service from the Prayer Book and a sermon from one of the prescribed collections.[12]

Rarely did a Virginia music master succeed financially. Charles Stagg and his wife arrived in Virginia as indentured servants. Stagg worked as an itinerant music teacher, prospered enough to open a theatre in Williamsburg, and ended his life comfortably well off. But he was the exception, in all probability because of his business acumen rather than any special musical ability. Indeed, few if any of the professional musicians who plied the roads of Colonial Virginia were of more than indifferent talent. Most had been trained in England or on the Continent, but found it prudent to emigrate because they could not compete in the more musically sophisticated cities of Europe.[13]

Cuthbert Ogle was the exception who might well have become a major fig-ure in Virginia music had he arrived earlier or lived longer. Ogle had played an active role in the London musical scene, staging concerts in his Soho rooms with some of the best players and singers of the day. His success and prosperity may be inferred from the fine wardrobe, music library, harpsi-chord, violin, and other instruments he arrived with in early 1755. Indeed, given Ogle's success in England, it is curious that he chose to move so late in life. It may well be that health concerns had forced him to seek a warmer climate. In any event, he set up in Williamsburg and placed a notice in the March 28 and April 11, 1755, issues of the *Virginia Gazette*, offering to teach keyboard and other instruments and "to play in Concert." But Ogle died on April 23, 1755, shortly after the advertisement appeared. Six months later Peter Pelham made an inventory of Ogle's music library. Among the thirty-eight items listed in the collection of both vocal and instrumental music are cham-ber pieces by Rameau, ensemble songs by Purcell, and works by Handel, as well as Hasse and Giardini, two composers popular at the time.[14]

In the last half of the eighteenth century, Peter Pelham (1721–1805) became the main musical figure in Colonial Virginia. Son of a Boston printer and artist, Pelham had been apprenticed to Charles Theodore Pachelbel at age eleven and followed his teacher from Newport to New York and thence to Charleston. Pelham arrived in Williamsburg sometime around 1750. A year later he was organist of Bruton Parish Church, playing what was probably a small chamber instrument either borrowed or rented by the vestry. In 1755, Bruton's new organ arrived, and Pelham set it up. He spent the rest of his life in Williamsburg, stitching together a living from church and theatre, teaching, and playing. Even then, to make ends meet he took such civic jobs as supervising the printing of the colony's currency (probably drawing on skills learned from his father, an engraver and artist) and acting as town jailer to take advantage of the living quarters that went with the job.[15]

MARYLAND

In 1632, Charles I granted Cecil Calvert, the second Lord Baltimore and his heirs as "absolute Lords and proprietors," some twelve million acres north of Chesapeake Bay as a refuge for Catholics. Baltimore named the territory

Maryland, in honor of Charles's Catholic queen, but decreed freedom of conscience for all Christians in the colony. In late 1633, some 200 settlers under Baltimore's younger brother sailed from England. Of the 200, twenty-five were gentlemen and the rest servants, farmers, artisans, and tradesmen, and many if not most were Protestant. They arrived in March of 1634 and planted their first town, which they named St. Mary's, on the north shore of the Potomac.

By the last quarter of the seventeenth century, the population had grown to some 20,000 and Maryland had settled into a cultural and social structure very much like that of Virginia. Tobacco plantations were worked by slaves and owned by rural gentry with winter houses in the capital, Annapolis, which like Williamsburg remained a relatively small city. Ties between the two were close, and the *Maryland Gazette* regularly reported news from Williamsburg. Maryland maintained freedom of conscience, but as in Virginia, Anglicanism was established as the tax-supported religion.

Amateur Music in Maryland

In Maryland, like Virginia, most music took place in private houses. A sampling of estate inventories between 1746 and 1759, containing something over twenty-four musical instruments, lists one trumpet, one spinet, four flutes, and the rest violins, doubtless because of their popularity for dancing. Occasionally, professional musicians were engaged for balls; more often, slave fiddlers played for dancing, and here as in Virginia musical talent was an identifying marker for fugitive slaves. The *Maryland Gazette* carried several notices for runaways; for example, in 1745, "Runaway . . . a Mullato Man John Stokes . . . plays very well on the Fiddle and formerly belonged to Dr. Charles Carroll of Annapolis." A slave named Toby ran away in 1748, taking a banjo and a violin, both of which he played. A year later another slave named Prince was reported as having run away with a violin.[16]

Eighteenth-century Maryland gentry, like their peers in England and Virginia, enjoyed music as recreation rather than serious art. Their preferences ran to popular songs, ballads, and dance tunes. Apart from a few operatic airs, most knew little and cared less about the major composers of Europe, and it is unlikely that more than a handful paid any attention to the rich musical life of the newly arrived Moravian settlers just to their north in Pennsylvania. As the prominent Maryland merchant and amateur gamba player,

Henry Callister, put it in a letter dated November 5, 1745, "we abound in Fiddlers but most wretched ones they are. Some of the better sort have a little of the true taste but they are content if they exceed the vulgar."[17]

Callister had recently been guest at a meeting of The Ancient and Honorable Tuesday Club. The club had been formed on May 14, 1745, at the home of Dr. Alexander Hamilton (1712–1756), Edinburgh-educated physician and prominent Annapolis citizen. Membership was limited to fifteen, each of whom had a pseudonym. They met on alternate Tuesdays in the home of a member for dinner, toasts, and intellectual discussion. But the members' primary interest was music; all of them played or sang, and a few even composed original music. Hamilton was the club's secretary from its founding to just before his death, and his manuscript history contains some of its music.[18]

Clergymen played a prominent role in the Tuesday Club. In 1748, Reverend Thomas Bacon (1700?–1768) wrote to Callister, "we are so improved in good company & music that it is worth-while to spend an evening with us." Three years later, the *Maryland Gazette* for October 2, 1751, gave notice, "This evening will be performed, by a Set of Gentlemen, a Concert of Music, in the Council Chamber, for the Benefit of the Tabot County Charity School." The "Set of Gentlemen" was largely made up of Tuesday Club members; for the school was a project of Bacon's, and his associates lent their support in raising funds for it. Bacon himself played the violin, gamba, and keyboard. He also composed a number of pieces under his pseudonym, "Signor Lardini," among them overtures and a 1751 *Ode*.

As a young man, Bacon had engaged in a variety of occupations from overseeing a coal depot and running a coffee house to editing his own newspaper in Dublin. In the latter capacity, he had reported on the first performance of Handel's *Messiah*, performed in Dublin under the composer's direction the afternoon of April 13, 1742. The next year Bacon abandoned his enterprises and began preparation for orders in the Church of England. He arrived in Maryland in 1745 and in due course became one of the colony's leading ministers.[19]

Another clergyman, composer, and member of the Tuesday Club, Reverend Alexander Malcom (1685–1763), had published a highly respected *Treatise of Musick* (Edinburgh, 1721) during his years as a schoolmaster in Scotland. Malcolm immigrated to New York in 1732 to teach school; however, in 1740 he was ordained and became rector of St. Michael's Church in Marblehead, Massachusetts. Hamilton met him in Marblehead in 1744, and the two men's shared Scottish background and love of music drew them into an immediate friendship. In 1748, Malcolm moved to Maryland to become rector of St. Anne's in Annapolis, where Hamilton was a prominent layman.[20]

Professional Musicians in Maryland

Like Virginia, Maryland's churches did not acquire organs until the mid-eighteenth century. St. Paul's Church in Baltimore installed its first organ, imported from England, in 1750. The Reformed Church in Annapolis received an organ in 1754, and St. Anne's, Annapolis, in 1759. Thus, professional musicians in the colony could not look to a church organist's post to provide them with a secure if meager income base. On the other hand, in Maryland as in Virginia, the popularity of amateur music making and dancing created a relatively steady demand for the services of music and dancing masters, and a number rode the circuit of Maryland plantations or waited on the planters at their seasonal homes in Annapolis. Between balls, the gentry's dancing skills could be honed at "two-penny hops," so-called because young people paid two pennies to practice their steps under the guidance of a dancing master.[21]

A few notices appeared in the *Maryland Gazette*. Typical was that placed by one John Lammond in the issues of November 21 and 28, 1750:

> John Lammond, Musician at the house of John Landale, Shoemaker in Annapolis, Hereby gives Notice, That if any Gentleman should want Music to their Balls or Merry-Making, upon Application made, they shall be diligently waited on by Their humble servant, John Lammond.

John and Mary Rivers offered to teach singing and dancing in the November 6, 1755, issue; and John Ormsby of Upper Marlboro advertised himself as a violin and dancing teacher in the *Gazette* for October 27, 1757.[22]

Individual performers and companies visited Annapolis from time to time. From June 22 to December 16, 1752, a touring company performed *The Beggar's Opera* along with other ballad operas and plays, assisted by local professional and amateur musicians, among them members of the Tuesday Club. Charles Love of New York performed for the Tuesday Club in May of 1755 and was accorded the sobriquet "Mons de l'Amour" by the members. He played the harpsichord, violin, and "all Wind Instruments," and taught dancing and fencing as well. The eminent Philadelphia organist and harpsichordist Giovanni (John) Palma was in Annapolis in the autumn of 1756. Thomas Bacon wrote Henry Callister on October 26 of that year,

> We had on Friday & Saturday last . . . the most delightful concert America can afford. My Honr. the B Fiddle being accompanied on the Harpsichord by the famous Signr. Palma who really is a thorough Master on that Instrumt. and his Execution surprizing.[23]

EARLY CAROLINA COLONISTS

In 1629, Charles I renamed the southern part of Virginia "Carolana" and granted it to Sir Robert Heath. Other than a few small farmers who moved south from Virginia in the 1650s, no colonization had taken place by 1663, when Charles II renamed the territory Carolina and bestowed it on eight political allies, designating them Lords Proprietor. One of the eight was Sir John Colleton, a Barbados sugar planter seeking to remedy the overcrowding and land shortage on that island by settling smaller planters and younger sons in Carolina. Settlers from Barbados attempted and then abandoned a colony at Cape Fear in 1665.

That same year, Charles reaffirmed and extended his grant, giving the eight proprietors extraordinary independence in legislating, conferring tracts of land, and even creating titles, all by way of recruiting colonists. The charter also offered absolute religious toleration. Although Anglicanism was established, other Protestant groups and Jews were welcome. The *Fundamental Constitutions of Carolina* of 1669 went so far as to allow slaves the same religious freedom "as all others . . . to be of what Church or Profession any of them shall think best."[24]

It was two more years before arrangements to establish a colony were complete, but in August of 1669, three ships finally departed England. The expedition stopped at Barbados to recruit still more settlers and reached the Carolina coast in 1670. They landed first at Port Royal, then moved north to the mouth of the Ashley River. In April, they planted their colony upstream, naming it Charles-Town in honor of the king. Ten years later, the town was relocated to its present site on a finger of land at the coast between the Ashley and Cooper Rivers, an excellent harbor.

Charleston (as it was renamed in 1783), already the colonial capital, thus became the only major seaport south of Philadelphia, and the colony's commercial capital. Within the first decade, French Huguenots, German Lutherans, Scottish Presbyterians, and Sephardic Jews mixed with the English and Barbadians making the city diverse and sophisticated. In 1713, North Carolina became an independent colony. By the early 1720s, the original proprietors had given up their grants, and both Carolinas had become royal colonies.

Charleston's earliest fortunes were made in trade and shipping. But the merchant aristocracy was soon joined by planters. Highly profitable rice could be cultivated in the tidal marshlands, so most plantations lay within easy travel distance of Charleston. In time, a few merchant families acquired plantations, while wealthy and leisured planters maintained luxurious summer homes in the city, at first to escape the malaria season from May to December. Planter families took to remaining in Charleston for most of the year, leaving their overseers and slaves to cultivate the rice and later the indigo crops that enriched them as they developed into "the most lordly and most leisured ruling class in America."[25]

The city's unique social and economic situation provided an environment in which culture in general and music in particular could flourish at a level unimaginable in Williamsburg or Annapolis. Whereas the Virginia and Maryland tobacco planters' lives and leisure activities centered in their country estates, except for brief periods in Williamsburg and Annapolis, the social and cultural world of South Carolina's rice and indigo planters and their families centered in Charleston. Similarly, whereas Virginia merchants were concentrated in Norfolk, the colony's seaport, South Carolina merchants had sumptuous Charleston mansions alongside the planters.' Accordingly, while the Virginia planters lacked the occasion or inclination to associate with the Virginia merchants and like contemporary English landed gentry came to consider them social inferiors, Charleston planter and merchant families socialized and intermarried. As a consequence, whereas Williamsburg and Annapolis remained somewhat provincial colonial capitals, Charleston became a cosmopolitan city-state, with a stable and wealthy population able to patronize theatres and concert halls and to maintain a goodly number of professional musicians.[26]

Private Music Making

As in other colonies, a significant portion of the income earned by professional musicians came from teaching. From January of 1732, when it began publishing, the *South-Carolina Gazette* carried insertions by music teachers.

John Salter (d. 1740), organist of St. Philip's Church, offered instruction in keyboard instruments. His wife ran a boarding house for young ladies where they were taught music by her husband. John Keen and Henry Makeroth taught the French Horn, and George Williams the violin and cello.[27]

As in Virginia and Maryland, most gentlemen and ladies of the upper class studied music in their own homes as a social grace. While gentlemen with some proficiency regularly took part in public performances, ladies generally performed only for their families, friends, and guests. In 1738, Eliza Lucas Pinckney, the daughter of a British army officer in the West Indies, had moved to South Carolina at the age of fifteen. While still in her teens she ran her own plantation and was among the first to begin the cultivation of indigo as well as rice. Her musical activity differed from other young women of her class only in her serious and thorough approach to it. In 1741, the eighteen-year-old wrote her father that she had "begun to learn music with Mr. Pacheble [Charles Theodore Pachelbel, Salter's successor as organist of St. Philip's]" and asked him to order music books for her from London. She had also studied music theory, for that same year she wrote her niece, Mary Bartlett, explaining the workings of the tenor clef. It became her custom to spend an hour a day after breakfast on music, and wrote a friend that music was her "own darling amusement . . . which I indulge in more than any other."[28]

Public Music Making

Whereas most musical activity in Virginia and Maryland took place in private houses, Charleston's urban, close-knit, and cosmopolitan society fostered a good bit of public music earlier than in other colonial cities. Concerts were given in the city's Council Chambers as well as churches. Similarly, dances were held in the ballroom of the city's Customs House and Exchange, rather than in private homes as in Virginia and Maryland.

Urban musical life was firmly established by the time the *South-Carolina Gazette* began publishing in January of 1732. Notice was given in the issue for the week of April 8–15, 1732, of a "Consort of Musick at the Council Chamber for the Benefit of Mr. Salter" to be given on April 19. On October 25, yet another concert was given under John Salter's auspices. The term "consort" indicates an ensemble of instruments. Virtually all such concerts were regarded as social events to be followed by dancing; indeed, the concert was probably regarded by most as a prelude to the main entertainment, the ball. A notice in the *Gazette* for June 24–July 1, 1732, announcing "For the benefit of Henry Campbell [a dancing master] . . . a Consort of Vocal and Instrumental Musick" in the Council Chambers, advised readers that it would be followed by "Country Dances for Diversion of the Ladies." The notices contained no programs indicating the music that was to be played; however, similar concerts in London usually consisted of pieces by such composers as Corelli, Vivaldi, Handel, and minor figures like Arne.[29]

Ballad opera made its appearance in Colonial America on February 8, 1735, with a lost work entitled *Flora, or Hob-in-the-Well*, written by one John Hippisley and performed in the Charleston Council Chambers. The genre, combining comic drama and even farce with simple melodious songs in popular style, would enjoy a huge following in America and England throughout the eighteenth century.[30]

Gentlemen amateurs often took part in public concerts alongside their teachers, or "professors." During October of 1760, the *Gazette* advertised "A concert of Vocal and Instrumental Music" to be followed, as was the custom, by a dance. The notice continued, "Gentlemen who are the best Performers, both in Town and Country are so obliging as to assist."[31]

In 1762, America's first musical association, the St. Cecilia Society, was founded in Charleston. The Society supported an orchestra of professional musicians supplemented by amateurs in a series of well-funded, high-quality subscription concerts, often featuring guest artists from Europe. The orchestra recruited professional musicians, especially wind players, through advertisements in northern newspapers. Attendance at the concerts and dances that followed them was restricted to the Society's membership: 120 gentlemen of the city's social elite, their ladies, and guests.[32]

Church Music

Churches played a major role in Charleston's musical life, though not for worship music, which was restricted to the usual metrical psalmody. Rather, they served as venues for musical events and as employers of community musicians. The city's prominent churches, especially St. Philip's and St. Michael's, were especially generous to their organists. Near the end of the eighteenth century, one prominent musician reported that his annual income, a considerable portion of which was related to his church work, reached

£450, the equivalent of approximately $90,000 in modern purchasing power.[33]

St. Philip's had procured an English organ in 1728, supposedly the very instrument used in the coronation of George II. Whatever substance there may have been to that particular legend, the instrument is worthy of some note for having been struck by lightning twice in the spring of 1744. It nevertheless went on serving the church until well into the nineteenth century. St. Michael's had borrowed or rented organs prior to 1768, when a large instrument by John Snetzler, the finest English builder of the era, was installed.[34]

The *Gazette* for October 29–November 5, 1737, gave notice of a "Concert of Vocal and Instrumental Musick" to be presented on November 22, St. Cecilia's Day, for the benefit of Charles Theodore Pachelbel (1690–1750). Pachelbel, musical mentor to Eliza Lucas Pinckney, among others, was one of colonial America's most talented and accomplished musicians. Born in Stuttgart, he was the son of the famed German organist Johann Pachelbel. No information has come down concerning his early life and years in Germany; however, a superb eight-part setting of the Latin *Magnificat*, dating from that period, suggests that his talent blossomed early.

Pachelbel first appeared in Boston in 1730, where he took as an apprentice the younger Peter Pelham, later organist at Bruton Parish Church in Williamsburg. In late February of 1733, the authorities at Trinity Church in Newport, Rhode Island, summoned him to assist in setting up and playing their new organ. He stayed there until late 1735, and then left for New York City, where he gave at least two concerts, on February 23 and March 9, 1736. He evidently moved to Charleston shortly thereafter, for a record exists of his marriage there on February 16, 1737. On Salter's death in early 1740, Pachelbel succeeded him as organist of St. Philip's, where he remained the rest of his life, evidently enjoying prosperity and appreciation. Pachelbel's successors at St. Philip's during the eighteenth century, Benjamin Yarnold and Peter Valton, were also highly acclaimed musicians.[35]

NORTH CAROLINA

North Carolina enjoyed no musical flowering comparable to its southern neighbor in the years before the Revolution. By the 1650s, some 4,000 settlers had moved from Virginia into what would become North Carolina. The Albemarle region had enough land for them to live at a distance from one another. At the same time, its coast had dangerous shoals, but no natural harbor to compare with Charleston to the south, and was more suited to smuggling and piracy than to shipping.

As a result, North Carolina's planters had to rely on ports to the north and south that were hard to reach over bad roads and through the coastal swamps. The colony remained rural, with no town like Williamsburg or Annapolis, let alone a vibrant cultural center like Charleston. Edenton, established in 1710, was the largest community, with about sixty houses in 1730. New Bern did not become the capital until 1765 and Salem was not founded until 1766. In other words, North Carolina had no wealthy urban class to foster music, and rural musical activity during the first six decades of the eighteenth century was much like that of Virginia to the north.[36]

Musical records from the 1750s are almost exclusively of the Moravians, a German-speaking religious community generally isolated from the English-speaking colonists. The Moravians produced a significant body of music, as will be discussed in another chapter; however, the linguistic and social barriers limited its influence on the music and musical life of the colony as a whole.

GEORGIA

Georgia was settled in 1733 as a buffer between the prosperous colonies to its north and the Spanish in Florida. Savannah was laid out in 1733 and inland Augusta in 1736. The colony had been conceived by a former general, James Oglethorpe (1696–1785), as a refuge for London's poor. He envisioned an egalitarian but highly structured community where productive labor was encouraged and both strong drink and slavery were banned, all enjoyed freedom of conscience, and land was held in trust and not bought and sold freely. Some of Georgia's original colonists were skilled craftsmen; others were educated professionals, and one was even a clergyman. None were convicts or refugees from debtors' prisons, but all were down on their luck and had emigrated at the expense of the colony's trustees.

The colony's promise of religious freedom attracted the first Moravians in the 1730s. They were pacifists, however, and refused to take up arms against the Spaniards. By 1740 they had abandoned Georgia for Pennsylvania and North Carolina. The Moravians and their musical traditions played no real part in Georgia's musical life, except to the extent that they influenced the great reformer John Wesley. Appointed minister of Christ Church in newly established Savannah, John sailed with his brother Charles in December of 1735. A group of Moravian emigrants was aboard their ship, and John found he preferred their more personal hymnody to the metrical psalmody of his own Church of England. He translated some of their hymns into English and had them printed in Charleston in 1737. Wesley's preference for such hymns rather than metrical psalms contributed to the problems that eventually caused him to flee Savannah for Charleston and to set sail from there for England in December of 1737, never to return to America.[37]

Early musical activity in Georgia is difficult to document, since many of the official records of the colony, such as probate inventories listing instruments, were lost after they were shipped out of Savannah ahead of the British occupying forces in 1778. Among scraps of information that survive is an account from January 26, 1733/34, describing a celebration of the marriage of six couples in Savannah, after which all "danc'd the whole night long." In a letter dated February 10 and 13, 1734/35, Elisha Dobree wrote the trustees back in London, "Although we are a poor Colony we have had of Late a great many marriages and Balls." As elsewhere, music for the minuets and country dances was played on the violin. During the 1740s, the visiting evangelist George Whitefield felt called on to reprimand the Reverend William Norris of Savannah, among other things because "he played on the Fiddle."[38]

During the 1740s planters began to move into Georgia from South Carolina, bringing their slaves with them, in spite of the colony's laws. Oglethorpe's noble vision quickly collapsed in the face of economic pressures, along with the prohibitions against alcohol and slavery. In 1752, Georgia became a royal colony like South Carolina, with plantations on which slave labor cultivated rice and indigo. By the mid-1760s, Augusta and Savannah were bustling urban centers.[39]

In April of 1763, the *Georgia Gazette* began publication, and over the next decade its pages carried occasional notices of musical performances, as well as advertisements offering instruction in music and dancing, and musical instruments, books of marches and dances, instructional manuals, and even blank lined music paper for sale, the latter indicating serious students of music theory and even composing in the colony. A notice in the *Gazette* for December 6, 1764, offered for sale copies of John Gay's *The Beggars Opera*, immensely popular in England and in the colonies. An insert in the issue for October 10, 1765, gave "Notice of the opening of a Dancing School for the tuition of young gentlemen."[40]

The first documented church organ in the colony was given to Christ Church, Savannah, late in 1765. The November 21, 1765, issue of the *Gazette* reported that Edward Bernard of Augusta gave the instrument, which "was opened by Mr. John Stevens, Jun., who is the appointed organist." Although the instrument was in service in 1770, according to a contemporary witness, it almost certainly was lost in the great Savannah fire of 1796.[41]

Stevens (1720?–1772) appears in the *Gazette* for May 21, 1766. "For the benefit of Mr. John Stevens, Jr. on Wednesday the 4th June next will be performed a Concert of Music at Mr. Lyons long room in Savannah. After the Concert, Musick will be provided for a Ball." Lyons and his wife kept a tavern in Savannah, and the "long room" was certainly its ballroom. As usual, no indication is given of the actual music programmed. In 1767, Stevens opened a school to teach "young ladies and Gentlemen in the Theory as well as the Practical Parts of Musick." The school was to meet twice a week. Stevens had to have been a relatively gifted and proficient musician, for the next year he was called from Savannah to Charleston where he became organist of St. Michael's Church, playing the fine organ built for the church by the great London builder John Snetzler.[42]

THE SCOTCH-IRISH

The Ulster Irish—or Scotch-Irish as they are often termed—arrived by the hundreds and thousands during the eighteenth century, as did Highland Scots, especially after the collapse of the Jacobite rebellion and defeat of Prince Charles Stuart at the Battle of Culloden in 1746. Most landed in Philadelphia or nearby New Castle, Delaware. Some of the latter remained in the coastal cities, particularly those who had come as indentured servants and bound themselves to an urban merchant or tradesman. In general, this group was absorbed into the prevailing English culture. The majority continued inland through the Cumberland, turning southwest along Shenandoah Valley and the spine of the Appalachians, and continued on as far as the Piedmont region of South Carolina. In single families and small groups, they settled this backcountry, from Pennsylvania to South Carolina, far from the urban coast. Here they maintained a hardscrabble, lonely, and often violent existence, gathering from time to time for fairs and after mid-century for religious meetings, and hanging fast to their own culture and customs.[43]

Few written accounts of their music have come down to us. The *Virginia*

Gazette for November 26, 1736, took note of a St. Andrew's Day festival in Hanover County, offering "divers and considerable prizes for dancing [and] singing" and "fine *Cremona* Fiddle to be plaid for by any Number of Country Fiddlers." The proper folk of tidewater Virginia who noticed these inland goings-on were on the whole unfavorably impressed. Some of the women, one onlooker reported disapprovingly, danced "without stays or hoops"; and Philip Fithian recorded his disdain for "the incessant scraping of the Caledonian Fiddle," as well as the skirl of bagpipes to which backcountry militia companies marched. Although the St. Andrew's Day festival, commemorating the patron saint of Scotland, was repeated in subsequent years, no further accounts of Colonial-era fiddling contests have surfaced.[44]

CONCLUSION

New England, with its numerous towns, coastal cities, and concentrations of mercantile wealth, might have quickly developed a truly vibrant musical culture, had the Puritan conscience encouraged amateur musical activity and permitted theatres, public concerts, and other venues where professional musicians might earn a living. In the Anglican South, on the other hand, no such religious scruples against theatres and public musical events existed. But in general, neither were there the numerous towns, coastal cities, and concentrations of mercantile wealth. Instead, the economy was based on large plantations and small farms, with relatively few towns. Plantation society fostered a good bit of music making, but it was overwhelmingly amateur and carried on in the ballrooms and music rooms of private homes, limiting in a precisely different way the opportunities for professional musicians. Their single significant source of income was as circuit-riding teachers for the rural gentry.

The only exception was South Carolina, where Charleston emerged as a commercial and cultural center for both wealthy merchants and planters. Of all the cities in Colonial America, only Charleston fostered a musical life comparable to that of London. A number of gentlemen amateurs were proficient enough to play with the professional St. Cecilia Society orchestra. As for the "professors" who taught them, church and theatre, concert hall, and ballroom provided generous income opportunities to sustain a large number in ample comfort.

The Middle Colonies

If New England was the cradle of American independence, the Middle Colonies—New York, Pennsylvania, New Jersey, and Delaware—can fairly be called the cradle of American diversity. England laid claim to the territory between New England and Maryland; however, the English were slow to settle the area. In spite of its moderate climate and vast tracts of rich farmland, no English colonies were planted there during much of the seventeenth century. Instead, Swedish and German immigrants settled what is now Delaware and New Jersey. The Dutch colonized New Netherlands, with its port of New Amsterdam at the foot of Manhattan Island. They also granted large tracts along the Hudson to a number of *patroons*, wealthy planters who agreed to bring tenant farmers to work the land and protect shipping on the river. New Amsterdam quickly attracted a flourishing commerce, and with it a diverse and polyglot population.

England reasserted her claims to the middle colonies in the 1660s, after the restoration of monarchy under Charles II. New Netherlands was renamed New York, and the settlements that Dutch governor Peter Stuyvesant had taken control of not long before became New Jersey. Delaware with its Swedish colonies was granted to William Penn in 1682 as part of his holdings in America. Under English domination, Pennsylvania's combination of religious freedom and rich farmland attracted settlers from the European continent, especially the strife-torn principalities that made up seventeenth- and

eighteenth-century Germany. These immigrants brought with them their languages, religions, and love of music and music, making the middle colonies
a tapestry of cultural diversity in contrast with the overwhelmingly English
colonial culture to their north and south.

NEW YORK

The Netherlands declared independence from Spain in 1581 and quickly
developed into a commercial sea power. Although the established church was
Dutch Reformed, the country adopted a policy of religious and intellectual
tolerance, and cities like Amsterdam quickly attracted a diverse and industrious populace. These same cities had produced the great composers of
Catholic church music a hundred years earlier; now prosperous Protestant
merchants and their families took pleasure in amateur music making.

Like the English Puritans, whose religious views they shared, the Reformed
congregations of the Netherlands refused to use organs in their worship; however, unlike the English, who removed and even destroyed the instruments,
the Dutch carefully preserved old organs and even built fine new ones for
their churches. These instruments took no part in the churches' worship. Indeed, they were city property, and their organists were city employees, paid
from municipal funds. Their duty was to present public recitals for all the citizens before and after services. They played variations and improvisations on
popular songs for the pleasure of their listeners, many of whom talked and
strolled as they enjoyed the music.[1]

By 1625, the Dutch West India Company had set up one trading post, Fort
Orange, at what is now Albany, and another, New Amsterdam, on the south-
ernmost point of Manhattan Island, thereby securing the mouth of the Hudson and its trading interests upstream. New Amsterdam's superb harbor
quickly made it a bustling seaport. At its docks rode vessels from many nations, and in its streets and taverns could be heard a dozen or more languages
and the songs of sailors and merchants from many lands.

Dutch influence expanded to the areas of New Jersey settled by German
and Swedish immigrants. In 1655, they submitted peacefully to the governor
of New Netherlands, Peter Stuyvesant. The atmosphere of cultural diversity,
so rare in the sixteenth century, continued after the English took possession
of the colony and fort in 1664 and renamed it New York. Successive waves
of French Huguenots, Scotch-Irish Presbyterians, Dutch and German Luther-

ans, Jews, and others continued to enrich the cosmopolitan character of New York, bringing with them their musical traditions.[2]

Amateur Musical Activity in New York

There is little documentary evidence of musical activity in early New Netherlands and New York, both the province and the town; however, we can be sure that the colonists took the same pleasure in singing and playing as their compatriots in Europe and elsewhere. Although the Dutch had submitted to British rule in 1664, they retained their religion, language, customs, and culture, including their psalmody and vernacular music. The musical give-and-take must have continued in the taverns and public houses of early New York, as seamen from various countries socialized with one another. Nevertheless, the earliest mention of any organized musical event appears in a letter of 1710, referring to a performance, probably a private gathering, "at Mr. Brayton's."[3]

Amateur musical activity in New York was doubtless enhanced with the arrival of the new Royal Governor, William Burnet (1688–1729), in 1720. Burnet was a cultured man with a love of music, whose friend and traveling companion on his voyage from London had been the musician and entrepreneur, Stephen Deblois. Burnet was the son of the bishop, intellectual and diplomat Gilbert Burnet, and had spent his childhood in the Netherlands. During his eight years in New York, he enjoyed an especially close relationship with his Dutch subjects and even married into one of New York's prominent Dutch families. Burnet was transferred to Boston as colonial governor of New England and died shortly thereafter. The inventory of his estate included a number of musical instruments, among them a harpsichord and a clavichord, a courtell or bassoon-like reed instrument, and a quartet of string instruments. Burnet also owned a trumpet, which one of his servants played for official ceremonies.[4]

In the mid-eighteenth century, a British traveler, the Reverend Andrew Burnaby, described the citizens of New York as "habitually frugal, industrious and parsimonious. Being, however, of different nations, different languages and different religions, it is almost impossible to give them any precise or determinate character." The ladies, he noted, enjoyed dancing; but Burnaby mentions no amateur musical activity in the context of the twice weekly "turtle feasts" he describes. "Thirty or forty gentlemen and ladies meet and dine together, drink tea in the afternoon, fish and amuse themselves until evening." Amateur music making must have existed, for a number of music and dancing masters taught in New York over the years; however, that activity was evidently not as popular—or at least, as visible—as in places like Virginia and South Carolina. Not until the 1770s, after James Rivington had opened a music shop, could enough skilled amateur musicians be gathered, along with local "professors," to form a "Harmonic Society" that gave regular concerts.[5]

New York Concert Life

Public concert life of record in New York began with the arrival of Charles Theodore Pachelbel in late 1735 or early 1736. The *Weekly Journal* for January 12, 1736, and *New-York Gazette* for January 6–13 gave notice of a concert he had organized:

> On Wednesday the 21st of January instant there will be a Consort of music, vocal and instrumental, for the benefit of Mr. Pachalbell, the harpsichord part performed by himself. The songs, violins and German flutes by private hands. The Consort will begin precisely at six o'clock in the house of Robert Todd, vintner. Tickets to be had at the Coffee House at 4 shillings.

Pachelbel advertised another concert in the *Weekly Journal* for March 8, 1736, to take place on March 9. However, in general few concert advertisements appeared in the New York press during the early eighteenth century. A Mr. Quinn announced a performance in the concert room at City Hall on October 19, 1749, and Charles Love organized an instrumental and vocal concert, to be followed by the usual ball on January 24, 1754, at the New York Exchange ballroom. No indication was given of the music played at these concerts.[6]

The leading figure in eighteenth-century New York's musical life was William Tuckey (1708–1771). Tuckey had been a singer in the choir of Bristol Cathedral and clerk of St. Mary-le-Port in that city. He arrived in New York in October of 1752.[7] Like the British émigré musicians who would follow shortly, Tuckey hoped to combine a number of musical activities, among them church music, into a relatively comfortable living. He advertised his professional skills in March of 1754, warning that he was prepared to leave the city if the patronage he anticipated and deserved did not materialize.[8]

Such warnings were a common device employed by musicians and artists seeking a clientele, and Tuckey probably had no intention of leaving New York. The previous January, he had been appointed clerk of Trinity Church, sharing the position with the incumbent, a Mr. Eldridge. In addition to his work with Trinity's charity school choir, to which he added some adult voices, he also established his own singing school using the parish's facilities two nights a week. He and another musician, William Cobham, gave the first of a set of benefit concerts for themselves on December 29, 1755, consisting of instrumental music and songs. Evidently, the authorities at Trinity disapproved of his musical activities outside the parish, for the next November he was dismissed as parish clerk. Nevertheless, he continued training Trinity's charity school children and directed the music for the dedication of St. Paul's Chapel in November of 1766.

Tuckey continued to perform on stage for several years. He sang the role of Mr. Peachum in John Gay's *The Beggar's Opera* on New Year's Day of 1769, and organized and directed numerous concerts of vocal and instrumental music. Perhaps Tuckey's most significant project was the first American performance of a sizable portion of Handel's *Messiah*, consisting of "the Overture and sixteen other Pieces," which took place in a private concert hall October 3, 1770, and again at Trinity Church in April of 1772. Tuckey was also highly regarded as a composer. Nine of his pieces are included in several American collections published during the second half of the eighteenth century. Trinity Church burned, along with a large part of the city, in September of 1776. The city was occupied by the British at the time, and the church was not rebuilt until 1781. Deprived of a major part of his living, Tuckey left New York in 1778 and settled in Philadelphia, where he became clerk at St. Peter's Church.[9]

During Tuckey's years in New York, several concert notices appeared in the papers. In 1760, a violin teacher and dancing master, William Charles Hulett, who had arrived the previous year and was part owner of an outdoor "pleasure garden," the Ranlegh, organized a series of subscription concerts. The repertoire was typical of sophisticated English tastes: music of Stanley, Avison, Handel, and Corelli, among others. The *New-York Gazette* for May 24, 1762, gave notice of a "public and weekly concert of musick" followed as usual by a ball.[10]

Church Music in New York

New York's oldest congregation was the South Dutch Reformed Church. Its worship was in Dutch, and its congregation sang metrical psalms from a Dutch translation of the Genevan Psalter. In 1727, the parish became the first church in New York and the first Reformed congregation in the colonies to acquire an organ, presented by Governor William Burnet. Although Burnet was an Anglican, he had married into an old New York Dutch family and often attended worship at the South Church. His young wife died just before they were to depart to take up his new duties as Royal Governor in Boston, and that is probably why Burnet presented his small residence organ to her church, rather than his own Trinity Church. On December 27 of that year, the consistory of South Church appointed Hendrick Koek organist. Since churches in the Netherlands had organs—although no use was made of them in worship—there was probably no inherent bias in the consistory against the instrument. But Burnet clearly intended that his gift be used in the services, so they grudgingly complied. Koek would play for "two years and no longer," at preaching services but not at communion.[11]

Trinity Church was established in 1696, and although early attempts were made to acquire an organ, it was not until 1739 that a contract was given to John Clemm (Johann Gottlob Klemm), a German immigrant and instrument maker. Trinity's organ was installed in July of 1741, and the builder's son, John Clemm Jr., was appointed organist for one year. Apparently, the arrangement did not work out, for in December of 1743, Trinity's vestry wrote to London seeking an organist. John Rice was chosen, and he served at Trinity until 1761.[12]

Trinity's music consisted of metrical psalms from Tate and Brady's New Version. Like a number of urban churches in England, the parish used children from its charity school to lead the congregational singing. The arrangement seems to have worked well. Dr. Alexander Hamilton of Annapolis attended services on June 17, 1744. Afterwards he noted, "There is a pretty organ att the west end of the church, consisting of a great number of pipes handsomly guilt and adorned, but I had not the satisfaction of hearing it play, they having att this time no organist, but the vocall musick of the congregation was very good." Lutheran missionary Henry Melchior Muhlenberg (1711–1787) visited New York in 1751, and wrote: "The English Church people know how to sing very beautifully and acceptably because they have a fine organ in their church and have been taught how to sing."[13]

Little is known of the music in New York's churches prior to the Revolution. Most of the earliest Lutherans in New York were Dutch; but Lutheranism was not the established church in the Netherlands, and they had none of the organized support from Europe that German Lutherans enjoyed. Hymnals were scarce, and singing was poor. A letter from Lutheran Pastor Wilhelm Christoph Beckenmeyer to the Amsterdam Consistory, dated October 21, 1725, described the situation bluntly: "The people are not capable of singing a hymn properly, and upon several occasions they have stuck in the middle of a hymn." Not until the 1750s, when the New York church joined Muhlenberg's Pennsylvania synod, did things improve. A more-or-less uniform liturgy was instituted, and the German tradition of congregational singing became standard.[14]

PENNSYLVANIA

In 1680, William Penn (1644–1718) received a grant of land between New York and Maryland from James II, as a refuge for Penn's fellow Quakers. Two years later, he received an additional grant of what is now Delaware, occupied at the time by Swedish colonists. Pennsylvania's "holy experiment" permitted absolute freedom of conscience and permitted no established church. By the end of the 1680s, a number of Quakers and others seeking liberty of conscience had found their way to the new colony and settled in the Philadelphia area.

The English Quakers represented an extreme wing of Puritanism that frowned on any kind of musical activity. Quaker missionary and elder George Fox called on his brethren to "cry out against all sorts of music." In his pamphlet entitled *A Musick Lector; or the Art of Music* (London, 1667), Solomon Eccles, who gave up being a professional musician after his conversion, described as "Musick that pleaseth God" the soundless music of the spirit alone.[15]

Although Pennsylvania's Quakers officially opposed public entertainments, many leading citizens, Quakers among them, enjoyed music and dancing in the privacy of their homes. Preachers at the Quakers' yearly meetings warned against the dangers of music and dancing, but a dancing master could be found in Philadelphia as early as 1710. By 1729, one Samuel Pierce was advertising for pupils in the gentlemanly skills of dancing and swordsmanship among the officially nondancing and pacifist Quakers. Private concerts were being presented before 1740.[16]

Music in Philadelphia

Dr. Alexander Hamilton visited Philadelphia in 1744 and attended a "Musick Club" where he heard a "tolerable *concerto* performed by a harpsichord and three violins." But Hamilton also observed that in Philadelphia, "There is no such thing as assemblies of gentry among them, either for dancing or musick." He attributed the situation to the influence of English evangelist George Whitefield who had preached in Philadelphia a short time before, although it could as well have been the city's Quaker tradition, even though Quaker influence on the city's cultural life had weakened by that time. Indeed, the practical issue of military defense finally caused the remaining Quaker proprietors to surrender political control of the colony to the Crown in 1756.[17]

Actually, Philadelphia's musical life picked up markedly by the mid-eighteenth century, thanks to the large number of music-loving German immigrants who had settled nearby. In 1748, four years after Hamilton's visit, the Philadelphia Assembly had organized the colony's first subscription series. In 1754, a touring company from London performed ballad opera in the city for the first time. The January 20, 1757, issue of the *Pennsylvania Gazette* gave notice of a public concert on the 25th by John (Giovanni) Palma. George Washington's journal mentions another concert by Palma, given on March 25. A bit of musical doggerel by a young gentleman of Philadelphia, written in 1768, alludes to "Corelli, Handel, Felton, Nares / With their concertos, solos, airs."[18]

James Bremner (?–1780), an English music master, arrived in Philadelphia in 1763 after a brief stopover in New York. His notice in the *Pennsylvania Gazette* for December 1, 1763, announced his readiness to teach "young ladies . . . the Harpsichord or Guittar" and "young Gentlemen the Violin, German Flute, Harpsichord or Guittar." In the years that followed, Bremner counted among his pupils Benjamin Franklin's daughter Sarah, and Francis Hopkinson, signer of the Declaration of Independence. On February 21, 1764, Bremner organized a concert to raise funds for the new organ to be built for Christ Church by the German immigrant organ builder Philip Feyring. The organ was completed in 1766, and the next January, Bremner became organist, holding that position, off and on, at least until 1774.[19]

On April 4, 1765, Bremner had organized and led yet another benefit concert of vocal and instrumental music, this one for the charity school sponsored by the College of Philadelphia (later the University of Pennsylvania).

The program included music by Stamitz, Arne, and Geminiani, as well as vocal pieces by Bremner himself. The *Pennsylvania Gazette* of April 18 reported: "The whole was conducted with great Order and Decorum, to the satisfaction of a polite and numerous audience. Thirty Pounds was raised for the Benefit of the Charity School belonging to the said College." A series of concerts organized by one John Gualdo from 1769 to 1771 included his own music along with works by favorite composers of the time such as Arne, Handel, and Geminiani.[20]

Amateur Music in Philadelphia

Although public concerts by professional musicians increased in the years leading up to the Revolution, most musical activity in Philadelphia, as elsewhere, remained amateur. Many upper-class homes had music rooms. Gottlieb Mittelberger, visiting the city in the early 1750s, reported having attended a harpsichord concert given in a private house by "some Englishman." Reverend Andrew Burnaby passed through Philadelphia in 1759 and observed, "There are some few persons who have discovered a taste for music."[21]

In the area of church music, James Lyon's (1735–1791) *Urania, or a Choice Collection of Psalm-Tunes, Anthems, and Hymns*, published in Philadelphia in 1761, was the first of many such collections that would appear in America during the late eighteenth and early nineteenth centuries. A talented musician and 1759 graduate of Princeton, Lyon was teaching a singing school in Philadelphia. The year *Urania* was issued, he left Philadelphia to return to Princeton for his M.A. degree and a thereafter gave up music to serve as minister of a succession of churches.[22]

Benjamin Franklin had some interest in music, along with his numerous preoccupations; indeed, he composed a string quartet playable by amateurs only on open strings. Around 1761, he invented an instrument called the glass harmonica, consisting of a set of nested glasses on a spindle, partially submerged in water and rotated by a pedal mechanism. Touching their wet rims produced a quietly eerie tone. The instrument enjoyed brief popularity in Europe; Mozart, Beethoven, and other composers wrote music for it.[23]

The single most significant figure on Philadelphia's musical scene during the 1760s and 1770s was Francis Hopkinson (1737–1791). A lawyer by profession; a patriot and signer of the Declaration of Independence; and a musician, poet, essayist, and sometime artist by avocation, Hopkinson composed

Francis Hopkinson (1737–1791). American political leader and writer. The Granger Collection, New York.

music and participated in concerts with other amateurs and professionals. Around 1759 he set Thomas Parnell's poem, "My days have been so wondrous free" for solo voice. On May 28, 1761, Hopkinson and his friends performed "an *Ode*, sacred to the memory of our late gracious Sovereign George II. Written and set to music in a very grand and masterly Taste by Francis Hopkinson, Esq, A.M."[24]

A vestryman in the combined parish of Christ Church and St. Peter's, Hopkinson also published a volume of sacred music for use in the two churches, in 1763. The collection consisted of thirty-seven pieces, most of them standard tunes from British sources, but including two of his own anthems, set for two and three voices and figured bass. He and William Young also took on the responsibility for training some children of the combined parish in "the art of psalmody." Vestry minutes for April 3, 1764, recognized the two men's "great and constant pains in teaching and instructing the children." That same year, the Dutch Reformed Consistory in New York engaged Hopkinson to prepare an English-language psalter for use in its bilingual services.[25]

By the 1780s, official duties had forced Hopkinson to curtail his performing activities. Nevertheless, he maintained an active interest in music throughout his life. In the years before his premature death, by now a highly honored national figure and Federal District Court judge, he seemed most proud to proclaim himself "the first Native of the United States who has produced a Musical Composition."[26]

German Immigrants and Religious Music

Many of the best amateur musicians came as refugees from the religious strife in Germany. In many cases, elaborate music was a part not only of their worship but of their daily lives and culture, and they played and sang it with as much zeal as they farmed the rich land of Pennsylvania, where most of them settled. The majority of the Germans who immigrated to Pennsylvania during the eighteenth century were either Lutheran or Reformed. The two groups sang many of the same hymns, in the same language, to the same chorale melodies traditionally associated with the texts. In fact, they shared a common and fully developed musical tradition dating from the time of Martin Luther in the sixteenth century.[27]

Luther and his successors had established a body of congregational song for his followers, the *chorales*. Some were newly composed, but most were either familiar vernacular sacred song, secular pieces fit with sacred words, or translations of Latin chant and hymns. Texts were adapted or newly written for use in the new liturgy. Unlike metrical psalm tunes, particular chorale melodies were identified with the specific words sung to them. In form, the chorale melodies usually consisted of four lines of music, the second being a repetition of the first.[28]

The earliest groups of German immigrants, however, were not of the major denominations, Reformed or Lutheran, but rather of smaller, breakaway pietistic groups, viewed by most Germans in much the same way as the Quakers were viewed by most English. Among the first immigrants were a group of mystics led by Jonas Kelpius (1673–1708), a university graduate who knew five languages, dabbled in science and the occult as well as music, and who dreamed of reuniting the Christian churches. Kelpius had arrived in 1694 and after a brief time among the colonists of Germantown, had relocated his community of forty men, "The Contented of the God-loving Soul," to the banks of the Wissahickon River in what is now Fairmount Park in metropolitan Philadelphia. There the Hermits of Wissahickon, as they were known, grew medicinal herbs and watched through their telescopes for early signs of the second coming.

The community's services attracted many outsiders, largely because of their music. The group played several instruments skillfully. Kelpius compiled a hymnal, which he called *The Lamenting Voice of the Hidden Love at the time when She Lay in Misery & Forsaken*, containing a dozen or so hymn tunes with texts in German and English on facing pages. The English translations were made by Christopher Witt (ca. 1675–1765), an English physician, musician and organ builder, and convert to Kelpius's sect.[29]

The first recorded use of an organ in a church service north of Mexico was by Kelpius's Hermits at the ordination of the Lutheran minister Justus Falckner (1672–1723) in Philadelphia's Gloria Dei Church on November 24, 1703. Falckner's ordination service began "with a voluntary on the little organ in the gallery by Jonas the organist, supplemented with instrumental music by the Mystics on the viol, hautboy, trumpets and kettle-drums." The Hermits in the front benches intoned the *Veni Creator* and the *Veni Sancte Spiritus* "to the soft strains of instruments." The organ was certainly owned by the hermits rather than the church, and loaned by them for the occasion.[30]

Of even more interest is the Ephrata Cloister, a celibate community of thirty-five women and thirty-six men, established in 1732 by Conrad Beissel (1690/91–1768), a German-born Seventh-Day Baptist minister. At its height in the 1770s, the Ephrata community numbered some 300. It had its own printing press from the mid-1740s to 1790 and produced its own hymnal, as well as tracts, poetry, and for one period during 1777/78, currency for the Continental Congress. At the same time, the sisters of the order produced some of finest examples of hand decoration and calligraphy, or *fraktur*. The group also ran schools to which some of the leading Pennsylvania families sent their children. Like other pietist groups in Pennsylvania, including the Moravians, the men of Beissel's community refused to take part in the War of Independence; however, the buildings at Ephrata served as a hospital after the Battle of Brandywine in 1777.

Initially, the Ephrata community's music appears to have consisted primarily of German chorales and at least some parts of the Lutheran liturgy. In February of 1735, Beissel and his group took part in the funeral of Alexander Moek, leader of the German Baptist or dunker community in Germantown. There they joined with the "Hermits of the Ridge"—the remnants, such as they were, of Kelpius's community—to chant the *De Profundis* antiphonally.[31]

But Beissel was also gathering and writing hymn texts on his own. An early hymnal, copied during the winter of 1733/74, contained a number of his original texts. Benjamin Franklin printed collections for Beissel's community between 1730 and 1736. The largest collection, however—entitled *Zion's Fragrant Censer (Zionitischer Weyrauchs Hügel)*—was printed by the recent immigrant, Christopher Saur, in Germantown in 1739. Its approximately 800 pages contained 691 hymn texts.

By that time, Beissel had begun to compose music as well as texts. He also took over direction of the order's choir from Ludwig Blum, a singing master he had engaged to train the group. The Ephrata choir had originally consisted of about fifteen women singing in four parts; however, Beissel added ten men singing two additional bass parts. He used no instruments as far as is known. Over a period of twenty years, he composed over 1,000 hymns and anthems as well as musical settings of whole chapters of the Bible and two settings of the Song of Songs.

Beissel had distinctive ideas about vocal production and the effect of diet on singers' voices and ability to learn. He prohibited meat and dairy products and restricted the choir members to vegetables and grains. Jacob Duché

(1737–1798), assistant minister at Christ Church in Philadelphia, visited the community in 1771 and described "the peculiarity of their *music*" in a letter dated October 2 of that year.

> [T]he sisters invited us into their chapel, and, seating themselves in order, began to sing one of their devout hymns. The music had little or no air or melody; but consisted of simple, long notes. The counter, treble, tenor and bass were all sung by women with sweet, shrill and small voices; but with a truth and exactness in the time and intonation . . . The performers sat with their heads reclined, their countenances solemn and dejected, their faces pale and emaciated from their manner of living . . . I almost began to think of myself in the world of spirits, and that the objects before me were ethereal.[32]

Beissel set forth his theories in the preface to the community's 1747 hymnal, *The Song of the Lonely and Forsaken Turtledove* . . . (*Das Gesäng der einsamen und verlassenen Turtel-Taube* . . .), containing 277 hymns. The overwhelming majority of them were by Beissel himself, in addition to his foreword, prologue, and epilogue, and characterized by Beissel as "a field of flowers, grown forth of many different colors, and of various fragrances as they were produced out of the *Mysterio* of God." Beissel's musical system was idiosyncratic in its notation, harmony, melodies, as well as singing style. His hymns and anthems were written in four to eight parts, with women's voices predominating, much doubling at octaves, parallel intervals, crude harmonies, and weak progressions. He rarely used dissonance or changed key. The rhythm followed the accents of the text freely, with strong syllables set to longer note values.[33]

Ephrata's press could only print text, and music had to be hand-copied. Israel Acrelius, the Swedish Provost, visited the cloister in 1753 and reported:

> The younger sisters are mostly employed in drawing. A part of them are now constantly employed in copying musical note-books for themselves and the brethren. I saw some of these upon which a wonderful amount of work has been expended . . . When they sing, each holds a note-book as well as a psalm-book . . . looking into each alternately.[34]

Although Ephrata's music forms an interesting cultural and historical entity, and the surviving music manuscripts of Ephrata are among the finest examples of *fraktur* art, when all is said and done the community's peculiar music is significant mainly as an artifact of the era. Sachse called it "virtually the outpourings of religious enthusiasts, whose nervous systems had been wrought up to a high pitch by incessant vigils, fastings and an abstemious mode of life. . . . So far as is known, no one connected with the community was a skilled musician."[35]

Moravian Music

The most distinctive contribution to eighteenth-century American music was made by the Moravian community, German followers of the fifteenth-century reformer Jan Hus. A number of Moravians had arrived in Georgia in 1734; however, many of the group found the Pennsylvania Quakers' commitment to religious liberty and pacifism more congenial and moved to Pennsylvania in 1740, where they established a colony called Nazareth on land owned by the evangelist George Whitefield. Within a few months differences arose with Whitefield, and in 1741 the Moravians bought land of their own nearby and established Bethlehem.

By 1757, Bethlehem was enjoying an active and sophisticated musical life, fully European in its tastes, standards, and repertoire. Its music impressed the artistically naïve George Washington when he visited; but it also excited the admiration of the far more cosmopolitan Benjamin Franklin. The Moravians organized numerous instrumental ensembles as well as choirs of various sexes, but the centerpiece of their sophisticated music establishment was their famed *Collegium Musicum*, an orchestra capable of playing the latest in European repertoire.

Moravian church music was equally sophisticated and involved the very same players and singers. As early as 1743, the Moravian church in Philadelphia had two organs, and its music was attracting attention among the English residents of the city. The hymnody they brought from Europe had roots that antedated Martin Luther. The singing of hymns was a part not only of the Moravians' worship, but also of their daily activities. In the freedom of Pennsylvania, if not before, the chorale tunes were often played from the church tower in four parts by trombone choirs to announce an event, or for special occasions.[36]

Congregational singing was promoted among the Moravians as a sacred duty. Often the minister would begin a hymn as the spirit moved him, and the congregation and organ joined in as they recognized the hymn. Texts and tunes were matched, and on occasion polyglot congregations sang the same hymn in different languages to its customary tune. At a love feast held in Nazareth in September of 1745, a single hymn is recorded has having been sung in thirteen languages simultaneously, including several Native American dialects.[37]

Among the community's finest composers were Jeremias Denke (1725–1791), Johannes Herbst (1735–1812), and Johann Friederich Peter (1746–1813) and John Antes (1740–1811). Herbst was a pastor of the congregation at Lititz, and almost all his surviving music is for church: sacred songs and anthems for special occasions. Peter, an organist and violinist, left over a hundred anthems in addition to concert pieces and chamber music. Antes, American-born and a maker of string instruments by trade, traveled in Europe where he met Haydn.

German and English Church Music

Several Pennsylvania churches acquired organs during the early eighteenth century, before most churches in other colonies. For most German congregations, organs were a natural and necessary part of worship, and any delay in providing an organ for a new church was purely a matter of economics. Meanwhile, the parish schoolmaster might be called on to lead the singing. Choirs were also organized to lead congregations; and in some cases amateur instrumental ensembles provided support, with varying degrees of success.[38]

St. Michael's Lutheran Church in Germantown, Pennsylvania, had a small organ in 1742, possibly built by Kelpius's disciple Christopher Witt. First Moravian Church in Philadelphia had an organ by 1743, and an otherwise unknown maker, one George Kraft, built a small organ for Holy Trinity Lutheran Church in Lancaster, Pennsylvania, before 1744. In May of 1751, St. Michael's Lutheran Church in Philadelphia dedicated an organ built by Johann Adam Schmahl of Heilbron, Germany. That same year Trappe (Augustus) Lutheran Church in Trappe, Pennsylvania, bought a small organ from John Clemm, builder of the organ in New York's Trinity Church.[39]

The German Lutherans, Reformed, and Moravians considered organs an indispensable part of worship. To the pragmatic English, an organ might be pleasant but it was by no means necessary. On the other hand, it seemed the easiest remedy for indifferent congregational psalmody. Christ Church in Philadelphia had an organ as early as 1728. Even among Presbyterians, resistance to organs had begun to weaken by 1760. With the introduction of an organ came the need for an organist, and several professional musicians were called from Europe to take charge of newly installed instruments in larger urban churches.[40]

Nevertheless, the general musical situation in German churches contrasted sharply with that in other churches of the middle colonies. German congregations in Pennsylvania imported the best hymnals from Europe, and their organists either compiled their own manuscript collections of tunes or used one of the several published chorale books from Germany.[41]

Henry Melchior Muhlenberg, who was a practicing musician as well as clergyman, had arrived from Germany in 1741, as pastor of all Philadelphia's Lutherans. He oversaw the construction of a new building, St. Michael's, during the years from 1742 to 1748. Immigration made a second building necessary, and Zion Church, the largest auditorium in the city, was built between 1766 and 1769.

Muhlenberg went on to assume responsibility for other Lutherans throughout the middle colonies. His accounts of travels through Pennsylvania and New York describe contrasts in music among the various churches. Of one preaching stop in Pennsylvania he reported: "The English were amazed at our singing and almost went into raptures over it, for some of the people had fine voices and knew how to sing in harmony." But when he preached to the Lutherans in New York, the situation was quite different. There was only one copy of a hymn book, and Muhlenberg was forced to resort to the distinctly distasteful device of lining out the hymns, such as was common in the Puritan churches of New England.[42]

The situation was much better in Muhlenberg's own Philadelphia churches. The quantity and quality of their musical activity resembled that of similar large city churches in Germany. On the other hand, the music in the city's English-speaking churches, like those elsewhere in America and in most British churches, was indifferent for the most part. German churches in Pennsylvania often maintained parish schools, and the position of schoolmaster and organist were often combined in the same person. By contrast, musicians in the English-speaking churches of Philadelphia, like those in other places, were forced to cobble together a living from teaching, theatre work, concert management, and music merchandising. They supplemented these activities with a church stipend, for which they usually did little more than play the organ on Sundays. Anglican churches, unlike the Lutheran, rarely expected these professional musicians to make a strenuous effort toward training singers, or composing or compiling church music for the parish. Nor were such general musician-organists usually involved with ongoing parish education or ministry. Few English churches maintained parish schools, and in the colonies as in England, skilled and dedicated amateurs like Francis Hopkinson who endeavored to work with charity students were few and far between.

When someone like William Tuckey prepared a compilation or taught singing, it was simply another musical enterprise, undertaken in the hopes of adding to his income. Late in life, Tuckey moved from New York and became clerk of St. Peter's in 1778. He may have taken on some of the didactic duties, in spite of his advanced age; but he was well past his prime by the time he arrived in Philadelphia, and as far as can be discerned, he had no influence on music in the city.

As a result, whereas German church musicians in America identified personally as well as professionally with their parishes, most English church musicians considered their congregations as clients and Sunday services as but another professional obligation. They felt no special loyalty to church music or to the parish that employed them. They moved from one church in a given locale to another and sometimes back again, freely and with no hard feelings on either side, according to circumstances, convenience, or whatever the period of the contract they and the church had agreed to. Nor was the standard to which they aspired especially high; American churches had no cathedral music establishments on which to model their service music. Not until the end of the century, and then only in a few churches, did choirs in non-German churches attempt elaborate music, and congregations sang metrical psalmody well into the nineteenth century.

CONCLUSION

Culture and music were far more diverse in the middle colonies than in the South, and far more so than in New England. In the years before British settlement began in earnest, continental Europeans had established trading posts in New York and farming enclaves in New Jersey and Delaware. By the time England reasserted political control over the territory, a number of con-

tinental cultural and musical traditions had taken root. Moreover, the tolerant atmosphere fostered by the commercial interests in New York and the
Quakers in Pennsylvania encouraged more settlement by non-Britons, especially fringe groups like Kelpius's hermits and Beissel's Ephrata commune,
and pietistic groups undergoing religious persecution in their homelands,
among them the Moravians.

All three groups have a distinctive place in American musical history; however, only the Moravians' contribution was to be lasting and significant. Imbued with the best of the central European art-music tradition which they
incorporated extensively into their religious practice and their day-to-day lives,
Moravian ministers, missionaries, farmers, and craftsmen, and their families, were skilled instrument makers, instrumental performers, singers, and
in many cases composers of beautifully wrought, highly sophisticated pieces
of ensemble music. The Moravian archives in Winston-Salem, North Carolina, preserve a large amount of this music for study and performance.

Meanwhile, commercial New York's shifting population and Philadelphia's
quasi-official Quaker aversion to music did not encourage the development
of public musical activity in the two cities, at least nowhere near the level of
Charleston in South Carolina, for instance, until after the Revolution. Instead,
urban music was cultivated privately by amateurs, especially in Philadelphia,
where public assemblies and concerts blossomed only after the Quakers had
surrendered political control in the mid-eighteenth century. It was out of this
tradition of private, amateur music making that there emerged such figures
as Francis Hopkinson, signer of the Declaration of Independence and better
known to history and his contemporaries as Founding Father of the Republic and political figure, as well as a skilled and talented performer, choir director, and published composer.

6

Music of the People

British men and women of all classes on both sides of the Atlantic Ocean shared a common body of traditional folk songs and ballads. Wealthy planters and merchants along the eastern seaboard cultivated what they considered to be a stylish and refined musical culture. But they also sang the same songs, listened to the same ballads, and danced to the same tunes as illiterate laborers rural farmers.[1]

Many of these English and Scottish folk texts and tunes dated back to the sixteenth century, or even earlier. They were generally transmitted orally, though some texts were copied down in manuscripts, and a number were later printed, either in pamphlets called chapbooks, or on single sheets called broadsides. During the late nineteenth century, Francis James Child, a Harvard English professor, collected and catalogued 305 traditional ballad texts from the English and Scottish oral folk tradition, and assigned a number to each one.[2]

By the beginning of the seventeenth century, new ballad texts that could be fit to the well-known tunes were being circulated, sometimes in chapbooks or periodicals, but usually on cheaply printed single sheets, or broadsides, to be sold on the streets and in taverns. Such "broadside ballads" usually enjoyed only a brief popularity and were quickly discarded once a new crop appeared.

In America, some communities of British settlers remained culturally isolated from colonial times to the beginning of the twentieth century. Colonists too poor to pay their passage bound themselves as indentured servants. On arrival, their labor was sold by the ship's master to the highest bidder, who paid the their costs in return for a period of service. Once that service was complete and they were free, many of them moved inland to carve out farms from the vast tracts of virgin territory. Some of these poor English, Scottish, and Ulster Irish immigrants settled in regions so isolated and out of touch with succeeding waves of taste and fashion that for generations their descendents kept eighteenth-century habits of language and music.[3]

When the English dancing master and folk music collector Cecil Sharp (1859–1924) visited communities in the southern Appalachians between 1916 and 1919, he found the speech and culture to be essentially that of rural Britain a century or more earlier. Ballads remembered only by a handful among England's oldest generation, including about a third of the ballads Child had collected, were still being sung by both children and adults in southern Appalachia. Sharp also discovered folk dances that predated the country dances in the first edition of John Playford's *The English Dancing Master* of 1651. Because these songs and dances, as well as their performance style, were preserved and passed from generation to generation as oral tradition, scholars like Sharp were able to document them and capture them on early recordings before the end of the 1920s, when the arrival of widespread radio broadcasting and phonograph records ended the cultural isolation of the southern Appalachian folk.[4]

FOLK SONGS AND BALLADS

During the colonial period, the term "ballad" was used for any kind of traditional or popular song. In practice, some songs were really folk lyrics, generally shorter than the ballad, and involving the singer as a participant in the text. "The Turtle Dove," or "The True Lover's Farewell," several versions of which survive from the eighteenth century in both Britain and America, is an example of a folk lyric.

> Fare thee well my dear, I must be gone
> And leave you for a while:
> If I roam away, I'll come back again,
> Though I roam ten thousand miles, my dear,
> Though I roam ten thousand miles.

Other texts were true ballads, lengthy narrative poems recounting a story. These ballad stories were often tragic, violent, or brutal. Warfare and murder, thwarted love, seduction, and betrayal are common subjects. Ballads were usually sung as unaccompanied solos, the singer having no personal role in the story, but rather simply retelling it for his or her listeners. Such ballads served not only as musical entertainment for listeners, but also as a sort of fictional, historical or moral literature for uneducated poor people, many of whom could not read.[5]

The ballad "Chevy Chase" (Child #162) for instance, considered a favorite of the common people by both Benjamin Franklin in America and Joseph Addison in England, tells of a bloody battle between two earls, one English and one Scottish, and their knights, over the right to hunt deer in a Scottish forest (see Appendix 4, Example 4). The theme of "Barbara Allen" (Child #84) is a tragically futile love affair. "The Cruel Mother" (Child #20) encounters the ghosts of her children, whom she has murdered. To be sure, some ballads like "Lord Bateman" (Child #53) have happy endings, and a few are even humorous. In practice the distinction between the lyric folk song and narrative folk ballad has always been blurred. The term "ballad" can therefore serve as a general term for both narrative and lyric songs.[6]

Generally, the stanzas of a given ballad have the same number of lines and the same rhythmic pattern, much like metrical psalms. A large number of ballads are in common meter; indeed, so frequently is it employed that the term "ballad meter" is sometimes used for the pattern. Each stanza in common meter contains four lines, the first and third having eight syllables, four of them accented; and the second and fourth lines having six syllables, three of them accented. Unlike the strict schemes of the metrical psalms, ballad texts often allowed for flexibility within a meter. An extra unaccented syllable might appear in a ballad text, subdividing a pulse. In the first stanza of "The Unquiet Grave," for example, the first pulse in the last line is subdivided into two syllables.

> Cold blows the wind to my true love
> And gently drops the rain.
> I've never had but one true love
> And in Greenwood he lies slain.

Another large group of ballads were in long meter, consisting of four-line stanzas, each with eight syllables and four accents.

> A wonder strange as e'er was known,
> Than what I now shall treat upon,
> In Suffolk there did lately dwell
> A farmer rich and known full well. . . .

Ballad texts in short meter are rare. The four-line stanzas contain two six-syllable lines with three accents, followed by a line of eight syllables and four accents, and another line of six syllables and three accents.

> The fit's upon me now,
> The fit's upon me now,
> Come quickly gentle lady,
> The fit's upon me now.

A large number of ballads do not fit into the three regular metric patterns. One such irregular meter, from as far back as 1549 in the text, "My lufe is lyand seik, send hym ioy, send hym ioy," can be seen 150 years later in a popular broadside ballad printed to mark the hanging of Captain Robert Kidd for piracy at execution dock in London, in December of 1701.

> Oh my Name was Robert Kidd as I sail'd, as I sail'd,
> Oh my Name was Robert Kidd as I sail'd.
> My Name was Robert Kidd,
> God's laws I did forbid,
> And most wickedly I did,
> As I sail'd, as I sail'd,
> And most wickedly I did,
> As I sail'd.

This particular meter pattern appears frequently in early American music; for example, the popular nineteenth-century folk hymn text, "What wondrous love is this, O my soul, O my soul."[7]

Ballad stanzas were sung to a repeated melody, usually by a single voice with no instrumental accompaniment. A body of popular and familiar folk melodies existed to which ballads were sung, but the pairing of a particular melody with this or that ballad text was by no means consistent. Some ballads were consistently paired with the same melodies; however, many ballad texts might be sung to any of several airs. Conversely, a particular air might be used for a variety of texts.

In general, ballad airs were a distinct and separate body of melodies from the tunes to which psalms were customarily sung, although there had been some overlap in the late sixteenth century, and instances are on record in the eighteenth century of metrical psalms being sung to popular ballad airs. Usually, psalm tunes were in clear major or minor, in the style of formal music by the era's leading composers. Ballad melodies, on the other hand, tended to be modal (based on scales other than major and minor) or pentatonic (based on five-note scales, rather than the usual seven notes) folk airs.[8]

Broadside Ballads

The broadside ballad first appeared in England in the sixteenth century. Both in England and the American colonies, some broadside ballads were published in periodicals or pamphlets called chapbooks, but most were printed in large quantities on single sheets of paper, or broadsides, and sold cheaply on street corners and in taverns, where common folk gathered and socialized.

Essentially, broadside ballads, like oral-tradition folk ballads, were sung to familiar melodies. The broadside sheets rarely contained any music, but they often listed the tune to which the ballad was intended to be sung. Many of those tunes have survived in other sources. A number of major English composers in the late sixteenth and seventeenth centuries wrote variations on popular airs, such as "The Carman's Whistle" and "Fortune My Foe." Keyboard manuscripts like the *Fitzwilliam Virginal Book* preserve these variations, and the melodies they were based on. Moreover, many of the ballad tunes served for country dancing. Among other books, John Playford's *The English Dancing Master*, published in numerous editions between 1651 and 1728, and used widely both in Britain and America, contains a large number of ballad airs. And finally, many broadside ballad airs were fit with new words and incorporated in the hugely popular stage works known as ballad operas, beginning with John Gay's *The Beggar's Opera*, introduced in London in 1728.[9]

Some broadside ballads were printed versions of earlier folk ballads. Others were parodies of well-known poems, or those earlier ballads. Still others were either serious or comical love stories. But most broadside ballads were timely and ephemeral. They reported and commented on current events, religious and political issues, and other matters of popular interest: for instance, the execution for piracy of Captain Kidd in 1701, mentioned above. In a sense, broadside ballads were the mass media of their time. A ballad held its popularity until public interest moved on to a new issue or event, whereupon it would be discarded as new ballads relating to that issue or event were printed and sold.[10]

During the Seven Years' War (or French and Indian War), numerous broadside ballads were published celebrating British victories over the French. One of the best known, for example, was David Garrick's poem "Heart of Oak," set to music by William Boyce for the theatrical production, *Harlequin's Invasion* in 1759, and still a favorite of the Royal Navy. "Heart of Oak" was issued as a broadside ballad that same year, in commemoration of several victories over the French, among them the capture of Quebec.

> Come cheer up, my lads! 'Tis to glory we steer,
> To add something more to this wonderful year;
> To honor we call you, not press you life slaves,
> For who are so free as the sons of the waves?
>
> Heart of oak are our ships, heart of oak are our men;
> We always are ready. Steady boys, steady!
> We'll fight and we'll conquer, again and again.

Not surprisingly, both the patriots and loyalists of the Revolutionary era also published broadside ballads, often setting them to well-known tunes. John Dickinson's ballad "The Liberty Song," for instance, was written to fit the melody of "Heart of Oak," a deliberate slap at British triumphalism. It was first published not in a broadside but rather in the preface to *Bickerstaff's Boston Almanack* for 1769.

> Come join hand in hand, brave Americans all,
> And rouse your bold hearts at fair liberty's call;
> No tyrannous acts shall suppress your just claim,
> Or stain with dishonour America's name.
>
> In freedom we're born, and in freedom we'll live,
> Our people are ready. Steady friends, steady.
> Not as slaves but as Freemen our money we'll give.[11]

Other melodies like "Yankee Doodle," the most popular and long-lasting tune to emerge from the Revolutionary War, provided music for a number of broadside ballads, written as propaganda by both patriot and loyalist camps.

A new Federal Song.

Tune.—*"Hearts of Oak."*

COME, rouse up my hearts, 'tis for Freedom we stand,
For Washington's fame, and the Peace of our Land!
Then let not the Antics our Forces divide ;
But, *charge them in Column*, and fight side by side.

Then for LAWRENCE we'll vote,
And we know he'll be found,
Steady, Boys, steady !
Then drink to his Health, Lads,
And push the Bowl round.

With the cry against Law, they keep dinning our ears,
And think to alarm with an old woman's Fears.
But in truth my brave Boys, they have no other aim,
Than to tickle our ears, whilst they light up a Flame.

Then for LAWRENCE we'll vote,
And we know he'll be found,
Steady, Boys, steady !
Lets drink to his Health, Lads,
And push the Bowl round.

Altho' Master Moses has made such a pother,
And parted with one *Goose* § to take up *another*.
We'll shew by our Zeal, our Numbers, and Spirit,
That the Vote of a Freeman is given to merit.

Then for LAWRENCE we'll vote,
And we know he'll be found,
Steady, Boys, steady !
Let's drink to his Health, Lads,
And push the Bowl round.

'Tis in vain, that the Antics their Cunning employ,
Our Fabrick of Freedom to sap and destroy ;
We know them too well, to permit any Tool
That's fashioned by them, our Councils to rule.

Then for LAWRENCE we'll vote,
And we know he'll be found,
Steady, Boys, steady !
Let's drink to his Health, Lads,
And push the Bowl round.

Whilst our Merchants, and Lawyers, and Tradesmen, are bound
In a firm Bond of Union, we'll still stand our ground ;
Our Commerce will thrive ; and the Antics shall see,
That in spite of their croaking, we're happy and Free.

Then for LAWRENCE we'll vote,
And we know he'll be found,
Steady, Boys, steady !
Let's drink to his Health, Lads,
And push the Bowl round.

§ I was 'a bit' of a Mechanic once myself.—Moses Oration.

One of many broadside ballads written to fit the melody of an already popular tune, "A New Federal Song" is to be sung to the tune of "Heart of Oak." Courtesy of the Library of Congress.

DANCING

Social dancing was one activity enjoyed both in England and America by men and women of the seventeenth and eighteenth centuries. To be sure, some Puritan ministers on both continents were wary of "promiscuous" dancing—men and women together—and warned against "lascivious danc- ing to wanton dities." But most Puritans, like other Englishmen, considered dancing a necessary and even desirable social grace.[12]

Britain was firmly under Puritan control in 1651 when John Playford (1623–1686) issued the first edition of *The English Dancing Master*. His prefa- tory note "To the Ingenious Reader" makes a case for dancing with which most English men and women, Puritans as well as others, would have agreed. "The Art of Dancing . . . is a commendable and rare Quality fit for yo[u]ng Gentlemen, if opportunely and civilly used . . . and much commend it to be Excellent for Recreation, after more serious Studies, making the body active and strong, gracefull in deportment, and a quality very much beseeming a Gentleman."[13]

This first edition of Playford's book contained 105 country dances. Subse- quent books and editions issued through 1728 raised the total to 1,053 sepa- rate dances, each with a tune and directions for steps and movements. Playford's dances were widely reprinted; and between 1730 and 1810, over 2,500 dance tunes with directions were printed in America.

Country dancing was the fashion among all classes of British, both in Eng- land and the colonies, from the seventeenth century until the early nineteenth century. Americans of the Colonial and Revolutionary eras danced country dances at urban assemblies, plantation balls, and impromptu gatherings of hardscrabble backcountry farmers and their women in rural taverns and barns.[14]

A country dance usually began with a number of couples in a formation. In some dances the formation alternated ladies and gentlemen in a circle or square. In others, they stood in a single line. In most, the two sexes faced each other in two lines "longways," sometimes for four, six, or eight (two, three, or four couples), but most often "for as many as will." Gentlemen and ladies did a sequence of steps and movements, sometimes together, but most often by couples in turn. The first couple would execute the movement, fol- lowed by each of the other couples.

The directions for each dance were printed with the tune, using abbrevia- tions and diagrams. These directions were for the benefit of the dancing master, rather than the dancers. He would use the book to teach his pupils the sequence of steps and movements. A country dance could be done at various levels of complexity. Urban and plantation gentry who were prosperous and fashionable enough to employ a dancing master to teach them were proficient at the more involved steps and movements. Those of more modest means, to say nothing of the rural and backcountry poor who had neither the time nor money to spend on dance instruction, would have kept to simpler steps: walking, skipping, skip-step, and so on.[15]

Consequently, and quite understandably, the colonial gentry took their dancing seriously, for dancing skills indicated status and social position in the community. William Byrd II of Westover (1674–1744) practiced his dancing most mornings and then carefully noted in his diary "Danced my dance." Dancing masters settled in cities on the coast and traveled the circuit of plantations in the South even during the Revolutionary War. British officers took the time to hone their dancing skills and form, engaging the local dancing master to coach them.

By the mid-eighteenth century, fashionable balls usually began with a set of formal minuets, often led, or "opened," by the most prominent gentleman and his lady. During and after the Revolutionary War, George Washington, who prided himself on his dancing skills, was invariably accorded the honor of "opening" any ball he attended. These opening minuets gave the more cultured and refined guests, those who could afford to hire a dancing master to coach them in the latest and most stylish dances, the chance to demonstrate their skill and style, and to impress the company who watched before joining in. Philip Vickers Fithian described a ball he attended in 1774 at the Virginia plantation house of Robert Carter as opening with minuets, followed by jigs, reels, and country dances.[16]

Dancing masters carried violins to accompany their students' lessons and dances. Plantations in the South often kept slaves who were proficient enough on the violin to provide music for their owners' balls. In some cases the violinist would be located in a gallery or on a platform in the ballroom; in others he would walk about the floor among the dancers as he played. The dance tunes in Playford and other collections were unharmonized melodies in regular tempo with a steady rhythm, clear phrases, and repeating sections or "strains." Playford included ballad tunes like "Upon a Summers Day," "An Old Man is a Bed full of Bones" (or "Cook Lorrel"), and "Sedauny, or Dargason," the latter better known today as "Irish Washerwoman" (see Appendix 4, Example 3). The even more popular ballad air "Greensleeves" appeared in

Playford's fourth edition of 1670, though the melody dates from much ear-lier. There are also tunes that are clearly for dancing, like "Kemps Jegge" [Jig], "Adsons Saraband," and "Irish Trot."[17]

CONCLUSION

The musical culture of folk ballad and country dance was probably one of the longest lived in Anglo-American music history. Country dancing main-tained its popularity well into the nineteenth century (as may be seen in Jane Austen's novels, for example). Indeed, it did not fall from favor until the 1840s, when dances like the polka and waltz changed the ballroom focus to individual couples. Even at that, figured and group dances like reels and quadrilles held their place at balls until well after the Civil War. And of course, country dancing persisted in out-of-the-way communities far longer. Cecil Sharp observed archaic country dancing in the Appalachians during World War I.

Most folk ballads gradually faded from public memory as nineteenth-century America developed its own vernacular song traditions, except in those isolated regions of Appalachia where hardy men and women preserved much of the colonial and revolutionary Anglo-American culture. The folk ballads and singing styles Sharp recorded during his trip to Appalachia were living artifacts of a style that had disappeared, even in its native England.

7

Music at the Margins: Native Americans and African Americans

The colonists, with their predominantly British outlook, had little interest in other cultures in general. They were especially contemptuous of the two groups at the margins of their own culture: the indigenous peoples of North America they sought to dispossess and the Africans they bought and sold as slave property. As a consequence, the very sources to which we turn for our knowledge of colonial and early American musical life, early newspapers, for instance, have little to say about the culture or music of these two significant but marginalized ethnic groups. However, Native American and African American music attracted the interest of some chroniclers, diarists, and letter writers for what they perceived as its "primitive" exoticism. On the one hand, these accounts provide us little more than a sketchy outline of Native American and African American music during those early years. On the other hand, however, a number of things they describe can be seen in traditional music played and sung today by both Native American and West African cultures.

NATIVE AMERICA

Experts disagree on the population in the Western Hemisphere at the time of Columbus's arrival in 1492; however, there is no question that a large num-

ber of tribes inhabited Native America, each with its distinctive customs, language, and musical culture. In the next few years, European weapons, and
especially European diseases against which the Indians had no resistance,
wiped out millions of people. By the time white chroniclers got around to es-
timating the size of the Native population in the seventeenth century, its numbers had probably been reduced by at least 80 percent. Whole tribal groups
had disappeared along with their culture and music.

The indigenous peoples themselves left no written records, let alone pieces
of music. Early European observers of Native music had little sense of, or interest in, its cultural contexts or customs; they considered Native traditions
to be ignorant and superstitious. Accordingly, early accounts focused on musical incidentals, describing the observers' impressions of the singing, dancing, and instruments they witnessed.

Early Accounts of Native Music

Europeans were especially fascinated by the natives' dancing. Thomas Har-
iot's description of the Roanoke colony, published in 1585, contained an illustrated account of the entire Native community dancing in a circle around
"three of the fayrest Virgins." Similarly, observers during the 1670s and
1680s took particular note of the Natives' religious songs and dances. A member of Marquette's expedition in 1672 compared the Indians' dancing to a
"very fine Entry of a Ballet"; in fact, exotically costumed "Indians" figured
prominently in several seventeenth-century French ballets.[1]

Native instruments and their significance also engendered a good bit of interest and commentary by early chroniclers. The use of rattles was especially
widespread. Alvar Nuñez Cabeza de Vaca (ca. 1490–1557), one of three sur-
vivors of a 400-man expedition to explore what are now the southern states
in 1528, was given a set of medicine rattles by one of the Native tribes he encountered as a sign of respect for his healing skills. Such rattles, he reported,
"which none dare touch but those who own them," were imbued with great
ritual significance, and Indian "physicians" of Mississippi tribes made use of
"their rattling calabash."[2]

One of the illustrations surrounding Captain John Smith's 1607 map of
Virginia shows a circle of Indians with Smith around a fire. The Natives are
holding rattles. Rattles are also prominently depicted in other images of
Powhatan, and Pocahontas, and of a Native priest. Smith's *The Generall His-*

torie of Virginia, published in 1624, depicts natives dancing with rattles. Smith comments,

> [T]heir chiefe instruments are Rattels made of small gourds or Pumpion shels. Of these they have Base, Tenor, Countertenor, Meane and Trible. These mingled with their voices sometimes 20 or 30 together, make such a terrible noise as would rather affright than delight any man.

William Strachey's *The Historie of Travell into Virginia Britania*, published in 1612, describes dancing to "rattles and shouts" in times of hardship or celebration. The native "priests" carried "every one his rattle for the most parte as a symbole of his place and profession. . . . Their devotion is mostly in songes, which the Chief Priest begyns and the rest follow him." In 1705, Robert Beverly reported Virginia Indians dancing and singing with rattles as well as a water drum, the latter consisting of a skin stretched over an earthen vessel half-filled with water. Years later, John Long's *Voyages and Travels*, published in 1791, describes Chippewas in the late 1770s and 1780s giving a small rattle to condemned prisoners, with which they sang their death songs. An account of 1776 tells of natives in California dancing with rattles made of animal hooves and tortoise shells tied to their legs, "so that all this ring and sounds with the movement of the body." Far to the north, French explorer Gabriel Sagard stayed with a group of Hurons during 1623–1624, writing down some of their songs and describing their dancing to the accompaniment of tortoiseshell rattles.[3]

Native flutes are similarly documented by explorers and colonists. As early as 1540, the viceroy of New Spain wrote to the Holy Roman emperor and Spanish king Charles V, describing flutes played by the Zuñi. These were of varied sizes and "had holes for the fingers. They make many tunes, singing jointly with those who play." That same year, Pedro de Castañeda, chronicler of Coronado's expedition in what is now the American Southwest, described Pueblos' "drums and flageolets, similar to fifes, of which they had many." Women ground corn meal to the music of "a small flute." The remnants of De Soto's expedition, sailing down the Mississippi in the spring of 1543, were attacked by Natchez Indians in large, fast canoes. Having killed a number of Spaniards, they finally broke off the chase, celebrating their success "with clamor and clatter of voices, trumpets, drums, fife, shells and other noisy instruments." Smith describes the natives of Virginia as playing "a thicke cane, on which they pipe as on a Recorder." In 1609–1610, the Virginia planter Henry Spelman described native dances with alternating men and women in a circle to the playing of "pipe and rattle."[4]

Accounts of string instruments among native tribes are rare. In *The History of the American Indians, particularly Those Nations adjoining to the Mississippi*, published in London in 1775, James Adair recalled seeing a ritual instrument resembling a banjo but about five feet in length, in 1746. The shaman playing it held the instrument between his feet while a second man assisted with the bowing.[5]

Native American Music Today

Many aspects of Native American music described by explorers and colonists in early accounts are still present in traditional music. It is thus possible to suggest a likely context for the bare elements described in those accounts. For instance, vocal music and dancing predominate in Native American culture, usually accompanied by rhythm instruments, especially drums and rattles similar to those observed by early explorers and colonists.

Today's Native American cultures attach a spiritual significance to music much in the same way early observers recorded. Even recreational dances and songs have a symbolic and spiritual significance. Native American music is not abstract art, but rather an integral and indispensable part of the events, ceremonies, and social occasions of daily life.

Some songs are for curing illness; others are for success in the hunt or harvest. Among some groups, songs are not composed by mortals, but rather inspired or even given as gifts by the spirit world. As such they are received and transmitted orally, generation to generation, with special care for accuracy. Some cultures consider particular songs the property of a particular family and forbidden to outsiders.[6]

Dance remains an integral part of Native American music. Percussion instruments are played along with the dancing to emphasize the rhythms. Rattles are especially common and may be either shaken in rhythm or swung in an arc to maintain a continuous rushing sound. Dancers often wear rattles on their legs to emphasize the rhythm as they dance. Drums are also common to Native American cultures. There are several types, some with wood or pottery bodies, and others containing water to keep the head wet and taut. Sizes vary from small hand drums to large floor and hanging drums. Some large drums are played by more than one person at a time. String instruments are relatively rare; however, numerous cultures employ flutes of various types, usually played in a meditative, free rhythm solo, or used to double or ornament a sung melody.[7]

Native Americans and European Music

Whether they thought of music conveying spiritual power or simply because of an affinity for it, American Indians quickly picked up bits of European music from the whites with whom they came in contact. The earliest recorded instance of English music in North America dates to the summer of 1579. Sir Francis Drake's vessel, the *Golden Hinde*, had been beached for repairs in California, and the expedition's chaplain, Francis Fletcher, would later report how fascinated the local natives were by the Englishmen's psalmody: "They took such pleasure in our singing of psalmes, that whensoever they resorted to us . . . they entreated that we should sing." Marin Mersenne's highly influential *Harmonie Universelle* (1636) included two of the Huron melodies written down by Gabriel Sagard in 1632. At the same time, Mersenne observed that the Indians were singing songs they had learned from French fur traders.[8]

Occasionally, music served a precautionary purpose for the Indians. During the sixteenth century, the Natives along the Florida coast used particular melodies to distinguish between the methodical and cruel Spaniards and the gentler French who enjoyed generally good relations with the Native Americans. Local tribes had learned some of the French Huguenot psalm tunes by rote and for years sang them to whites they encountered to ascertain whether the newcomers were French or the more dangerous Spanish.

In general, the British colonists had no real interest in converting the Natives or incorporating them into a social structure, as the Spanish had in Central and South America. Nevertheless, there were a number of missionary efforts by individual clergy. During the 1760s, Eleazar Wheelock, working in Connecticut, taught his Native congregation to sing psalmody in parts. At about the same time, a Montauk Indian covert and missionary, David Fowler, was teaching psalmody to the Oneidas in upstate New York. In 1774, Samson Occum, another Native convert and missionary, published a compilation of hymn texts, including his own poetry along with that of Watts and Wesley.[9]

AFRICANS IN AMERICA

The Portuguese had set up trading forts on the west coast of Africa as early as the fifteenth century. However, it was the discovery of America that led to the mushrooming of an Atlantic slave trade, for neither indigenous Native Americans nor Europeans were able to withstand the rigors of working the mines and fields of Spanish America. By the late sixteenth century, slave traders from a number of European nations were plying the seas between West Africa and the Americas.

The first recorded sale of slaves in North America occurred in August of 1619, when a Dutch vessel dropped anchor at Jamestown. For some years, Africans were regarded as indentured servants, and freed after a set number of years' service. As late as the 1650s, blacks were being emancipated after a period of servitude; however, during the 1660s, the English colonies, influenced by the slave codes of the Caribbean sugar planters on Barbados, legislated a permanent state of slavery for Africans.

Over the next two centuries or more, the Atlantic slave trade removed large numbers of Africa's youth. The traffic engendered tribal warfare solely to take captives for sale, dislocated and displaced ethnic groups, and wiped out whole cultures. Although Britain outlawed the slave trade in 1807 and used its formidable navy to suppress the traffic by other nations over the next few decades, the Atlantic slave trade did not come to an end, once and for all, until 1883 when Argentina and Brazil finally ceased importing human chattel.

African Music

Africa's wide expanse south of the Sahara Desert includes a range of languages and cultures with a great deal of musical diversity. Nevertheless, some characteristics are common to many traditions. Although there are numerous differences among the musics of various cultures, certain common musical characteristics may be distinguished, many of which appear in early accounts of slaves' music.[10]

Like Native Americans, many African cultures consider the creation of music to be supernaturally inspired, a message from the spirit world that is often received in a dream. Once composed, pieces are passed down aurally.

Because there are no authoritative written versions, improvisation is freely practiced and existing pieces may be recomposed into a new ones.

In African cultures, music is an accompaniment to the routines and passages of life. Children learn of their traditions and mark their coming of age through songs. Music sets the pace for labor, glorifies rulers, accompanies prayer and praise, and celebrates a successful harvest or hunt. Music is also a tool of practical communication, and its character may be closely tied to speech. Talking drums, for example, imitate vocal inflections by the manner in which they are struck and the tension on the cords holding their drumheads.[11]

Vocal music, usually accompanied by dancing, predominates in all African cultures, and instrumental pieces are frequently derived from songs. A song may be strophic—that is, it may consist of stanzas of text sung to a repeated melody—or it may be declamatory, sung line by line, often in free rhythm, with pauses in between. An accompanying instrument may play a repeating figure, or ostinato, even during the pauses. In general, group vocal music is responsorial, or call-and-response, alternating lines, or "call," by the leader or soloist and responses by the group, either with or without accompaniment.

African dance and music are inseparably linked. Dancing tends to be dramatic and symbolic, active and highly gestured. Dancers may accompany themselves on drums, rattles, or even wind instruments, or they may be accompanied by instruments, the singing of a repeated melodic pattern, or the simple clapping of hands. Complex rhythms and rhythmic variety are among the most striking traits of African music—in contrast with Native American music, in which rhythms tend to be simple and regular. A given piece of African music may contain several independent rhythmic lines and cross rhythms.[12]

Instruments and Ensembles

In general, African music makes use of a variety of instruments. Percussion instruments are especially prominent and include rattles of metal, gourd, skins, wood, or shells; as well as clappers, rhythm sticks, slit and log drums, and bells. Wood-keyed xylophones in a variety of sizes and configurations are a prominent feature in African music of many cultures. The instrument is widely used, both as a solo instrument and in ensembles. Indeed, sometimes two or more performers play the same instrument simultaneously. The *kalimba* or *mbira*, sometimes referred to as the "thumb piano," is a distinctively African instrument. It consists of a varying number of narrow metal tongues fastened to a resonating board, gourd, or wood box that are snapped with the fingers of both hands to create repeating melodies and rhythms.

A number of drums in a variety of shapes and sizes are used not only as musical instruments, but also to communicate over long distances. Drum bodies may be made of wood, gourd, or clay; and barrel, conical, goblet, and waisted shapes are common. Drums may be double-headed or single-headed, with open or closed bottoms. Heads may be tacked or laced to the body. Pitch and timbre may be varied by striking different points on the drumhead with different parts of the hand, or by tightening or loosening laces that maintain the head's tension. Drums may be struck with the hand or with sticks; employed singly, in pairs, or in tuned sets requiring two or more players. Individual dancers sometimes carry small hand drums to accompany themselves.

African music also employs string instruments, both plucked and bowed. These include zithers, lutes, and viols with two to five strings, and harps and lyres with five or more strings in various sizes and shapes. Wind instruments include flutes of bamboo, cane, wood, clay, and occasionally even metal pipe. Flutes may have as few as two holes, but three to six holes are more common. They may be played alone, in groups, or along with other instruments and with voices. Reed instruments are generally found in areas with strong Arab- and Muslim-influenced cultures, but trumpets and horns made of elephant tusk, wood, or gourd are common everywhere.[13]

African American Music

American slaves came from a number of African tribal traditions, none of which were of the slightest interest to their white overlords, who considered African culture, like Native American culture, worthless. Indeed, the whites took time to "season" newly arrived slaves so they might forget their former lives and accept their state of permanent servitude. Although aspects of African culture managed to survive seasoning, over the years specific and distinctive African tribal customs largely blended into a new African American culture.

Slaves adapted African musical practices to their American existence. African call-and-response style was carried over into several aspects of their daily life. The familiar pattern of a solo leader singing short one-line stanzas or "call," and the group singing a refrain or "response" after each such call found its way into the slaves' distinctive style of Christian worship and into the work songs that drivers and the slave gangs themselves used to coordinate the effort and exertion required for particular group tasks.[14]

Africans also carried their love of dancing into captivity, and it became their only group recreation. Aboard slave ships, captains compelled their often unwilling captives to dance on deck as exercise. Many vessels carried both African and European instruments to accompany the dancing. Mid-seventeenth-century slaves in the Antilles sang and danced for hours to the playing of an upright drum and rattles. Many whites enjoyed watching and even joined in the dancing on occasion. Some of the more thoughtful among them, however, worried that such occasions presented slaves with an opportunity to plot or attempt insurrection. As early as 1654, planters on the Caribbean island of Martinique moved to curtail slave gatherings; in 1678 they chastised one of their number for allowing drums and dancing at a slave wedding. French and Spanish planters in Louisiana had the same concerns; however, they generally allowed their slaves to continue gathering and dancing to the sound of drums and an African instrument with four strings and a gourd body, a precursor of the banjo.[15]

Clergymen in seventeenth- and eighteenth-century Virginia and South Carolina remarked disapprovingly on similar slave dances held on Sundays, the only day the blacks were allowed for recreation. On January 30, 1774, Philip Fithian, Presbyterian clergyman and private tutor to the Carter children on their father's Virginia plantation, noted in his diary, "This evening the Negroes collected themselves into the School-Room & began to . . . dance. I went among them, *Ben & Harry* [Carter] were in the company—Harry was dancing with his Coat off—I dispersed them however, immediately." On May 29 of the same year another Virginian, Nicholas Cresswell, "went to see a Negro Ball . . . Dancing to a Banjo," which he described as "a Gourd . . . with only four strings." In Albany, New York, during the same period, black slaves celebrated well into the night a late spring holiday they called "Pinkster" (from *Pfingsten*, Dutch for Pentecost), dancing to the pounding of a drum.[16]

Most Europeans were quick to acknowledge—indeed, to stereotype—what they perceived to be Africans' special affinity for music. As early as 1623, the English sea captain and slave trader Richard Jobson wrote of the West Africans, "[N]o people on earth [are] more naturally affected to the sound of musicke." Jobson goes on to describe the xylophone, terming it "their most principall instrument." Olaudah Equiano, a former slave living in Britain, wrote of his fellow Africans, "We are almost a nation of dancers, musicians and poets."[17]

Many owners encouraged their slaves' musical talents. Thomas Jefferson wrote, "[Blacks] are more generally gifted than the whites with accurate ears for tune and time." Several masters had their slaves taught to play European instruments, especially the violin, which was favored for dancing by whites. Such proficiency offered a slave respite from field labor and at the same time increased his value to his owner. Advertisements offering slaves for sale or giving notice of runaways made prominent mention of any musical accomplishment. A notice in the *New-York Gazette-Post-Boy* of June 21, 1748, offered "A Negro Indian Manslave, about forty years of age, well known in town, being a fiddler"; and a similar insert in the *South-Carolina Gazette* for April 19, 1770, sought the return of a runaway named "CAESAR . . . plays well on the French Horn."[18]

Black Christianity

In the south, conversion to Christianity among African Americans increased noticeably during the revivals of the Great Awakening that began in the 1740s. Black preachers worked effectively among the slaves and with little white opposition, at least for a time. As late as the 1790s, slaves were reported to walk as far as twenty miles to attend religious "praise" meetings. In many places, this religious tide suppressed the slaves' Sunday recreational gatherings, while channeling some aspects of those gatherings into religious activities. Left to their own devices and worshipping by themselves, they turned to the African call-and-response song and to their accustomed dancing, restructuring it to express their new faith.[19]

White clergy were especially put off by one of the blacks' most distinctive religious practices, the so-called ring shout. John Fanning Watson, a white Methodist, provided one of the earliest descriptions of a ring shout, which he witnessed at a camp meeting in 1817. Some of the blacks moved round and round counterclockwise in a circle as others in the group sang

> short scraps of disjointed affirmations, pledges or prayers, length-
> ened out with long repetitive choruses. . . . With every word so

sung, they have a sinking of one or [the] other leg alternately, producing an audible sound of the feet at every step. . . . [Others,
seated,] strike the sounds alternately on each thigh.[20]

Other blacks, especially in the North, attended services along with, but separated from, whites and learned to sing traditional psalmody. Delighted by
the sound of black voices singing Watts's psalms, the Reverend Samuel Davis
rhapsodized, "The Negroes above all Human Species that I ever knew have
an Ear for Musick."[21]

Indeed, several Africans developed a special skill for psalmody. Against the
prevailing tide of racism, a number of black singing masters taught schools
for whites in the eighteenth century. One such African American, known only
as "Frank the Negro," had been a pupil of the white singing master Andrew
Law. He went on to establish himself in New York during the 1780s, and Law
ruefully acknowledged his former disciple to be a formidable competitor. Another African singing master, Newport Gardner (1746–1826), had arrived in
Newport as a slave around 1760. His owners enrolled him one of in Law's
singing schools, and he became skilled as both a singer and composer. A win-
ning lottery ticket enabled Gardner to buy his freedom in 1791, and he opened
his own singing school, where he taught whites and blacks with the same demanding discipline. He became a deacon in the Congregational church and
at age eighty returned as a missionary to Africa, where he died shortly after
his arrival.[22]

CONCLUSION

Relatively little can be known with certainty about the actual music of Native Americans and African Americans during the Colonial era. Nevertheless,
it is clear that music played an important role in the day-to-day lives of both
groups. Most Colonial-era Native American cultures had neither written
records nor written music; accordingly, what little information there is must
be gleaned from accounts by white explorers and colonists. These accounts
focus for the most part on the Native Americans' dancing and on their musical instruments.

African Americans have figured in America's musical life from their first
arrival in America as slaves. Africans brought with them distinctive African

musical practices, especially the "call-and-response" style of singing and their dancing. As with the Native Americans, the Africans' dancing was of particular interest to white observers. Whites regarded blacks as having a special aptitude for music. As a result, many slaves were given training on the violin so that they could play for their masters' dancing or be rented out to play for other whites. In the north, a few slaves became singing masters and taught schools for whites.

8

The Revolutionary Period

In some ways, the basic pattern of musical activity continued during the Revolution much the same as it had been in prior years. If anything, the influence of the singing school movement grew as singing masters ranged far and wide, from Massachusetts throughout New England and into the Middle and Southern Colonies during the 1770s and 1780s. The classes they trained and left behind stayed together to form choirs, rather than returning to their old places to lead congregational singing. As for the singing masters themselves, the Revolutionary generation that included men like William Billings, Daniel Reed, and Andrew Law had begun composing their own music, rather than simply compiling music from English collections. The singing masters had evolved into composers, or "tunesmiths," as they are often called.

Private music making among the gentry also seems to have carried on much as before, except, of course, in such battle zones as the Carolinas during 1780 and 1781. Even as they struggled for independence from England, most of the colonists remained English in their cultural outlook. If, as one scholar has observed, eighteenth-century America had no musicians of a stature equivalent to painters like John Singleton Copley, that ought not to surprise us. It simply reflected the contemporary English tendency to value the arts in proportion to their economic usefulness.[1]

Music was generally regarded as entertainment or a popular amateur pastime, whereas painting, for instance, was considered a serious professional craft. Portraits were in demand as tangible possessions and genealogical icons, so to speak, for prominent families both in England and America. Moreover, the eighteenth century had a keen sense of history. Letters of men like John Adams and Thomas Jefferson show how concerned they were about their image for posterity. Consequently, even moderately skilled professional artists were accorded a measure of respect, both in England and America, for rare indeed was the amateur whose work could approach that of even a mediocre journeyman portraitist, let alone a Copley or Stuart, a Gainsborough or Romney.

Music, on the other hand, was but ephemeral entertainment as far as most English and American gentry were concerned. After all, not even the finest professional performance could be possessed as property. Accordingly, music was seen as a harmless amateur occupation with which to while away one's leisure hours, or as a necessary adjunct to the mandatory social skill of dancing. If some among the propertied classes on both sides of the Atlantic had a relatively critical eye for painting, far fewer had anything like a critical ear for music. Consequently, even the most enthusiastic amateurs were quite well satisfied with their own, their friends', or even their servants' modest musical capabilities. The majority would have agreed heartily with British composer and author Charles Burney's characterization of music as "an innocent luxury, unnecessary indeed, to our existence, but a great gratification and improvement of the sense of hearing."[2]

To be sure, music in the colonies suffered the effects of the war. New York, for instance, was garrisoned by the British and largely populated by loyalists from 1776 to 1783. Throughout those years, its prominent citizens and the regimental officers quartered in the city maintained an active round of concerts, balls, and theatrical performances. In other cities, like Philadelphia, public concert life was sparse during the war years, especially after Congress adopted a resolution in 1778 urging the several states to curtail such entertainments.

In a real sense, the British regiments that began arriving in the late 1760s added new dimensions to American musical life. Although many if not most of the colonials resented, and a smaller number resisted, the presence of British soldiers, at the same time they enthusiastically embraced the regimental bands. In due course they formed similar bands of their own. At the same time, that very resentment and resistance found its outlet in the numerous patriotic ballad texts, for the most part anonymous, that appeared on printed broadsides and in newspapers. By the end of the war numerous song-sters, collections of such broadside ballad texts written to be sung to well-known tunes of the time, were being printed in Massachusetts. A few of the song texts from the era, particularly the traditional words, still sung to the tune "Yankee Doodle," have survived to the present as musical artifacts of the American Revolution.

AMATEUR MUSIC

Whatever their regard for music as an art, amateur musical activity con-tinued to be a popular pastime among many of the colonial gentry, urban and rural, throughout the Revolutionary period. Women sang and played the guitar; men favored the flute and violin, and both played keyboard instru-ments, the harpsichord, and the newly fashionable pianoforte. The *Virginia Gazette* of September 28, 1769, observed, "Musick was never so much in vogue," and attributed the fashion to Queen Charlotte who played the harp-sichord.[3]

Men whose names would soon be synonymous with patriotism and inde-pendence honed their musical skills alone or in chamber ensembles. In Williamsburg, Virginia, Thomas Jefferson and his mentor in legal studies and fellow violinist, George Wythe, met weekly to play chamber music with John Tyler as cellist and Robert Carter at the harpsichord. Their fellow Virginian, Patrick Henry, was also an amateur violinist. In Philadelphia, Francis Hop-kinson composed and performed on the harpsichord. Benjamin Franklin in-vented the glass harmonica, popular enough in Europe and America, albeit briefly, to attract the attention of such composers as Mozart and Beethoven. Franklin also wrote a string quartet playable on open strings by far less skilled amateurs than a Jefferson or Wythe.[4]

Instruments and music by such composers as Handel and Corelli, along with lesser figures like Arne, could be purchased in American cities and most towns, either from specialized music merchants, most of whom were them-selves musicians who taught and performed, or from booksellers and print-ers who carried musical merchandise as a sideline. Music masters, usually English or German immigrants, continued to make the circuit of rural plan-tations or eked out a living in towns and cities from a combination of teach-ing and performing, much as they had before the war and would continue to do afterwards.[5]

American amateurs, like their counterparts in Britain, subscribed to *Gent-leman's Magazine*, or bought it from a local bookseller. Issues included dances and musical numbers from the London stage. During the early 1760s, advertisements in New York and Philadelphia offered locally printed collections of songs by fashionable English composers, with titles like *The American Cock Robin* and *The Wood-Lark*. Although dealers and individuals continued to import instruments, more and more amateurs turned to local craftsmen, most of them immigrant journeymen, who were making violins, harpsichords, pianos, and even pipe organs, of a quality comparable to European instruments, and at a far lower price. By the 1770s, the harpsichord was giving way to the piano as the favorite amateur keyboard instrument.[6]

Dancing masters continued to teach amateurs in private homes as well as the taverns that served as meeting places for clubs and centers for public gathering and socializing, even in Puritan New England. In Boston, Harrison Gray Otis was an enthusiastic dancer. John Adams, on the other hand, disapproved of the activity. "I never knew a good Dancer," he wrote, "good for anything else." But in Virginia, George Washington, like his fellow tidewater aristocrats, prided himself on his dancing skills. And at six feet, two inches of height, he cut an impressive figure. After his appointment by Congress to command the Continental Army in 1775, Washington was invariably accorded the honor of opening the dancing when he was in attendance at a ball.[7]

Philip Vickers Fithian, a Princeton-trained Presbyterian minister who was engaged as a tutor to the children of Robert Carter, provides an illuminating glimpse into the rich musical life of the Carter family at their Virginia plantation, Nomini Hall, between October of 1773 and October of 1774. Fithian's observations run the gamut from the young girls of the household dancing to the fiddle playing of "John the serving man" to a volume of sacred music shown him by Carter, "set in four parts for the Voice; he seems much taken with it & says we must learn & perform some of them . . . with instruments." Fithian took notice of John Stadler, "a man of great skill in music." Stadler had worked in New York and Philadelphia before coming to Virginia. Among other activities, he taught music to Washington's stepchildren at Mount Vernon in the years between 1766 and 1771. During the summer of 1774, Stadler visited Nomini. On August 11, Fithian noted, "*Mrs Carter & Mr Stadley* [sic] performed both on the [glass] harmonica." The next day "*Mr Stadley* played on the Harpsichord & harmonica several Church Tunes & Anthems, with great propriety."[8]

CHOIRS AND CHURCH MUSIC

By the middle of the eighteenth century, some Protestant churches had begun using hymns, particularly those of Isaac Watts (1674–1748), in their worship, in addition to the customary metrical psalms. Beginning in the 1720s, a series of religious revivals had swept through the colonies culminating in the Great Awakening of 1730s and 1740s. From the first, congregational song played a major role in these revivals, arousing the emotions of congregations and making them more receptive to the preachers' words. The old metrical psalmody was ideally suited to the tightly reasoned scriptural expositions of the strict Calvinist Puritan ministers; but the passioned exhortations of "new light" revivalists called forth hymn texts with more personal sentiments.

The first great evangelist in America, George Whitefield (1714–1770), brought with him the hymn poetry of John and Charles Wesley, as well as hymn texts by Watts. This poetry was written so as to fit the familiar tunes of congregational psalmody. The Watts texts quickly gained favor with many congregations, and several editions had to be printed. In 1741, Jonathan Edwards had an edition of Watts's *Psalms of David Imitated* (1719) printed in Boston for use in his Northampton church, but only as a supplement to the psalter. The congregation embraced the new texts with great enthusiasm. On his return from a journey the next year, Edwards discovered, much to his dismay, that his church had all but stopped singing the old metrical psalm and was now using only Watts's hymn texts.[9]

At about the same time, during the 1730s, music published in England for parish choirs took on a more complex character, with melodic ornaments, varied textures, and especially imitative, or "fuging," sections. By mid-century, collections of music in the new style, composed and compiled by such men as William Knapp (1698/69–1768), John Arnold (ca. 1720–1792) and especially William Tans'ur (1700–1783), had found their way to the colonies. Similar collections by Americans appeared in the 1760s, beginning with James Lyon's *Urania* in 1761. These collections were printed in oblong-shaped books that opened from the end. These books customarily contained introductory essays on singing and rudimentary music theory. Many of the pieces were clearly not intended for congregations, but rather for singing classes to display their prowess at graduation concerts. Moreover, graduates had begun insisting that they be allowed to sit together as a choir in a loft or separate area of the church. The choir led congregational singing, but also cultivated its own distinctive repertoire of music, usually sung before or after the regular services.[10]

In other words, even as the singing school movement began its most active phase during the 1760s and 1770s, with singing masters expanding their endeavors from New England into the other colonies, it had turned away from its original purpose of promoting congregational psalmody. Intentionally or not, singing masters were fashioning classes of singers into choirs. By the end of the 1750s, many city churches had established choirs, and over the next two decades they appeared in rural churches as well. Far from New England, in tidewater Virginia, Philip Fithian was surprised by the singing of a choir in a church where he preached. In a diary entry dated September 25, 1774, Fithian wrote, "it is seldom in the fullest Congregations that more sing than the Clerk & about two others—I am told that a Singing Master of good abilities has been among this society lately."[11]

Not surprisingly, still another controversy ensued in and among New England's churches, this one over the seating of choirs, as well as their proper role in the worship service. The Second Church in Worcester, some forty miles west of Boston, waited until August of 1779 to abandon the practice of lining out congregational psalmody. At the same time, the church voted to allow the singers to sit together in a front gallery. The next Sunday, the deacon stubbornly stood and began reading out the first line of the psalm as usual. The choir singers responded by singing the psalm without the customary pause between lines, drowning him out. The poor man stubbornly attempted without success to shout the lines over the din, then stormed out of the meetinghouse in tears.[12]

There was yet another serious consideration, apart from anything having to do with the singing. Puritan meeting houses were "seated" each year by a committee of the congregation. Women and children were separated from the men, and church members deemed more pious or prominent were allocated better pews, in accordance with their perceived degree of piety or prominence. Disturbing this custom by seating the singers together in the congregation or a choir gallery, with none of the usual regard for age, social class, or sex, brought objections from some of the more conservative members.

> The Meeting House was Seated as much in favour of promoting
> the Singing as could be convenient with decency as to Age and

Birthright, . . . Now Seats are Shifted, Some of the males have
Stretched a Wing over upon the Female Side and have intruded
upon their Right.[13]

And the new music aroused at least as much indignation, especially the so-
called fuging tunes: sections in which the individual voice parts introduced
the melody one after the other in imitation, rather than the usual homophonic
chordal texture of melody and harmony.

When our singing wanted to be revived, . . . they so suddenly ex-
changed old tunes for New ones . . . it was but a few could bear a
part in the delightful part of Divine Worship.[14]

Instead of those plain and easy Compositions . . . away they get off,
one after another, in a light airy jiggish Tune . . . [T]he matter of
the Psalm has very little Share in their Attention.[15]

The momentum was not to be stopped, however. Choirs demanded more
anthems, and entrepreneurial singing masters and compilers supplied them.
During the remainder of the century, about a thousand pieces of choral music
were printed. Numerous collections, heavily derivative one from another,
were imported from London or published in America. The term "anthem"
first appeared in America applied to a simple three-voice setting in James A.
Turner's psalm-tune supplement of 1752. A manuscript by Francis Hopkinson, now in the Library of Congress, contains "An Anthem from the 114th
Psalm" signed "F. H. 1760," for two treble voices, bass voice, and keyboard.[16]

The first American collection of choir anthems was James Lyon's
(1735–1794) *Urania*, published in Philadelphia in 1761. Lyon graduated from
the College of New Jersey (now Princeton) in 1759 and may have taught a
singing school in Philadelphia the year after. In 1764 he was ordained a Presbyterian minister. He evidently abandoned his musical activities and from
then on devoted himself to his churches in Nova Scotia and from 1772 on, in
Machias, Maine.[17]

Urania contained a twelve-page introduction with a clear explanation of
musical fundamentals, followed by 198 elegantly engraved pages of music.
The ninety-six pieces, most of them by non-Americans, included twelve
choral works for two, three, and four voices. The six fuging tunes in *Urania*
are the first published examples of that sort of music in America. Among the
composers represented in the collection were William Tuckey (1708–1781), a

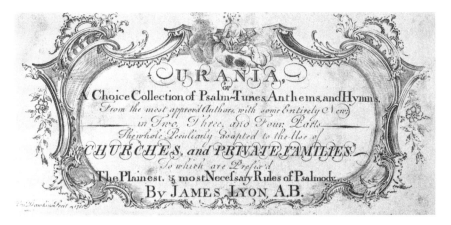

Engraved title page by Henry Dawkins for the first edition of James Lyon's *Urania*, Philadelphia, 1761. The Granger Collection, New York.

native of Bristol who had emigrated to New York and taken charge of the music at Trinity Church; Giovanni (John) Palma (fl. 1757), who worked in Philadelphia at the time; Lyon himself; and Francis Hopkinson.

Hopkinson's own publication, *A Collection of Psalm Tunes with a few Anthems and Hymns . . . for the Use of the United Churches of Christ Church and S. Peter's Church in Philadelphia*, appeared in 1763. He was a vestryman and warden of Philadelphia's combined Anglican parish, Christ Church and St. Peter's. That year a new organ had been installed in St. Peter's, and Hopkinson's collection included pieces set for two treble parts and bass with keyboard. His own setting of Tate and Brady's text, *The Twenty-Third Psalm*, for the same combination was smooth and graceful, in the cultivated English style influenced by Italian opera, popular in England at the time.[18]

SINGING MASTERS AND TUNESMITHS

During the years after 1760, the singing masters who organized and taught singing schools developed into a distinctively American musical profession. Most of them carried on their teaching and compiling part-time and in conjunction with trades they practiced at least part of the year. Some, popularly termed "tunesmiths," began composing their own music, instead of, or in addition to, compiling collections of music by others.

Josiah Flagg (1737–1795), a Boston jeweler and engraver, bandmaster and singing master, compiled *A Collection of the Best Psalm Tunes . . . to which are added some Hymns and Anthems, the greater part of them never before printed in America*, which he had printed in Boston by Paul Revere in 1764. Flagg's aim, as he put it in his introduction, was to "extract the Sweets out of a Variety of fragrant flowers." The collection included the psalm tunes as well as two brief anonymous anthems. Most of the music was European in origin. Flagg drew on Lyon's *Urania* as well as several English tune books. He was one of the earliest promoters of Handel's music in America; among the tunes in his collection is a march from Handel's 1728 opera *Riccardo Primo*. Two years later Flagg himself engraved and printed a collection of anthems by English composers, *Sixteen Anthems, collected from Tans'ur, Williams, Knapp, Ashworth & Stephenson. To which is added, a few psalm-tunes*. The twenty-five pieces, none of them by American composers, included seventeen anthems for four voices and the remainder for two or three.[19]

Even as some singing masters like Flagg were compiling collections, others had begun writing their own congregational tunes, anthems, and fuging tunes. Preeminent among these tunesmiths was an eccentric, one-eyed tanner with a withered arm, a stunted leg, and a booming voice, William Billings (1746–1800) of Boston, America's first professional composer.[20]

Although he may have had occasional bits of instruction from Flagg, Billings appears to have taught himself music, using as his guide the introductions from English collections by Tans'ur and others. By 1769, he had begun to teach singing schools in the Boston area, Providence, and as far away as Maine, and form community singing societies and church choirs. He went on to publish six major collections of his own music, in addition to psalm tunes and individual anthems in pamphlet form. Over his thirty-year career, Billings composed at least 340 pieces. About a third of them are for a trained choir, including fifty-one fuging tunes, fifty-two anthems, and four canons, or "rounds." Billings's anthems are sectional, with the sections governed by the text. Passages written as solos were actually intended to be sung by small groups rather than individual singers.[21]

Most of Billings's pieces were hymn tunes for congregational singing, along with the choir. They are arranged in parts, with the melody or "air" in the tenor. A bass line provides harmonic support, the soprano a secondary or countermelody, and the alto fills out the harmony. In practice, Billings generally divided his sopranos and tenors between the air and countermelody, so that both parts were doubled at the octave. Billings's harmonies tend to be simple, but he frequently uses open chords, as well as distinctive and irregular doublings and progressions.

Billings's *The New-England Psalm-Singer,* which appeared in 1770, was the first such collection given over entirely to the work of a single American composer. The collection's "Introduction to the Rules of Musick" relied heavily on Tans'ur. In it, Billings declared the independence that characterized his distinctive compositional style at the very beginning.

> Perhaps it may be expected by some, that I should say something concerning the Rules for Composition; to these I answer that *Nature is the best Dictator,* for all the hard dry studied Rules that ever was prescribed, will not enable any Person to form an Air any more than the bare Knowledge of the four and twenty [*sic*] Letters, and strict Grammatical Rules will qualify a Scholar for composing a Piece of Poetry, or properly adjusting a Tragedy, without a Genius. But it must be Nature, Nature must lay the Foundation, Nature must inspire the Thought.[22]

The New-England Psalm-Singer contained 126 pieces, most of them four-voice psalm tunes. The year 1770 was filled with tensions between the British soldiers garrisoned in Boston and the city's patriots. Billings made his sympathies clear with his most famous work, "Chester," included in this first publication with one stanza of its fiery text, beginning "Let tyrants shake their iron iron rod,/And slavery clank her galling chains." Billings would reprint it with four additional patriotic stanzas in *The Singing Master's Assistant,* eight years later, at the height of the Revolutionary War (see Appendix 4, Example 6). There were also five anthems and three "rounds" or canons, including the hauntingly beautiful "When Jesus Wept."

For whatever reason (probably to enhance sales of the new collection), Billings wrote harshly of *The New-England Psalm-Singer* in the preface to his next publication, *The Singing Master's Assistant,* published in 1778.[23]

> After impartial examination, I have discovered that many of the pieces in that Book were never worth my printing, or your inspection; therefore in order to make you ample amends for my former

intrusion, I have selected and corrected some of the Tunes which were most approved of in that book, and have added several new pieces which I think to be very good ones . . . I make no doubt but you will readily concur with me in this sentiment, viz. that the *Singing Master's Assistant*, is a much better Book, than the *New-England Psalm-Singer*.[24]

The Singing Master's Assistant was very popular and went through four editions, the last of them in 1786. It contained seventy-one compositions, sacred and patriotic, including nine anthems for choir. More to the point, *The Singing-Master's Assistant* introduced some of Billings's best and most famous works, among them his Christmas carol, "A Virgin Unspotted," the elegant and poignant "David's Lamentation," and especially the defiant call to arms, "Chester," by now a rallying cry for the New England minutemen, recycled from *The New-England Psalm-Singer* with four additional stanzas.

Issued in the heat of Revolutionary fervor, *The Singing Master's Assistant* also contained a parody of Psalm 137 written and set to music by Billings. His "Lamentation over Boston," beginning "By the waters of Watertown we sat down & wept when we remember'd thee, O Boston" referred to the city's occupation after the Port Act of 1774, in retaliation for the Boston Tea Party in December of the previous year. But the British had been gone from Boston since March 17, 1776, so it is likely that Billings included the song in his 1778 collection to keep alive the fires of patriotism among Bostonians, even though by that time the Revolutionary battleground had shifted from New England to the Middle and Southern colonies.[25]

Billings's next publication, *Music in Miniature*, which he printed and sold himself in 1779, contained seventy-two congregational psalm tunes in four voices without texts, including ten rearranged from English sources. The latter constitute his only publication of music not his own. The book's size and shape indicate that it was intended to be bound with a metrical psalter. In 1781, the year Cornwallis surrendered to Washington at Yorktown, effectively ending the War of Independence, Billings published *The Psalm-singer's Amusement*, a collection clearly intended for the recreation of experienced singers rather than students. Billings's activities would continue beyond the end of the war, but the popularity of his music would fade, along with his fortunes, as American tastes at century's end turned more and more to European fashions introduced by immigrant musicians from the Old World.

CHURCH ORGANS AND ORGANISTS

Many if not most professional musicians gravitated to the coastal cities, where a concentration of resources and population supported a combination of enterprises. A number of churches had organs by the 1760s, and several immigrant musicians earned a part of their living playing for services. In Puritan Boston, the Anglican parishes of King's Chapel, Trinity Church, and Christ Church (more popularly known today—though not then—as Old North) had organs, as did Christ Church in Cambridge, across the Charles and close by Harvard. The Congregational church in Providence was the only New England Puritan parish to make use of an organ in worship during the 1760s.

In Charleston, both St. Philip's and St. Michael's had organs, and the city was an exceptionally profitable place for organists. Charles Hartley, who had returned to Charleston in 1770 after a term as organist of King's Chapel in Boston, estimated his income from teaching, performing, and church work at £500 a year, possibly as much as $100,000 in modern purchasing power. But Charleston and Hartley were exceptional. Bruton Parish Church in Williamsburg, Virginia, had an organ; however, its organist, Peter Pelham, eked out a living as a printer, engraver, and even town jailer. In New York, Trinity Church had an organ, as did the old Dutch Reformed Church, although the latter instrument, given by Governor Burnet in 1727, had evidently fallen out of use by mid-century. In Philadelphia, Christ Church and St. Peter's had organs, as did St. Mary's Catholic Church.[26]

Some instruments were targets for vandalism by American troops, especially in Anglican churches in Puritan New England. Christ Church in Cambridge was used as a barracks by Connecticut militiamen during the spring of 1775, and the soldiers melted the pipes of its organ into musket balls. When Washington worshiped there on New Year's Day of 1776, a viola and clarinet supported singing, while what was left of the organ sat mute in the gallery. In spite of the patriotic role its steeple played in the events of April 1775, Christ Church in Boston was forced to close its doors from 1775 to 1778, and put the pipes of its organ into storage to spare them from being recast into bullets. King's Chapel also closed, but its organ was not damaged.

Outside of New England, instruments survived with little or no damage, especially in cities with a strong Anglican presence. In Charleston, Philadelphia, and Williamsburg, they escaped relatively unscathed. In Pennsylvania, Henry Melchior Muhlenberg arrived at the Lutheran church in Trappe to officiate at the funeral of a child in September of 1777, and was dismayed to find the building occupied by soldiers, one of whom was playing popular songs and marches on the organ to the delight of his comrades. Nevertheless, the organ was not seriously damaged. In New York, the great fire of September 21, 1776, destroyed Trinity Church and its organ. Burnet's organ in the Dutch Reformed Church disappeared during the British occupation of 1776–1783, and its fate is unknown.[27]

POPULAR SONGS AND PROPAGANDA

Broadside ballads, poems printed on single sheets and in newspapers for singing to well-known tunes of the day, were popular among all classes. They often served as a means of commenting on current events and expressing opinions. Well before the fires of Independence were kindled in the city, the *Boston Evening Post* for July 4, 1737, worried, "A few ballad singers uncontroll'd, if their ditties be but tolerably droll and malicious, are sufficient to cause disaffection in a state, to raise dissatisfaction in to a ferment and that ferment into a rebellion."[28]

Indeed, as tensions between the colonists and England escalated, the ballad was seized on by both patriots and loyalists as an effective means of spreading propaganda among the large proportion of the colonial population who had not taken sides in the conflict. New ballads appeared regularly on broadsides and in newspapers. In Philadelphia, the *Pennsylvania Evening Post* published both patriotic and loyalist ballads. Occasions such as the Stamp Act and the Boston Tea Party brought forth numerous new ballads on single broadsides and in newspapers.[29]

Evidently, the first printed patriotic ballad was Pennsylvanian John Dickinson's "Liberty Song," published in 1768 to be sung to the tune of a favorite British Royal Navy anthem, "Heart of Oak," a melody by the famous English composer William Boyce (1711–1779). First issued as a single broadside, "The Liberty Song" was subsequently reprinted in the *Pennsylvania Gazette* and later in New York and Boston papers. In a diary entry dated August 14, 1769, John Adams described a dinner with the Sons of Liberty in Dorchester. "The Liberty Song" was sung, "and the whole company joined in the Chorus." Most ballads were anonymous, for instance, "Come jolly Sons of Liberty" to the tune of "Come jolly Bacchus." Indeed, Benjamin Franklin and Francis Hopkinson probably authored a number of anonymous ballads that appeared in Philadelphia.[30]

In 1770, the Boston physician and patriot Dr. Joseph Warren published "The New Massachusetts Liberty Song" under his own name, to be sung to the tune, "British Grenadier." In 1775, the year Warren died in the Battle of Bunker Hill, another ballad, "War and Washington," appeared, fit to the same melody. "War and Washington" quickly caught on among Continental troops. On January 28, 1779, a British prisoner of war in Delaware complained in his diary of "the noise of the American soldiers who vociferate their songs so loud that the whole house rings with War and Washington, a favourite ballade."[31]

"Yankee Doodle" is certainly the best known and longest lasting of the numerous Revolutionary-era melodies, although more as an instrumental march than in association with any particular patriotic text. The origins of the tune are obscure. It has been dated as early as the seventeenth century, as a melody for texts such as "Lucy Lockit lost her pocket." It has also been dated at about 1755 and attributed to a British army surgeon during the French and Indian War; however, a manuscript book of dance tunes known to date from as early as 1730 contains a version of the tune, headed "Yankey Doodle." When all is said and done, we cannot tell for sure how old the tune is. All that can be said for certain is that it was a popular march for British troops in the 1760s. In fact, the first redcoats who arrived in Boston on October 1, 1768, to enforce the British customs laws made a point of marching from the waterfront to the common with their fifers playing "Yankee Doodle," clearly intending the gesture as an insult to the city's population.[32]

As it turned out, "Yankee Doodle" changed sides after the battle at Bunker or Breed's Hill on June 17, 1775. Heartened by their own valor against British regulars, the continentals commandeered what had been a British taunt and turned it into an American march. At the same time they embraced the British epithet "Yankee" as well, proudly claiming the title for themselves. Thereafter a number of ballads to be sung to the tune of "Yankee Doodle" were printed. The one most often associated with the melody, beginning "Father and I went down to camp along with Captain Goodwin / And there we saw the men and boys as thick as hasty pudding," was written by Edward Bangs (1756–1818). Burgoyne's surrender at Saratoga, October 17, 1777, brought forth yet another text to taunt the defeated general, "As Jack the King's Commander / was going to his duty." A similar parody appeared after Cornwallis's surrender at Yorktown, October 19, 1781, beginning "Cornwallis led a country dance, / the like was never seen, Sir," and ending with a taunt to native loyalists, "That while your hopes are danc'd away, / tis you must pay the piper" (see Appendix 4, Example 5).[33]

THEATRE MUSIC

The first commercial theatre opened in Williamsburg in 1716. By mid-century, theatres could be found in most cities and towns, Puritan-rooted Boston being the most conspicuous exception. Like taverns, they served as places both for socializing and for entertainment. Theatres, like churches, were a source of relatively steady income for city musicians. But if the employment was reliable, it could also be harrowing.

All sorts of men attended the theatre, as well as women of the streets who were known to entertain clients in a gallery set aside by the management for the purpose. Audiences were quick to voice and vent their dissatisfaction with hoots and well-aimed fruit and stones. Vendors moved freely and noisily through the throng selling food and drink. Music for which the mob did not care was shouted down with demands for popular marches, patriotic songs, and dance tunes. Musicians, for their part, felt free to take a break from playing during the course of an evening and slake their thirst at a nearby tavern.[34]

Troupes of actors toured colonial cities in the years leading to the outbreak of war. The ballad opera was especially popular. Essentially, it was a play with spoken dialogue into which were inserted numerous short "airs," consisting of original texts sung to well-known melodies. The plots were comical and the characters were usually disreputable figures from London's streets and alleys, often petty criminals.

John Gay's *The Beggar's Opera* is the best known of the ballad operas and a good example of the genre. It was first performed in London in 1728 and became an immediate success because of its popular melodies, satirical plot, and familiar underworld characters, among them a highway robber named Macheath, the buyer of his loot, Peachum, and a miscellany of thieves and prostitutes. The numerous songs include such texts as "Our Polly is a sad slut" set to the folk air "Oh London is a fair town," and "Let us take the Road. Hark! I hear the sound of Coaches" to a march by Handel from the opera *Rinaldo*.[35]

The Beggar's Opera was first performed in 1750 in New York City, and subsequently staged in Annapolis in 1752 and Philadelphia in 1759. Not until

1770 was *The Beggar's Opera* finally presented in Boston, the presence of the British garrison having trumped both stubborn Puritan opposition and a city ordinance of 1750 against theatrical productions. Maria Storer, who played one of the leading characters, Lucy Lockit, had a song collection named for her and published in Virginia in 1772, entitled *The Storer: or the American Syren*. Although *The Beggar's Opera* was especially popular in America throughout the century, other such musical productions enjoyed brief celebrity. Thomas Arne's *Love in a Village* merited a favorable notice in the *Pennsylvania Gazette* of January 22, 1767.[36]

Musical entertainments included other ballad operas besides *The Beggar's Opera*; pasticcios, which borrowed serious music by other composers rather than popular tunes and dances; and pantomimes, theatrical dance productions similar to ballet. Serious plays were almost always presented with musical overtures and interludes containing familiar melodies from popular songs, dances, and marches. And usually a brief musical work, aptly termed an afterpiece, followed the evening's dramatic presentation.[37]

During the Revolutionary War, the British military presence supported theatres, balls, and concerts in cities they occupied. New York, though second in population to Philadelphia, was the most cosmopolitan and diverse of the coastal cities; however, New Yorkers' interest was in commerce, and public arts were a distinctly secondary concern. A modest theatre opened as early as the 1730s; and the city's status as the military headquarters for the British army in America and a center of loyalist sympathies fostered the establishment of such places of entertainment during the Revolutionary period. The John Street Theatre, known as the Theatre Royal during the British occupation of 1776–1783, opened in 1767. At the same time, two pleasure gardens began offering theatrical entertainment as well as music and dancing. The Ranlegh Gardens, named for a similar place in London, opened in 1762, providing food, entertainment, dancing (including instruction by a resident dancing master, John Trotter), and a band that played evenings from Monday through Thursday. A competing establishment, the Vauxhall Gardens, also named for a London pleasure garden, opened in 1767.[38]

Outside of British control, the situation was more restrained. On October 24, 1774, the Continental Congress meeting in Philadelphia passed a resolution against entertainments in view of the political and economic conditions caused by the rising tensions. Congress had departed the city when some 18,000 British soldiers entered Philadelphia in October of 1777, and their presence made that winter a lively one for plays, concerts, and balls. But the

British left in June of 1778, and austerity returned, along with Congress. In October of that year the delegates urged individual states to legislate against theatrical productions for the duration and prohibited "any person holding office under the United States" from patronizing such entertainments. In response, the Pennsylvania legislature passed an act in 1779 prohibiting theatrical entertainments. Pennsylvania did not repeal its prohibition against theatres until 1789. Indeed, American theatre in most cities did not mature as an art or entertainment until the years after the Revolution.[39]

CONCERT ACTIVITY

In general, public concert activity declined during the Revolutionary War years. On the other hand, the war brought musicians from England and the Continent, among them several who would emerge as America's musical leaders during the early years of Independence, for example William Selby (1738/39–1798) in Boston and Peter Van Hagen (1755–1798) in Charleston and later New York.

Among the colonial cities, Boston was the least hospitable to public concerts; it was also the first American city to feel the British military yoke, in the autumn of 1768. Nevertheless, Boston's leading singing master, Josiah Flagg, was able to organize a series the next year and his concerts continued until 1773, when Flagg left the city. In spite of his apparently good relations with British band musicians who regularly took part in his concerts, Flagg was an ardent patriot who subsequently fought as an officer in the Continental Army. Ironically, the Boston loyalist Stephen Deblois did not fare as well as Flagg in his relations with the British. Some young British officers became disorderly in his concert hall and went on to assault Deblois himself. He angrily cancelled the remainder of his concert series, but relented after their regimental commander assured him that in the future they would "behave with decency."[40]

The British evacuated Boston once and for all in March of 1776. From September of that year until November of 1783, the British commander General Howe made his headquarters in New York. That city harbored a good deal of loyalist sentiment, and New York merchants were eager for the profits from supplying the British troops. A fire on September 21, 1776, shortly after Howe's arrival and possibly set by patriots, destroyed about a third of the city including Trinity Church; however, thereafter there was little real danger from the Continental Army. Secure in their New York headquarters, the British officers, their ladies, and the city's Tory families maintained a round of gatherings, dances, and other entertainments throughout the season from autumn to spring. Amateur dramatic and musical events were organized, and band musicians joined with local "professors" and gentlemen amateurs to perform in concerts.[41]

In the interval between the American victory at Yorktown in 1781 and the final British evacuation of New York in late November of 1783, conditions in the city deteriorated. Nevertheless, a series of subscription concerts were presented during those last years of occupation. The loyalist printer James Rivington's *Royal Gazette* for April 27, 1782, advertised "a *Concert* of Vocal and Instrumental *Musick* for the benefit of two distressed Refugee Families" including works by Haydn, Stamitz, Vanhall, J.C. Bach, and then popular but now lesser known composers of the period. The program offered a varied selection of music for string ensemble, songs, and a succession of solo pieces for flute, clarinet, oboe, and violin. The program was precisely what would have been performed in that day for a sophisticated London audience.[42]

Except for the brief period from October of 1777 to June of 1778, during which the city was occupied by the British, Philadelphia had no significant public concert life during the Revolution. The Continental Congress, meeting in the city, had formally pronounced against public entertainments in 1774; and on its return to Philadelphia in 1778 after the British departure had voted to prohibit its members and employees from attending them. It is thus not surprising that dances and entertainments in Philadelphia came to a sudden end when the city was abandoned by Howe's army in 1778. Concerts did not resume in Philadelphia until the autumn of 1783, when John Bentley established a biweekly subscription series.[43]

Although Philadelphia had a limited public concert activity at best, several of its churches maintained fine musical establishments. St. Mary's Roman Catholic Church, built in 1763, drew Protestants as well as Catholics to its musical events. In October of 1774, John Adams made note of a vesper service he had attended at St. Mary's, along with George Washington and several others, describing the assembly's chanting "most sweetly and exquisitely." Nearly five years later, in 1779, Congress and other dignitaries gathered at St. Mary's for the first Fourth of July religious service.[44]

Large Lutheran churches in Pennsylvania had fine organists and choirs of boys who had been rigorously trained in the school maintained by each parish. Unlike English congregations of the era who sang the metrical psalms in unisons and poorly if at all, German Lutheran congregations were used to singing their chorales in parts, often alternating stanzas with the choir in the gallery. Zion Church, within an easy walk of Independence Hall, was the largest indoor space in Philadelphia. During the brief occupation of 1777–1778, the British had used it as a hospital. By 1781, however, it had long since been restored to religious and occasionally civic purposes. On October 24, 1781, after Cornwallis's surrender at Yorktown, Congress, the French minister, and other dignitaries gathered there for a public service of thanksgiving, at which the music was sung by "German school children" to an instrumental accompaniment "by a few virtuosos."[45]

In Charleston too, public concert life diminished during the Revolutionary years. Violinist and organist Peter Van Hagen arrived from Rotterdam in the Netherlands during 1774, and the *South Carolina Gazette* of October 24 gave notice of his debut in a "Grand Concert of Vocal and Instrumental Music" to be presented on October 27. No program survives for the evening; however, Van Hagen shared the stage with a "Signora Castella," possibly his sister, who sang and played the glass harmonica. This was apparently the last public benefit concert until after the end of the war. Charleston fought off the British in 1776; however, Clinton took the city in May of 1780, and proceeded to occupy it with a heavy hand. The St. Cecilia series was suspended until 1783, and the *Royal Gazette* gave notice of only three public concerts during the years of British control.[46]

MILITARY BANDS

On October 1, 1768, units of the British army landed in Boston to enforce the collection of the highly unpopular British customs duties on imports. One witness recorded their march to the Common "with drums beating, fifes &c, playing . . . The Yankee Doodle Song was the Capital Piece in their Band of Music." Their mission and the generally boorish manner in which they behaved toward Boston's residents made the British unwelcome guests; however, most Bostonians enjoyed the British regiments' bands, even if the Puritan ministers were angered by their habit of playing loudly outside meeting houses during Sabbath services.[47]

A typical British regiment consisted of eight infantry companies and a company of grenadiers. Each company was allowed two drummers who beat calls, kept cadence during marches, and signaled formations and commands via

Three men playing two drums and a fife. Courtesy of the Library of Congress.

drumbeat patterns during battles. Dragoons, or cavalry, were allotted trumpets rather than drums for signaling. In addition to its drummers, the grenadier company had two fifers, usually boys, who played popular airs over the drummers' cadence during marches. These juvenile fifers had no role in battle.

Officially, no other regimental music was authorized; however, most regiments also had bands of wind instruments, privately paid for (like the pipers in the Scottish regiments) by regimental officers. Such bands usually contained two oboes, two bassoons, two clarinets, and two horns. Eight of the nine British regiments in Boston in 1775 had bands. In fact, the majority of the fifty-six British regiments that fought in America had regimental bands, as did the regiments of Hessian mercenaries that fought beside them and the French regiments that fought with the American army. Bands supplied dinner music for regimental officers and ceremonial music for regimental affairs. A number of collections of band music, consisting of popular marches and airs, were published in London between 1695 and the end of the Revolution, with titles like *XXIV Favourite Marches in Five Parts, as They are Perform'd by His Majesty's Foot and Horse Guards* (London, 1770).[48]

British military bands also performed for civilian events, public assemblies, and even hangings. In Boston, where the British presence was most resented, British band musicians nevertheless took part in concert activity, playing alongside locals and under the direction of such local musicians as Josiah Flagg and William Morris. In loyalist New York, visitors to the Ranlegh Gardens were serenaded on summer evenings by a complete band made up for the most part of British musicians. The band of the British 18th Regiment of Foot, or Royal Irish Regiment, participated in the College of Philadelphia's 1773 commencement ceremonies. And of course, individual bandsmen gave concerts for their own benefit, like other professional musicians of the time.[49]

Bostonian Josiah Flagg, that erstwhile jeweler, engraver, singing master, and subsequently an American military officer, claimed to have formed the first colonial band in 1769, but his concert notices suggest that he used musicians from the British bands, particularly that of the 64th Regiment. Boston newspapers carried notices of Flagg's concerts for the next four years, initially without listing the music to be performed. On May 16, 1771, *The Massachusetts Spy* advertised an evening of "vocal and instrumental musick accompanied by French horns, hautboys, etc. by [sic] the band of the 64th Regiment," scheduled to take place the next night and listing a program containing the Overture to Handel's *Ptolemy*, a Stamitz symphony, a sinfonia by J. C. Bach, pieces by Stanley, Abel, and others, and various vocal and instrumental solos. The repertoire suggests a highly proficient group of musicians and a relatively sophisticated audience. The program for another Flagg concert on October 4, 1771, included selections from Handel's *Acis and Galatea* and the overture to the same composer's *Il pastor fido*. Flagg's last Boston concert took place in the autumn of 1773. He had left Boston by May 9, 1774, when the *Boston Post* advertised the last such "Grand CONCERT of Vocal and Instrumental MUSIC accompanied by the Band of the 64th Regiment."[50]

Following the example of the British regiments, the American army quickly began employing drummers and fifers for marching and signaling. George Washington would have gone further, for he was an advocate of military bands. "Nothing is more agreeable, and ornamental than good music," he wrote. "Every officer, for the credit of his corps, should take care to provide it." Yet for most military units under his command, Washington's order was more easily received than obeyed. Qualified players were hard to find; and in any case, Continental Army officers, unlike their British counterparts, could rarely afford to underwrite the cost of outfitting and maintaining a regimental band of musicians. Consequently there is no official record of Continental military bands until 1777. Enemy prisoners and defectors were sometimes pressed into service. Two complete Hessian bands were captured at the Battle of Trenton, and a British band was seized at Cowpens.[51]

Records exist of at least seven bands in the Continental Army by the end of the war. The 3rd Regiment of Continental Artillery had a band that continued to give concerts after 1783. A Philadelphia artillery regiment, a Connecticut regiment, and General Henry "Light Horse Harry" Lee's corps had bands. Nevertheless, there was evidently no American band at the last major battle of the Revolutionary War. Witnesses at Yorktown in 1781 recorded that only British and French bands took turns performing for the troops on both sides while their commanders negotiated the surrender of Lord Cornwallis's army.[52]

Nobody really knows what tune was piped as the defeated British soldiers marched out of Yorktown to lay down their arms. Tradition, fed by later legend, names the air associated with a seventeenth-century ballad, "The world turned upside down." That melody would certainly have been in the musicians' repertoire along with the other popular ditties the troops had enjoyed marching to in happier times. And in fact, the British might well have derived some consolation from its equally popular association with another set of words, beginning "When the King enjoys his own again" (see Appendix 4, Example 7).[53]

CONCLUSION

Ardent patriot, steadfast loyalist, and all shades of sympathy in between, most Americans retained their British tastes. If in the end, destiny decreed political independence for their land, they still looked to London to dictate fashions in music and culture. As a result, music in America changed very little during the Revolutionary era. Perhaps the main musical consequence of the war was the number of professional musicians who arrived as bandsmen in the British and Hessian regiments, and who remained in America. They and their successors laid the foundations of the cultivated musical tradition that grew up in the cities alongside the vernacular work of tunesmiths like William Billings during the last two decades of the eighteenth century.

9

Church Music in the Federal Era

By 1783, the British colonies in North America had gained their political independence and formed a new nation. Culturally and musically, however, that new nation was still very much a British colony. Immigrant professional musicians, most of them from England, dominated all aspects of musical life in America.

Although native-born, self-taught, and semi-amateur singing masters flourished for some years after the Revolution, European professionals gradually displaced them in the city churches. More and more, their singing schools and psalmody were relegated to smaller churches in cities and towns, and to rural congregations. Sophisticated urban congregations came more and more to prefer the agreeable harmonies and sensitive melodies of the cultivated European style, rather than the rough-hewn, open harmonies and folk-like melodies of native tunesmiths like William Billings. Many churches had formed choirs, and after the War of Independence, they begun acquiring organs as well, most of them imported from England. Immigrant British musicians were thus able to supplement their weekday teaching and other endeavors by playing the organ on Sundays.

Churches continued to be the cultural centers of most communities. Moreover, since they were generally the only large public auditoriums, churches became the venue for concerts of "sacred music" (as distinct from "church music") presented by amateur singing societies, usually organized and directed by the immigrant musician who served as organist. Such concerts were often called "oratorios," although they were in fact miscellaneous programs of airs and choruses from a variety of oratorios, especially those of Handel, along with a scattering of instrumental pieces. Sacred music was thus kept clearly distinct from church music. Sacred music was sung on special occasions in concert by musical societies; whereas church music, consisting of psalms, hymns, and now and then an anthem, was sung regularly for worship services by church choirs.

SINGING MASTERS

Even as they faded from musical prominence, especially in the cities, the singing masters and their schools, as well as the "tunesmiths" and the music they composed, continued to play an active part in American music during the last years of the eighteenth century. Most tried to keep in step with changing tastes. Only William Billings, the best known of the New England group, attempted to mount a rear-guard action against the incursion of the new and fashionable church music, with its delicate, florid melodies and simple, consonant harmony.

Billings had been in his prime when the Revolutionary War ended. In 1781, the year Cornwallis surrendered at Yorktown, he published *The Psalm-Singer's Amusement*, its relatively difficult pieces clearly intended for proficient and experienced singers rather than singing school beginners. His *Suffolk Harmony* followed in 1786. But in 1792, the *Massachusetts Magazine* had carried an appeal for subscriptions to underwrite the printing of "a Volume of Original American Musick, composed by William Billings, of Boston . . . The distressed situation of Mr. Billings' family has so sensibly operated on the mind of the committee as to induce their assistance in the intended publication." Billings was ill and in financial straits when his last collection, *The Continental Harmony*, appeared in 1794. In its introduction, Billings defended his rustic native style in the face of the public's increasing preference for the more refined, less demanding European idiom. *"Variety is always pleasing*, and . . . there is more variety in one piece of fuging music, than in twenty pieces of plain song."[1]

Many of Billings's colleagues, on the other hand, were quick to adopt the new musical style. Andrew Law (1749–1821) of Cheshire, Connecticut, was a graduate of Brown University, an ordained minister and singing master who taught singing schools as far afield as Pennsylvania, Maryland, and the Carolinas. A teacher and compiler, rather than a composer, Law declared his preference for quality European music and refined singing voices.

> In a word, our [American] singing in general is extremely harsh; and this harshness produces its natural effects, it renders our psalmody less pleasing and less efficacious; but it does more; it vitiates our taste and gives currency to bad music. . . . Hence the great run it has taken to the exclusion of European composition.[2]

In contrast to the educated and ordained Law, Daniel Read (1757–1836) was a humble New Haven shopkeeper who occasionally taught singing schools but seems to have been interested more in composing and compiling. His earlier collections, such as *The American Singing Book* (1785), contain old-style fuging tunes, angular melodies, and open harmonies. But by 1795, the year he issued the last volume of *The Columbia Harmonist*, he, like Law, had embraced the cultivated European style. In a letter dated February 3, 1829, Read characterized his earlier music as "chiefly ephemeral," and in another letter, dated May 2 of that same year, recorded his preference for European musical style as based "on the broad ground of settled principles, rather than the narrow one of individual taste" (see Appendix 4, Example 8).[3]

The Massachusetts Compiler (Boston, 1795) prepared by a Danish immigrant, Hans Gram, and two native New Englanders, Samuel Holyoke (1762–1820) and Oliver Holden (1765–1844), contained seventy-eight pieces, at least seventy of them by non-Americans. The best composers of the day were represented, including the Englishmen Arne, Burney, and Purcell; the continental masters Handel and Haydn, and the immigrant British musicians George K. Jackson and William Selby, both of Boston. Holden, Holyoke, and Gram each contributed one piece. The preface, signed by the three men, declared:

> Many American votaries of sacred music, have long since expressed their wishes for a compendium of the genuine principles of that science. At the present period it becomes necessary that greater attention be paid to every means for improving that important part of divine worship, as good, musical immigrants are daily seeking an asylum in this country. . . . With respect to the selection of music, it is necessary to observe, that several of the pieces were not originally composed for sacred words; they were chosen

and adapted for furnishing a variety of style from the most modern compositions.[4]

Holyoke and Holden clearly represented a new generation of musicians
who looked to fashionable European composers not only for inspiration but
also for material. Their practice of adapting European music from all sources,
sacred and secular, to church use would become widespread in America during the first half of the nineteenth century. Holden was a native of Shirley,
Massachusetts, who made his home in Charlestown, near Boston, from 1787
on. Holyoke was born in Boxford, Massachusetts, of an old family, and was
a graduate of Harvard. Both men taught singing schools. Holyoke was the
better educated of the pair, and a more prolific composer than Holden.
Holden, however, is the better known of the two, primarily because his tune,
"Coronation," appears in virtually every denominational hymnal and on the
list of almost every congregation's favorite hymns (see Appendix 4, Example 10).

In Philadelphia, Andrew Adgate (1762–1793), a native of Norwich, Connecticut, and pupil of Andrew Law, founded an Institution for the Encouragement of Church Music in 1784. The next year the institution changed its
name to the Uranian Society, and declared its aims: teaching psalmody to any
and all churches and sponsoring concerts of sacred music. By 1787 the society, again renamed as the Uranian Academy of Philadelphia, was firmly established, with Adgate as its president, and such patrons as Benjamin Rush
and Francis Hopkinson. Between 1785 and his premature death during the
yellow fever epidemic of 1793, Adgate organized and led several concerts of
sacred choral and orchestral music. He also compiled several collections and
published a primer, *Rudiments of Singing*. It is an indication of Adgate's influence in the city that he was able to recruit an impressive 230-voice chorus
and an orchestra of fifty for a "GRAND CONCERT of vocal and instrumental music" given May 4, 1786, in Philadelphia's German Reformed Church.[5]

These men and most of the other singing masters who flourished in the
last decade of the eighteenth century and the early nineteenth century, moved
away from Billings's fuging tunes and rough-hewn native idiom and toward
a smoother, more refined, European-based style. But Billings and others less
well known had given American church music a distinctive voice. Even
though many of them, like Daniel Read, later turned away from that distinctive voice and adopted the smoother, more cultivated idiom of the immigrant
European musicians who were arriving in increasing numbers as the century

waned, that distinctive voice with its open harmonies, modal counterpoint, and angular melodies would survive as a distinctive folk tradition in rural churches of backcountry America.

ORGANS IN LATE-EIGHTEENTH-CENTURY CHURCHES

By the 1780s and 1790s, choirs were flourishing in several New England churches. On the other hand, the Puritans' historic aversion to organs was still evident in the region. Boston's Park Street Church, for example, had a fifty-voice choir but no organ. Support for the singers and congregation was provided by an ensemble of flute, bassoon, and cello. Smaller New England churches got along with a wooden pitch pipe to set the pitch for congregational psalmody or at most a cello or bass viol, sometimes called a "church viol," to etch a bass line under the psalm tune.[6] Of New England's numerous congregational churches, only First Church in Providence had dared use an organ in worship in the years before the Revolution. Ezra Stiles, president of Yale, recorded in his diary on July 10, 1770, "Last month, an organ of 200 Pipes was set up in the Meeting-house of the first Congregational Chh. in Providence: and for the first time it was played upon in divine Service last Ldsday, as Mr. Rowland the pastor tells me. This is the first organ in a dissenting presb. Chh in America."[7]

Not much had changed by the last years of the century. In Boston, only the Anglican parishes and the progressive Brattle Square Church had organs. All the instruments had been imported from England, except for the one in Christ Church (Old North), built by a local craftsman, Thomas Johnston, in 1753. Brattle Square Church's situation was especially tense. The congregation had declined founder Thomas Brattle's bequest of his own organ in 1712, and it had thereupon been given to King's Chapel, giving that congregation the distinction of owning the first church organ in the colonies. In 1790, Brattle Square Church finally installed an instrument by the London builder Samuel Green. So bitterly had this most liberal of Boston congregational churches been divided over the issue that even as the ship bearing the organ hove into view, a conservative member of the congregation offered to reimburse the church its cost if the instrument were thrown overboard outside Boston harbor.[8]

In 1756, King's Chapel replaced Brattle's little organ with a much larger instrument by Richard Bridge of London, whose 1733 organ was still in use in

Trinity Church, Newport. Trinity Church in Boston had bought an organ from yet another London builder, Abraham Jordan, in 1744. During the 1750s, Anglican churches in Cambridge and Salem, as well as Middletown and Stratford, Connecticut, acquired organs. Trinity Church in New Haven bought an organ from the London builder Henry Holland, in 1785.[9]

In New York, the organ given to the Dutch church by Governor Burnet in 1727 had disappeared during the British occupation of 1776–1783, the building having been commandeered for use as a hospital. Trinity Church had burned in September of 1776, along with its new organ, built in 1764 by the greatest of London's master makers, John Snetzler. Trinity Church was rebuilt in 1789–1790, and a year later a new organ arrived from London, the work of a fine if less celebrated—and doubtless less expensive—builder, Henry Holland. In the South, larger Anglican churches acquired organs rather early. St. Philip's in Charleston had used an organ since 1728. Bruton Parish Church in Williamsburg, St. Paul's in Baltimore, and St. Anne's in Annapolis all purchased organs during the 1750s. St. Michael's in Charleston received its Snetzler organ in 1767.[10]

Most of these imported organs were the work of England's finest builders and provided excellent models for the handful of American craftsmen who were beginning to try their hand at organ building. The finest examples were those of John Snetzler. Sadly, the large Snetzler organ in New York's Trinity Church was destroyed in the fire of 1776, and a smaller one in Christ Church, Cambridge, was stripped of its metal pipes. But at least two other Snetzlers were intact, in St. Michael's Church Charleston, and in Boston's Deblois Concert Hall.

Although New England churches furnished a limited market for organs, a few organ builders worked in the area, probably nourished by the modest market among wealthy amateurs for small home instruments. As the century came to its end, notices began to appear in newspapers announcing the contracting of a church organ. The *Columbian Centinel* for February 8, 1792, announced the completion of an organ by Josiah Leavitt for the "Universal[ist] Religious Society of Boston. For compass and sweetness of sound, and elegance of construction, it is exceeded by but a few imported Organs." The next November, Leavitt had completed an organ for the Congregational church ("Meeting House") in Worthington, Connecticut. Another New England builder, Henry Pratt (1771–1841) of Winchester, New Hampshire, built over forty small organs, twenty-three of them for rural churches.[11]

Surprisingly, New York lagged behind Boston in developing an organ-building trade. Not until 1798 did the first builder of any significance appear.

John Geib (1744–1818), a native of Stauderheim, Germany, had moved to London in 1760 and set up as a piano maker. Geib's pianos, equipped with his patented "grass-hopper" escapement action, gained a respectable portion of the market; however, in 1797, he closed his London shop and immigrated to New York with his family. In 1798 he began building both pianos and organs there, and his descendents carried on the piano-making portion of his enterprise until the 1850s. Geib's first organs were built in 1798 and 1799, for Christ Lutheran Church and Christ Episcopal Church, both in New York. Over the next two decades, Geib built organs for churches in New York and New Jersey, and as far afield as Massachusetts, Rhode Island, and Pennsylvania. Unfortunately, none of his organs have survived; however, Geib's work was highly respected in his time.[12]

America's first great organ builders worked in Pennsylvania, where there was a strong market for church organs. Although Philadelphia's Quakers had no use for any music, the city's oldest Anglican parish, Christ Church, had an organ as early as 1728, as did Gloria Dei Lutheran Church at some time between 1737 and 1741, and St. Joseph's Catholic Church between 1748 and 1750. The German churches, of course, had no scruples against organs, and only financial considerations delayed the purchase of an organ for a new Lutheran or Reformed church even in rural areas.[13]

It was in this context that David Tannenberg (1728–1804) emerged as the leading American organ builder of the eighteenth century. Only Philip Feyring (1730–1767), another German émigré, approached him in quality and reputation. Feyring had set up in business making and repairing keyboard instruments in Philadelphia around 1755. Over the next few years, he built large instruments for St. Peter's (1763) and Christ (1766) churches in Philadelphia. Feyring's premature death in 1767 removed the only serious competition Tannenberg might have had in Pennsylvania.[14]

Tannenberg was the son of a Moravian shoemaker who had been jailed for his faith. The family immigrated to Bethlehem, Pennsylvania, in 1749, and the young man took up his trade of joiner, married, and began a family. Tannenberg worked for a time with John Clemm, builder of the first organ for Trinity Church in New York. After Clemm's death, Tannenberg moved to Lititz, where he made his home for the rest of his life.

Tannenberg built forty-one organs for churches as far afield as North Carolina. Most of his work was done for Pennsylvania German congregations, and most of his instruments were quite small and similar one to another. Eight survive, six of them playable as of this writing. As his reputation grew, it is probable that the elders of the Moravian community became concerned about his frequent absence from the community, for at one point pressure was brought to bear on Tannenberg to give up organ building and return to cabinet making. He resisted successfully, however, and a number of his late organs, among them his largest instruments, went to non-Moravian churches. He was finishing the organ in Christ Lutheran Church, York, Pennsylvania (1804), when he suffered a stroke from which he died a few days later.[15]

David Tannenberg's largest organ was built between 1786 and 1790 for Zion Church in Philadelphia. So great was the interest that a special private showing of the organ was given September 3, 1790, for President Washington and other dignitaries of government, and three dedication services, on October 10, 11, and 17, were required to accommodate the crowds, even though the building seated 2,500 to 3,000. Pastor Helmuth wrote a cantata text for the occasion, set to music by Zion's organist and parish schoolmaster David Ott. Both organ and event received wide notice in newspapers. The organ served Zion's congregation for only a brief time. Building and instrument were destroyed by fire on December 26, 1794.[16]

CHURCH MUSIC IN BOSTON

If William Billings represented the native tunesmith tradition in Boston, his contemporary and counterpart in the cultivated tradition of church music was the British immigrant William Selby (1738–1798). Selby was a significant figure on the Boston musical scene during the last years of the eighteenth century, and the main figure in Boston church music and amateur sacred music, especially in the years between 1786 and 1794.

Selby's arrival was preceded by that of his brother John (1741–1804). He landed in Boston in the early autumn of 1771 to take up his duties as organist of King's Chapel, and apparently left the city when the British evacuated it in March of 1776, settling in Halifax. John Selby made no mark on Boston's music, probably because his talents were far more modest than his brother's, and possibly because his years in the city coincided with political unrest and widespread anti-British sentiment.[17]

Between 1756 and 1773, William Selby had gained a small measure of success as a composer and organist in London. In October of 1773, he resigned his London posts and immigrated to Newport, Rhode Island, to take up his duties as organist of Trinity Church. In January of 1774, he placed a notice in the *Newport Mercury*, offering to teach a number of instruments, including violin and guitar, as well as dancing. Clearly, William did not share his brother's political opinions, for during the late summer or early fall of 1776, only months after the British evacuation and his brother's departure, he settled in Boston as organist of Trinity Church. For whatever reason, he was replaced as Trinity's organist in 1780, and for the next year or two made his living running a wine shop. In 1782 he was made organist of King's Chapel and held that post for the rest of his life.[18]

Unlike his contemporary and friend William Billings, Selby's career in America flowered in the years after the Revolution, and he remained a significant figure in Boston's musical life during the early years of the republic. The *Massachusetts Gazette* for January 2, 1786, advertised a "Concert of *Sacred Music*" for voices and instruments under Selby's direction to be presented January 10 in conjunction with the regular 11:00 A.M. Sunday service at King' Chapel. The program included the overture to Handel's *Occasional Oratorio*, solos from Handel's oratorios *Messiah* and *Samson,* an overture by J. C. Bach, and anthems and pieces by Selby himself. Selby organized a similar concert given on January 16, 1787, at King's Chapel, again within the framework of a regular church service.[19]

Yet another "Oratorio, or Concert of Sacred Music" at King's Chapel was advertised for October 27, 1789, to commemorate the occasion of George Washington's visit to Boston. The performance "in the presence of the PRESIDENT of the United States" was to have included a concerto and an anthem by Selby, selections from *Messiah* and *Samson,* and a now-forgotten oratorio, *Jonah* composed in 1775 by a minor British musician, Samuel Felsted. The choruses were to be sung by the Independent Musical Society and accompanied by an instrumental ensemble consisting of "gentlemen" amateurs and players from a British naval band. Unfortunately, the concert had to be postponed until December 1, 1789, due to the "indisposition of several singers," by which time Washington had departed Boston.[20]

Selby's concert activities extended to other towns around Boston. On November 25, 1790, he performed at St. Peter's Church in Salem "on the Organ, with the BAND from Boston . . . for the purpose of raising money for repairing the Organ." As usual, the program included a mix of vocal and instrumental music.[21]

Few of Selby's compositions have survived, but those that have are in the clear melodic and harmonic style typical of English music at the time. His setting of Psalm 100 appeared in a number of collections and was apparently popular. An anthem, "Behold He is My Salvation," also appeared in several collections, including Oliver Holden's *Union Harmony* of 1793.[22]

It is probable that only in Boston were the circumstances such that two such dissimilar men as Billings and Selby could work not only in close proximity but also in such harmony. Indeed, Billings ran a singing school at King's Chapel (known at the time as the Stone Chapel) in 1785, during Selby's tenure as music director. Selby often included Billings's music in his programs, and was probably the director of a concert for the benefit of Billings "whose distress is real," advertised in the December 8, 1790 *Columbian Centinel* and presented in King's Chapel on December 21.[23]

CHURCH MUSIC IN PHILADELPHIA

Philadelphia was the largest city on the East Coast during the eighteenth century. As late as 1790, when it was the nation's capital, its population of about 42,000 outnumbered New York's 33,000. Philadelphia's German immigrants, both Lutheran and Reformed, brought with them a strong tradition of church music, especially the vigorous congregational singing of hymns or *chorales*. Even in rural Pennsylvania, some congregations developed the strong musical programs that characterized larger churches in their native Germany. Parish organists who also frequently served as parish schoolmasters drew on boys in their schools to form choirs that provided special music for the services and led the congregational singing.

Music was as integral a part of the curriculum in Lutheran parish schools in America as it was in Germany. Like their European counterparts, ministers in America frequently wrote texts for special occasions, which were then set to music by their parish organist-schoolmasters. Organists played preludes, interludes, and free accompaniments to congregational hymnody. Congregations sang numerous hymns they had known since childhood, in parts and antiphonally or responsorially with the choir or soloists.[24]

Justus Heinrich Christian Helmuth (1745–1825), pastor of Philadelphia's two Lutheran churches, Zion and St. Michael's, was an amateur musician as well as a writer of hymn texts. Between 1781 and 1817, he produced some sixty collections of poems and hymn and cantata texts. Under his leadership, the combined parish became the largest and most influential German-speaking congregation in the country, with a music program fully equal to that of large-city churches in Germany. Zion Church, which had Philadelphia's largest auditorium and was within easy walking distance for members of the government, became a sort of official church, in spite of the fact that its regular Sunday worship and preaching were conducted exclusively in German. English was used for public observances like the service of thanksgiving for the surrender of Lord Cornwallis, held in Zion Church on October 24, 1781.[25]

Where music was cultivated to any degree in an English church, such was usually at the instigation or through the efforts of an interested layman or the rare clergyman with a commitment to music as a part of worship. Nor was the standard to which they aspired especially high; Anglican, or Episcopal, churches had no cathedral music establishments in America on which to model their service music. Rarely did their choirs, where such existed, attempt anything elaborate. At best, congregations sang nothing but metrical psalms and a sprinkling of Watts and Wesley hymns to the same few tunes.

The rector of the combined Episcopal parish of Christ Church and St. Peter's in Philadelphia, and later bishop of Pennsylvania, William White (1748–1836), had little if any interest in elaborate music and tolerated only metrical psalmody in services he led. Nor did White think a congregation should learn any more than twenty tunes. "I am convinced," he wrote, "that no circumstance impedes good singing in our churches so much as the great diversity of tunes." Doubtless at his instigation, the Vestry of Christ Church and St. Peter's directed, on April 3, 1785, that only familiar tunes be sung and that no new tunes be added, "the singing of other tunes, and frequent changing of the tunes being . . . generally disagreeable and inconvenient."[26]

Francis Hopkinson (1737–1791), lawyer, patriot, and signer of the Declaration of Independence, and an accomplished amateur musician, was a member and former vestryman of the combined parish of Christ Church and St. Peter's. Throughout the 1760s and early 1770s, he was active in Philadelphia's musical life, joining with local professionals in concerts and even composing music for their performances. In 1763, he published a volume of sacred music for use in Christ Church and St. Peter's, including two of his own anthems. He and William Young also took on the responsibility of training some children of the combined parish in "the art of psalmody." Vestry minutes for April 3, 1764, cited the two men's "great and constant pains in teaching and instructing the children."[27]

Hopkinson remained an enthusiastic musical amateur throughout his life. In the years before his premature death, he was proud to proclaim himself "the first Native of the United States who has produced a Musical Composition" as he wrote in the dedication of his *Seven* [actually, eight] *Songs For Harpsichord* (Philadelphia: J. Aitken, 1788). Nevertheless, by the 1780s, Hopkinson's duties as a Federal District Court judge had long since forced him to curtail his musical efforts with the children of the combined parish.

William Tuckey (1708–1781) left without a church position after the fire of 1776 had destroyed Trinity Church in New York, where he had had charge of the music, and was appointed clerk of St. Peter's in 1778. He may have tried to continue Hopkinson's work with the boys in spite of his advanced age. Tuckey died in the late summer of 1781; however, not until December of the next year did the parish get around to forming a committee to "regulate the singing at St. Peter's." Matthew Whitehead was employed "to instruct twelve persons in singing to accompany the organ," and early in 1783, Andrew Law was engaged to conduct a singing school at St. Peter's.[28]

White continued turning to Hopkinson for musical advice and even deferred to him on more than one occasion. In 1785, Hopkinson prepared the eight-page music supplement to the proposed *Book of Common Prayer*. White went along, though he took a dim view of the whole business, as he wrote to his fellow minister, William Smith: "Mr. Hopkinson . . . is desirous of inserting a page of chants; and if I comply with this it will be to gratify him, as he has taken so much trouble in the matter."[29]

Hopkinson was just as tactful with White. Sometime before 1787, he framed a lengthy letter to White concerning the use of an organ in church. Graceful as always, Hopkinson carefully acknowledged the subordinate role of music, emphasized its purpose as "adoration," and taking David as his example, affirmed metrical psalmody as the most proper sort of music. The organ, wrote Hopkinson, could heighten the musical praise, but only when that use was carefully regulated and the organist made no attempt to show off his skill or to entertain the congregation. Organ interludes between verses of a psalm should give the congregation a chance to take a breath while reflecting on what has just been sung. In general, Hopkinson sums up, the organ should ever be dignified and the organist should not attempt to entertain with tuneful "airs," and still less "lilts and jiggs."[30]

The Catholics of Philadelphia, most of them German immigrants, had long enjoyed good church music. As far back as Christmas day of 1749, Lutheran minister Peter Kalm noted in his diary that he had attended Catholic services at St. Joseph's in Philadelphia which, according to Kalm, had the only functioning organ in the city.

> [T]hat which contributed most to the splendor of the ceremony was
> the beautiful music heard today. It was this music, which attracted
> so many people. . . . The officiating priest was a Jesuit, who also
> played the violin, and he had collected a few others who played the
> same instrument. So there was good instrumental music, with
> singing from the organ-gallery besides.[31]

St. Mary's, a much larger church, was built in 1763, and the next year its
trustees resolved to establish a singing school for the choir. Sixteen years later,
the *Pennsylvania Packet* for July 10, 1779, reported that various dignitaries and
the members of the Continental Congress gathered at St. Mary's on July 4,
1779, at the invitation of the Minister of France, whereupon "a *Te Deum* [was]
solemnly sung by a number of good voices accompanied by the organ."[32]

In 1787, John Aitken, a Scottish immigrant who worked as a silversmith,
engraver, and publisher of piano music, issued a collection entitled
*Compilation of Litanies and Vesper Hymns and Anthems as they are Sung in the
Catholic Church*. The volume contained music for the Mass, a requiem, litanies, and English- and Latin-text "anthems," most of the pieces by European
composers. The collection was successful enough for subsequent editions to
be issued in 1788, 1791, and 1814.

Benjamin Carr (1768–1831) became organist of St. Joseph's Catholic
Church shortly after his arrival in Philadelphia in 1793. Carr was born in London and had studied there with Samuel Arnold as well as Samuel and Charles
Wesley, sons of the great hymn writer and highly regarded both as organists
and composers. His brother, Thomas, and their father, Joseph Carr, immigrated in 1794. Benjamin settled in Philadelphia and opened a business, the
"Musical Repository," importing, selling, and publishing music. He subsequently opened a Baltimore branch, run by Thomas and Joseph, as well as a
branch in New York.

Like other expatriate English musicians, Carr was active in a variety of musical endeavors. He taught music, took part in concerts, and composed,
mostly popular songs, keyboard music, and stage works. St. Augustine's
Catholic Church was completed in 1801, and in June of that year Carr was
appointed its organist. During his tenure, which lasted until his death thirty
years later, he established an active program, performing, among other
things, abbreviated versions of Handel's *Messiah* and Haydn's *Creation*. Carr
also compiled and published a collection of music for Catholic worship,
Masses, Vespers, Litanies, Hymns & Psalms, Anthems & Motets (1805), contain-

ing anthems, masses, and other music for two treble voices and bass. Carr's own music made up the lion's share of the collection, including a remarkable if not especially original Christmas anthem, made up of disjointed fragments from Handel's *Messiah*, Haydn's *Creation*, and music by Corelli.[33]

The most heavily represented composer in Carr's collection after Carr himself was his older colleague, fellow church musician, and fellow English expatriate in Philadelphia, Rayner Taylor (ca. 1747–1825). Taylor may well have been the most talented composer of his time in America. His earliest musical training was as a chorister at the Chapel Royal in London. By the 1770s and 1780s, he had achieved a measure of success as theatre musician and stage composer in London. A number of his pieces were published and well received.

Taylor arrived in Baltimore in October of 1792, served briefly as organist of St. Anne's Church in Annapolis, gave a few performances in Virginia and Maryland, then moved to Philadelphia. In 1795, he became organist of St. Peter's Church, and in 1813 moved to a similar post at St. Paul's Church. Although there is little doubt that Taylor could have enjoyed as much success composing for the stage in America as he had in England, for whatever reason, he devoted himself for the most part to the far less lucrative occupations of teaching and church music. His contemporary, John Rowe Parker, observed: "The drudgery of teaching and a scanty organ salary have been his only recompense." Taylor was also a prolific and highly respected composer of Episcopal service music. William Smith's *The Churchman's Choral Companion to His Prayer Book* (New York, 1809) contains eleven of his pieces, and his music continued to appear regularly in similar publications up through the mid-nineteenth century.[34]

CHURCH MUSIC IN NEW YORK

Music was not a priority for New York's Anglican and Reformed churches as they slowly recovered from the effects of the September 1776 fire and the British occupation of the city (1776–1783), during which military units commandeered church buildings as hospitals and in one case a riding school.

As late as the 1790s, there are but a few comments on New York's church music by European travelers. Henry Wansey attended an afternoon service at the North Dutch Reformed Church on June 1, 1794, to hear a sermon by the renowned Presbyterian minister William Linn, one of the handful of English-speaking preachers licensed by the narrowly conservative Dutch authorities in New York. Wansey seemed most interested in use of Watts's hymns in addition to the metrical psalms that were the only music officially and customarily employed in the Dutch Reformed liturgy.[35]

Moreau de St. Méry attended Trinity Church in October of 1794 and observed only that "the hymns are sung to an extremely well-played organ." Moreau's remark is noteworthy, for Trinity's organist at the time was John Rice, who—assuming he was the same John Rice first employed by Trinity in 1741—was well over seventy and might reasonably be expected to have passed his prime by the time Moreau heard him. Some three months later, Rice was retired and his place taken by John Christopher Moller (1755–1803).[36]

Moller was German by birth, but had relocated to London around 1780 and published a considerable amount of his own music there. He arrived in New York in 1789 and took part in a city concert later that year, performing on the harpsichord. But Moller's attention seems soon to have focused on a more promising locale for his skills. He had followed with interest the publicity surrounding the completion of Tannenberg's organ for Zion Church in Philadelphia. Perceiving an extraordinary opportunity, he presented himself to the parish authorities in 1790 as a candidate for the post of organist and was quickly appointed.

Unlike other musicians in Pennsylvania's German Lutheran churches, Moller did not undertake the duties of parish schoolmaster. Instead, he pieced together a living, engaging in the usual variety of musical activities in addition to his church work. He was active as a composer, teacher, performer, and manager of a city concert series, and proprietor of a music store. When the December 26, 1794, fire at Zion rendered his services as organist unnecessary and his income was reduced, Moller returned to New York and was promptly appointed organist of Trinity Church, which had just installed its new organ. As in Philadelphia, he supplemented his modest income from playing in church by teaching, performing, composing, and publishing. In the eight or nine years left him, Moller made little if any mark on Trinity's music.[37]

Perhaps because of its role in their liturgy and tradition, New York's Lutherans were the exception to the city's torpid church music scene. They published an official English-language Lutheran hymnal in 1795, mainly through the efforts of Johann Christopher Kunze, who had left Philadelphia in 1784 to become pastor of Christ Lutheran Church in New York. Although Kunze's mother tongue was German, he encouraged the use of English out of concern for the younger generation. He even tried to preach in English, but his command of the language was so imperfect that he had to engage an English-speaking assistant, George Strebeck.[38]

The two men prepared the collection, which contained 240 hymns, over half of them translated from the German, and several other English texts from the 1789 Moravian hymnal. No music was included; the chorale melodies that went with the texts were as well known to most Lutherans as their catechism. Each text had a number that indicated one of sixty chorale tunes named in a list at the end of the volume.[39]

CHURCH MUSIC IN CHARLESTON

Although Charleston was the largest southern city, its population—only 16,359 by 1790—in no way approached that of New York, Boston, or Philadelphia. Nevertheless, its two Anglican churches, St. Philip's and St. Michael's, paid their organists relatively generously, and as a result were able to attract a string of skilled musicians during the eighteenth century.

In 1769 the Reverend Henry Purcell (1742–1803), graduate of Oxford, came to the city as assistant at St. Philip's and chaplain to the Second South Carolina Regiment. Unlike many of his fellow Anglican clergymen, he took the patriot side during the Revolution and had to flee during the British occupation. On his return to the city after its evacuation by the British in 1782, he was appointed rector of St. Michael's Church, where his organist was the highly talented Peter Valton (1740?–1784), who had at one time been deputy organist at the Chapel Royal, Westminster Abbey, and Handel's own parish church, St. George's, Hanover Square.

Valton was also a composer of modest talent whose anthems, glees, and keyboard sonatas (with violin obbligato, as was usual at the time) were in the typical correct British style. Valton had served as organist of St. Philip's from 1764 to 1780, and he and Purcell had doubtless come to know each other during that period. Purcell was an amateur musician of some accomplishment, a composer and advocate of good church music, and he immediately began to take steps to enhance the music at St. Michael's. He and Valton composed new tunes for the congregational psalmody. By 1786, records mention a male choir singing regularly.[40]

Unfortunately, Valton had but a year at St. Michael's and two years or less of life left by the time Purcell arrived. Meanwhile, Purcell himself had begun training a choir of boys from the church orphanage. His efforts were evidently successful, for not only St. Michael's but also St. Philip's soon had a functioning choir; and in 1793 there is record of the boys being engaged to sing at a local theatre.[41]

In 1801, the training of the boys for use at St. Michael's was stopped, probably because Purcell, now in his sixtieth year and nearing the end of his life, was finding the added responsibility of rehearsing the boys beyond his strength. In any event, a set of instructions to the organist, dated February 27, 1803, suggests the musical conditions at St. Michael's only a short time after Purcell's death. The organist was directed to chant along with the clerk, to receive the selected psalm and hymn texts and choose appropriate tunes for them, and to "play a solemn & well adapted Voluntary preceding the first Lesson."[42]

By 1805, efforts were underway to form another choir of boys, this time from within the parish. And shortly after, St. Michael's began another period of musical growth under the leadership of Jacob Eckhard (1757–1833), a musician of German Lutheran rather than English extraction. Born in Hesse-Kassel in 1757, Eckhard came to America in 1776 as a musician in the Hessian army. After a brief time in Richmond, Eckhard immigrated to Charleston in 1786. On April 15 of that year he was appointed organist, clerk, and schoolmaster by the German-speaking congregation of St. John's Lutheran Church. Eckhard quickly became a leading figure in Charleston's musical life, and in 1809 was appointed organist of St. Michael's, where he remained until his death in November of 1833.[43]

CONCLUSION

The years after the Revolution were a period of professionalization for American music. Nowhere was the result more pronounced than in church music. In the cities, immigrant European musicians steadily displaced the domestically trained singing masters, especially as those churches acquired organs and found themselves in need of trained organists.

Music in urban American churches became more and more like that in city churches of England and—in the case of Pennsylvania's German congregations—Germany. Even the later generation of singing masters adopted the fashionable musical styles of European church music. The distinctively American style of the Revolutionary-era singing masters was gradually restricted to rural parishes and small-town congregations.

Theatre, Concert, and Amateur Music in the Federal Era

In the 1780s and 1790s, American urban music and culture, both cultivated and vernacular, were firmly anchored in the British tradition that most citizens of the new nation shared. The seeds of the rich diversity that characterizes American vernacular culture and the arts in our time were sprouting in places like backcountry Appalachia, Southern slave quarters, the German farming communities of inland Pennsylvania, and the still-modest ethnic enclaves of the coastal seaport cities. The full flowering of that diversity, however, would have to wait until well after the mid-nineteenth century, when emancipation, successive waves of immigration, and ultimately the rise of media transformed American culture and music forever. But at the end of the eighteenth century, America was still a cultural tributary of Britain.

In the late eighteenth century, most Americans, city merchants as well as rural tradesmen and farmers, had mixed feelings about music. On the one hand, most viewed cultivated music and drama as at best the idle pursuits of a dissolute aristocracy, and at worst as temptations to immorality. Even the thoughtful John Adams, who had earlier claimed to be a student of war and politics so that his grandchildren could freely indulge in an appreciation of the arts, now dismissed them as relics of decadent European culture. Much of the disdain focused on fashionable European music and the professional musicians who played it. William Billings reflected an attitude shared by many when he declared his preference for "a few wild uncultivated sounds from a natural singer clientele" over "a Concert of Music performed by the most refined artificial singers on earth."[1]

On the other hand, amateur music was even more popular as a pastime for more and more Americans with the leisure to pursue it. Wealthy and educated Americans had pursued music as a serious pastime before the Revolution, and music professors had managed to cobble together a living in the colonies as teachers, performers, and dealers. With postwar prosperity came a new and increased demand for those activities. The growing number of prosperous merchant and planter families carefully followed the fashions and manners of the very English gentry from whom they had fought to separate themselves only a short time before. In these social circles, periodic attendance at concerts and the theatre was a sign of refinement, and a modest degree of skill in playing or singing came to be considered a necessary social grace, especially for marriageable daughters.

A new generation of British and European musicians was on hand to supply the demand for musical instruction, performance, and merchandising. A number of these men were British and Hessian bandsmen who had stayed behind when their units returned home. Most of them immigrated from England and the Continent in hopes of gaining fame and fortune, or at least of making a comfortable living. They were largely musicians of modest talent at best, and they knew it. They also knew that America's audiences would be far less critical and the communities far less competitive for them to make their way in than the musically sophisticated cities of old Europe. As it turned out, many of these immigrant musicians found a measure of success in America, though some had to move from one place to another before they found the right market for their skills. As theatres opened and concert activity resumed in the coastal cities, professional musicians had ample opportunities to supplement their incomes from private teaching with public performances. Several prospered as music publishers and dealers. Still others composed music for the amateur market, churches, and especially for the theatre.[2]

IMMIGRANT MUSICIANS

Most of the European musicians who sought their fortunes in the America come down to us, at best, as little more than names in early city directories or newspaper notices. A few were clever, talented, or industrious enough to make their mark on American musical activity in the early republic. Peter Albrecht van Hagen (1755–1803) had arrived from the Netherlands in 1774, on the eve of the Revolution, and spent the war years in Charleston. In 1789 he moved to New York with his wife Elizabeth (1750?–1810) and their eight-year-old son Peter Albrecht van Hagen, Jr. (1781–1837). In New York, van Hagen conducted a theatre orchestra, organized a subscription concert series, and taught a number of instruments, while his wife also taught keyboard and voice in their home, particularly to young ladies of prominent families. In 1796, the family moved to Boston, where the elder van Hagen again conducted a theatre orchestra and sold sheet music and imported pianos. His wife taught privately, as did his son, who had already developed into a composer and string player of some proficiency, though still a teenager.[3]

Alexander Reinagle (1756–1809) was probably the most active and prominent figure, and, except for Rayner Taylor, the most gifted composer in American music during the years after the Revolution. Reinagle had enjoyed a measure of success in Edinburgh and in London as a composer and performer. In 1782 he published *A Collection of Scots Tunes with Variations* for piano, and in 1783, a volume of piano sonatas. By the early summer of 1786, he was in New York, and on June 20 of that year he took part in a concert. In the autumn of 1786, he settled in Philadelphia, where he taught, composed, performed, and conducted both for concerts and the theatre. His celebrity attracted a number of pupils from prominent families, among them George Washington's adopted daughter. Although Reinagle returned briefly to New York during 1788 and 1789, and gave concerts in Baltimore in 1791 and Boston in 1792, his musical life centered in Philadelphia, where he lived until 1803. His last years were spent in Baltimore.[4]

In 1790, Philadelphia was both the fledgling nation's capital and its largest city. If concert and theatre life were not yet flourishing in Philadelphia, they were at least beginning to bloom. Quaker resistance and wartime austerity was fading from memory, concerts and theatre were beginning to attract audiences, and music dealers were finding a ready clientele. In 1791, Reinagle joined with Thomas Wignell to establish a new theatre company in Philadelphia. The next year, Reinagle became director of the music at the Chestnut Street Theatre and Wignell traveled to England to recruit performers for their company. In the years that followed, a flood of English and continental musicians crossed the Atlantic to seek their fortunes in Philadelphia and the other cities of the new republic. By 1794, the Wignell and Reinagle's Chestnut Street Theatre boasted an orchestra "superior to what any other theatre in America ever did or does now possess," according to one writer.[5]

Rayner Taylor (1747–1825) had been Reinagle's teacher in England. Trained as a choirboy in the Chapel Royal, Taylor had gained considerable acclaim as a composer, conductor, and performer at the Sadler's Wells and Haymarket theatres in London. Indeed, his sudden emigration to America in 1792 is somewhat puzzling, given his successes in England. The cause may have been an illicit love affair with a singer much younger than himself. In any event, Taylor performed in Richmond and Annapolis before settling in Philadelphia, where he became organist of St. Peter's Church in 1795. Although he occasionally wrote for the stage, Taylor's work in America centered for the most part on teaching and keyboard performance, rather than the theatre music that had won him such acclaim during his London years.[6]

Taylor had been associated with Benjamin Carr (1768–1831) in London. Carr was a pupil of the Wesleys and Samuel Arnold, and had enjoyed a modest degree of success as a theatre composer. His opera *Philander and Sylvia* was presented at the Sadler's Wells Theatre in 1792. Carr's father was a music publisher and dealer in London; and it is likely that the son emigrated in 1793 in order to take advantage of the growing number of composers and musicians in America by setting up a similar business.[7]

Carr opened a music dealership and publishing house in Philadelphia in 1793. In 1794, his father and brother Thomas joined him to run a Baltimore branch of the enterprise. A second branch in New York was sold to another immigrant musician and entrepreneur, James Hewitt, in 1797. Benjamin Carr remained in Philadelphia where he ran his publishing and merchandising enterprises and carried on as a performer, impresario, church organist, and composer. As early as February of 1794, his *The Caledonian Frolics* opened at the Chestnut Street Theatre under Reinagle's direction.[8]

James Hewitt (1770–1827), who bought out Carr's New York operation in 1797, had arrived in New York in the late summer of 1792. He and the group of "professors" with whom he arrived soon gave a concert and announced a subscription series for the next year. Hewitt also opened a teaching studio and like other immigrant musicians, stitched together a living from a number of activities, among them composing, conducting, and performing in theatre orchestras. Hewitt's anti-Federalist political opera, *Tammany; or The Indian Chief*, opened March 3, 1794, not without some physical danger to its composer, to be described presently. Three years later, Hewitt led the orchestra in the first performance of Carr's popular opera, *The Archers*. In 1811, he moved to Boston to become organist of Trinity Church and conductor of the orchestra at the Federal Street Theatre. He also continued to compose and teach. In his last years, he divided his professional life between New York and Boston, traveling back and forth.[9]

Gottlieb Graupner (1767–1836), an oboist and German by birth, had established himself in London and may have played in Salomon's concerts under Haydn's direction in 1791–1792. Graupner immigrated to Charleston in 1796 and moved to Boston in 1797, having married a singer from that city. Like other immigrant professors, he cobbled together a living from a number of endeavors. He ran a music store and publishing business, performed, conducted, and taught woodwinds, keyboard, and strings. In 1809, he formed the Philharmonic Society; and in 1815 along with Thomas Webb, Graupner established the Handel and Haydn Society, still in existence.[10]

THEATRES AND MUSIC

Most proper gentlemen and ladies of the late eighteenth century regarded theatres and actors with a mixture of disapproval and fascination. Actors were considered immoral and dissolute. Theatres stank of unbathed crowds, tobacco smoke, and the alcohol that flowed freely either in the lobbies or nearby taverns to which men of the audience, as well as the musicians in the orchestra, repaired during intermissions. Prostitutes solicited openly and entertained clients in a balcony set aside for them. Audiences carried on noisy conversations and expressed themselves freely and loudly during performances. Patrons who were willing to pay for the privilege had seats on the stage. They and other respectable folk in the pit were often targets, along with the actors and musicians, for the rowdy spectators in the less expensive gallery seats.[11]

Nevertheless, theatres increasingly became popular gathering places and many were built in the years after the war. Performances, lasting four hours or more, were presented on Monday, Wednesday, and Friday evenings, and sometimes Saturdays, beginning after sunset: six o'clock in winter and eight o'clock in the summer. Although Charleston's largest theatre, built in 1773, had burned in 1782, two new ones were competing for patronage by the 1790s. Three theatres flourished in Philadelphia after the 1789 repeal of anti-theatre laws passed ten years earlier during the war years. A theatre opened in Newport in 1794; Baltimore had two theatres by 1795. Boston had finally repealed its theatre prohibition in 1793, and by 1796 two theatres were vying for audiences there.[12]

All these theatres required capable orchestras; for as in England, plays of all kinds customarily included a goodly amount of music. Songs and dances were interpolated in the evening's principal play, or "mainpiece." The orchestra, or "band" as it was termed, played "waiting music" before the first act. Audiences expected musical entertainment during the intermissions between acts, as well as a farce or lighter play, the "afterpiece," which was staged after the mainpiece, again preceded by music. The number of musicians in the band varied from fewer than a dozen to twenty-five or more in the larger cities. As was common with orchestras during the eighteenth century, control was divided between the director, who set the tempo from the keyboard, and the leader, who controlled the players from his chair in the first violin section.[13]

Theatres thus provided steady employment for professional musicians, but that employment was often demeaning and could frequently be hazardous. Audiences felt free to demand the popular music they wanted to hear and to express their displeasure when it was not forthcoming by shouting down the music being played, throwing fruits, vegetables, and even stones, and generally making an uproar. On March 4, 1794, in New York, James Hewitt, conductor of the American Company's theatre, was physically abused by members of the audience at a performance of his own opera *Tammany; or the Indian Chief,* for refusing to play the political air they were demanding. Henry Wansey attended the Federal Street Theatre in Boston in May of 1794, and afterward recorded in his journal, "Between the play and the farce . . . the gallery called aloud for Yankee-doodle which after some opposition was complied with." A Philadelphia newspaper reported on January 31, 1796, that a theatre orchestra had declined to play Philip Phile's popular "President's March."[14] The spectators were boisterous in their insistence, whereupon the orchestra refused to play at all. In the end, the musicians gave the audience the tune it wanted, and the situation was calmed, except for two people in the gallery who were arrested.[15]

Louis Hallam's London Company, which had toured the colonies since 1752, finished its 1774 season in Charleston and then retreated to British Jamaica because of the rising tensions in the North American colonies. Once the war was ended, the troupe renamed itself the American Company and returned to Philadelphia in 1784. In 1785, the American Company moved on to the John Street Theatre in New York.

French refugees from the slave uprising in Santo Domingo brought Italian opera to America in 1794. Paisiello's *Barber of Seville* was performed, in English translation, in Baltimore, Philadelphia, and New York. By 1796, a French company was mounting Italian and French opera at the John Street Theatre in New York to a mixed reception. A year later, Gretry's *Richard the Lion-Hearted* was presented at Boston's Federal Street Theatre. But American audiences preferred English "operas," with their commonplace characters, earthy plots, spoken dialogue, and familiar music. In Boston, the Board Alley Theatre successfully mounted fifteen different English operas during the 1792–1793 season.[16]

English plays and operas both included spoken dialogue and music; however, in opera, as the term was understood by English and American audiences, music was more important than the plot and dramatic content. In a real sense, eighteenth-century English opera was essentially what we would term "light opera." Ballad opera had appeared in London in the 1720s as a middle-class reaction against the aristocratic fashion for Italian operas, composers, and performers. The earliest and best known ballad opera was *The Beggar's Opera* by John Gay, with familiar characters from London's underworld and song lyrics set to popular airs that were familiar to the audience. The pasticcio differed from ballad opera in that it drew on the works of celebrated composers, such as Handel and Arne, rather than popular tunes, for music to fit the opera's song lyrics. The usual English ballad opera or pasticcio opened with an overture, either a three-movement, fast-slow-fast form typical of Italian operas, or a medley of the music to be heard in the opera, similar to mid-twentieth-century American musical comedy overtures. The vocal numbers consisted of solo airs, duets, and ensembles.[17]

The first production by an American composer to be performed by a professional company was Benjamin Carr's *The Archers*, presented at New York's John Street Theatre on April 8, 1796. The opera, revised from an earlier work entitled *The Patriot, or Liberty Obtained*, was built on the story of William Tell. Its strong political overtones would certainly have pleased a late-eighteenth-century American audience. Interspersed with the dialog were songs, dances, and ensembles, all of which are now lost. Only the rondo with which the overture ended has survived.

Dance pieces, especially pantomimes, were also popular, both as afterpieces and full-length mainpieces. Continuous music accompanied acrobatics, dances, gestures, and stylized movement in pantomime; although by the 1780s, songs and spoken dialogue were also employed. Whereas characters

The John Street Theatre in eighteenth-century New York. Courtesy of the Library of Congress.

in ballad opera were usually familiar, those in pantomime were often mythological or allegorical, and elaborate costumes, scenery, and stage effects were common. *Melodrama* appeared at the end of the century. Music alternated with dialogue, or was played as a background to it to heighten its emotional impact, much like modern film music. The first American melodrama was apparently Victor Pelissier's *Ariadne Abandoned on the Isle of Naxos*. First presented in 1797 and now lost, it was characterized as follows: "between the different passages spoken by the actors will be full orchestral Music expressive of each situation and passion."[18]

CONCERT MUSIC

Concert activity resumed in the new nation during the years after the Revolution. The repertoire was similar to what had appeared on prewar concert programs; however, the quality of playing certainly improved during the late 1780s and 1790s, as more and more immigrant "professors" arrived, established themselves in the cities, and began organizing new concert series and societies. The majority of these professional performers, composers, and entrepreneurs were from London; however, there was also a liberal mix of French musicians fleeing the Reign of Terror and the colonial slave uprising in Haiti. Between 1793 and 1796, a company of French musicians from Santo Domingo toured the coastal cities.[19]

In Philadelphia, America's capital and its largest city, John Bentley established the biweekly City Concert series in the fall of 1793. Each performance was to be followed by ballroom dancing. The concerts were presented until April of 1784. The *Pennsylvania Packet* for September 9, 1784, announced a similar series for the season of 1784–1785, and yet another series was begun in the fall of 1785; however, the concerts came to a temporary halt in the winter of 1785–1786. The next year, Alexander Reinagle reestablished the City Concerts, programming a somewhat more sophisticated level of repertoire.[20]

As before, the programs were varied. Reinagle's first concert, presented October 19, 1786, included symphonies by Vanhall and Haydn, as well as a Haydn piano sonata, along with violin, cello, and flute solos, an aria (termed a "song") by the French operatic composer Gretry, and a "glee," presumably for vocal ensemble. Other concerts in Reinagle's series of 1786–1787 featured a Mozart piano sonata, an overture by J. C. Bach, a Corelli concerto, and various songs, solos, and ensemble works by lesser figures like Martini, Vanhall, and Reinagle himself. Several of the pieces, particularly the demanding ones, were repeated in subsequent concerts of the series. The Bach overture, for instance, appeared on the concert programs for January 25, February 8 and February 23. The next year, in the 1787–1788 series, Reinagle programmed a "Grand Symphony" by Haydn, along with pieces by Corelli, Stamitz, and C. P. E. Bach interspersed with the usual scattering of instrumental solos and songs, among them "Tally Ho," in the December 6, 1787, concert, sung by a Mrs. Hyde.[21]

Reinagle returned to New York in 1787, and the series was discontinued. He was back in Philadelphia in 1792 and made an attempt at another series; however, it was suspended in the spring of 1793, either because of the yellow fever outbreak or, more likely, because of Reinagle's involvement with Wignell and the Chestnut Street Theatre. Nevertheless, he evidently had the distinction of programming the first complete Haydn symphony; number 85 ("La

Poule") was performed December 29, 1792. Reinagle conducted a concert to celebrate the theatre's opening on February 2, 3, 4, and 7, 1793. The program contained pieces by Haydn and Stamitz, along with Reinagle's own music. In the spring of 1794, even as he was planning the first operatic production at the theatre, Samuel Arnold's *The Castle of Andalusia*, Reinagle took time away from his theatre activities to organize a new series of weekly concerts, in collaboration with Carr and others. Professionals and amateurs joined in performing pieces by Haydn and Stamitz; however, most of the music was by English composers.[22]

Between the concert series with an orchestra made up of professional and amateur musicians, and the public interest in theatre music that followed the opening of Wignell's and Reinagle's theatre, there was little community support for a subscription concert in Philadelphia during the season. On the other hand, the less formal summer concerts given in outdoor pleasure gardens gained in popularity. The May-through-October series at Gray's Gardens, combining popular and patriotic pieces with works by such composers as Stamitz and Haydn, ended in 1793; however, George Esterley's Harrowgate concerts, begun in 1789, ran through 1796. Other outdoor pleasure garden series continued into the nineteenth century. Typical of the repertoire programmed were pieces like Carr's *Federal Overture* of 1794, a medley of nine popular political tunes, among them "Yankee Doodle," the "Marseillaise," and "O dear, what can the matter be."[23]

The fire of 1776 and the British occupation of New York between 1776 and 1783 had depleted the city's resources. On the other hand, New York was British military headquarters during the Revolutionary War, and numerous cultivated loyalists and their families sought refuge there. Together with members of the similarly cultivated officer corps, they had organized and patronized a variety of concerts and dramatic productions, contributing their own amateur talents to play alongside professional musicians from the regimental bands.

Reinagle organized three New York concerts in 1788 and three more in 1789. The programs were generally similar to his Philadelphia concerts; however, they contained a larger number of solos and songs and a less ambitious selection of ensemble pieces. Reinagle's concert of September 28, 1788, for example, presented opening and closing ensemble "overtures"; however, the remainder of the program was made up of songs, instrumental solos, and a Trio by Boccherini, played by Reinagle and two string players. Reinagle also provided music for George Washington's inauguration ceremonies.[24]

During the early 1790s, Peter van Hagen and his wife took over management of the series. They performed a large proportion of the solo music themselves, and drew heavily on the works of Pleyel for the relatively small amount of ensemble music they programmed. Other musicians in New York also organized programs, sometimes in competition and other times in collaboration with one another. One of the van Hagens' main rivals was a group of English musicians including James Hewitt, who arrived in New York in early September of 1792. They immediately attempted to organize subscription concerts in competition with van Hagen's. As it turned out, the newcomers were plagued by problems, and their series failed. In December of 1794, Hewitt and the van Hagens collaborated in organizing three concerts for the winter and early spring season. The next year Hewitt withdrew from the arrangement, to be replaced by Frederick Rausch (1755–1823), a keyboard virtuoso who had at one time been employed at the Imperial Court in St. Petersburg, Russia, and who had arrived in New York in 1793.[25]

John Christopher Moller (1755–1803) had emigrated from London in 1790 and lived in New York for a brief period before moving to Philadelphia, where he taught, conducted, and played the organ at Zion, the city's largest church. But Zion burned in late December of 1795, and early in 1796, Moller was back in New York as organist at Trinity Church. That year, the van Hagens moved to Boston, and Moller took over the van Hagens' subscription concert series. As in Philadelphia, however, public support for subscription concerts waned as the theatre gained in popularity.[26]

In New York, again as in Philadelphia, the shift in public interest from subscription concerts to the theatre did not carry over to the lighter summer concerts in such outdoor pleasure gardens as the Vauxhall, Ranlegh, and Columbia Gardens. New York had these concerts as far back as 1766, and the events held their popularity through the end of the century. Similarly, amateur musical societies continued to flourish. Most of them were choral societies devoted to the performance of "sacred music," solo and chorus movements from oratorios, rather than orchestral music. The St. Cecilia Society, founded in 1791, was an exception, as was the Harmonical Society, established in 1796. Both focused on instrumental music. In 1799, the two organizations joined to form the Philharmonic Society.[27]

By century's end, James Hewitt was the most prominent musician in New York. His endeavors flowed with the current of public taste. Ever on alert for the promising business opportunity, he bought out the local branch of Benjamin's Carr's music store and publishing house in 1797. He led concerts at the Vauxhall Gardens and conducted the orchestra of professional musicians at the Park Street Theatre, and at the same time cultivated an amateur clientele through his music store and studio.[28]

In Charleston, the St. Cecilia Society resumed its activities after the Revolution, and concert activity by other musicians, itinerant and resident, began again. As in other American cities, musical theatre made its appearance in Charleston during the last years of the century. In 1787, Harmony Hall, outside the city, opened for theatrical productions, which were advertised as concerts because of the prejudice of most respectable citizens against plays and actors. The state legislature promptly passed a law prohibiting "theatrical representations," and Harmony Hall was forced to curtail its season. For the next two years, it functioned as a school for the teaching of amateur music, social dancing, and swordsmanship. By 1790, theatre was legal and in fashion, with English opera and a scattering of French and Italian opera presented by a refugee troupe from Santo Domingo.[29]

With the French immigrants, Charleston had a concentration and diversity of musicians sufficient to do the best European music of the era. In 1794, a second concert association, the Harmonic Society, was formed. Charleston audiences were treated to works by Haydn, Mozart, and Gluck, along with pieces by lesser figures such as Pleyel, Gretry, and Gossec, performed at as high a level of proficiency as could be had in most European cities. A benefit concert presented by singers and instrumentalists of the city on March 9, 1797, presented a symphony by Mozart—who was considered extreme by connoisseurs of the day, in comparison to Haydn—and the overture to Gluck's *Iphigenie en Aulide*. By century's end, Charleston had its pleasure gardens with their concerts of lighter fare, like other cities.[30]

Boston's concert life also saw a surge in the 1790s, though not at the level of Philadelphia or New York. The historical aversion of many, if not most, New England churches to organs deprived professional musicians of what in other places was a major source of income. On the other hand, the city developed a strong tradition of amateur music. As early as 1786, Boston had a mixed professional and amateur musical society. The *Columbian Centinal* for November 21, 1792, gave notice of a concert to be presented on the 27th, by a combined ensemble of professionals and amateurs skilled enough to manage the ambitious program consisting of symphonic works by Pleyel and Haydn, along with songs and solo on the glass harmonica and "a Quintetto, composed by Pleyel, and performed by the Gentlemen Amateurs of Boston." Graupner assembled a mixed group of amateurs and professionals for his concert in nearby Salem on May 15, 1798, including vocal and instrumental works by Pleyel, Haydn, the popular British composers Samuel Arnold and James Hook, and others.[31]

AMATEUR MUSIC AND THE MUSIC TRADES

Such combined ensembles of "professors and gentlemen" were in a real sense only the surface of amateur music making in the early republic. Amateurs who shared the stage with professionals generally had to possess a fairly high level of skill on their instruments. Obviously, not many amateur musicians could lay claim to such proficiency. Most amateurs cultivated no more than a modest amount of skill as an appropriate and laudable attribute in fashionable circles of the planter or merchant class. And of course, the majority of working Americans, farmers and craftsmen, had a measure of disdain for the performing arts as somehow immoral and of no practical use, much as had been the case before the Revolution.[32]

Men played the violin or flute, and both men and women played the guitar or keyboard instruments. Singing was enjoyed by men and women of all classes, as was ballroom dancing. Moreau de St. Méry noted, during his visit in 1789, that dancing was "less a matter of self-display than it is of true enjoyment. . . . Each one dances for his own enjoyment and not because it is the thing to do."[33]

A French visitor to Boston in 1788 captured the spirit of musical activity among the gentry in a letter he wrote home.

> Music, which their teachers formerly proscribed as a diabolical art, begins to make part of their education. . . . This art, it is true, is still in its infancy; but the young novices who exercise it are so gentle, so complaisant, and so modest that the proud perfection of art gives no pleasure equal to what they afford.

Peter van Hagen's wife especially solicited women as pupils for her instruction in theory, keyboard, and singing, "as motives of *delicacy* may induce parents to commit the tuition of young Ladies in this branch of education to one of their own sex."[34]

The piano was rapidly displacing the harpsichord as the most popular amateur keyboard instrument; however, a number of wealthy families' music rooms also boasted chamber organs, small pipe organs that were popular

Upright piano, called the "Portable Grand," by John Isaac Hawkins, Philadelphia, 1801. The Granger Collection, New York.

among the upper classes in England. Most pianos, organs, and other instruments were still being imported from England by local agents and music merchants. John Jacob Astor (1763–1848) had worked with his brother George in London, making flutes and other instruments. In 1786, his attention already turning to the fur trade with which he would lay the foundation for his massive fortune, Astor had opened a music store in New York, selling a variety of instruments imported from England. A small organ once owned by singing master Oliver Holden and now in the old State House in Boston bears an Astor Brothers label.

At the same time, however, an increasing number of American craftsmen were turning out pianos, organs, and other instruments of a quality to comparable imported ones. Samuel Blyth of Salem, Massachusetts, was making keyboard instruments as early as the 1780s. Benjamin Crehore, a stage carpenter for Boston's Federal Street Theatre, began making pianos in 1792. In New York, John Geib, who had enjoyed great success as a piano maker in London, began building pianos and organs in 1798. Thomas Dodds announced his arrival from London in the *Independent Journal* for August 13, 1785. He set up shop a few doors down from Astor's store on Queen Street, offering to make and repair keyboard instruments as well as string and wind instruments. Dodds formed a partnership with Christian Clause, another immigrant and guitar maker, and the pair began manufacturing pianos and guitars. In 1789, Washington bought one of their pianos for his stepdaughter.[35]

Most of all, colonial musicians, amateur and professional, needed sheet music and music books. In general, they had depended on imported sheet music, either ordered from London or purchased from a merchant importer; however, in the years after the Revolution, a fledgling publishing industry blossomed in America. For this clientele of musical amateurs at various stages of skill and sophistication, American publishers provided songs and piano pieces, most of them light and engaging, ephemeral and undemanding. The songs were usually the same sort of simple strophic airs—that is, two or more stanzas to the same melody—that were fashionable in England, or popular Scottish ballads. Sentimental songs were coming into fashion on the stage, and were frequently reprinted for home use.[36]

Local composers, many of them highly skilled, supplied the music. In Philadelphia, Benjamin Carr published his own music as well as Reinagle's and Rayner Taylor's. Piano pieces included medleys of songs, or "potpourris," like Carr's *Federal Overture*, originally for orchestra but arranged by the composer for piano; and variations on well-known tunes; for example, Carr's variations on "Yankee Doodle," published in 1796. Arrangements of airs from the popular stage for piano were also much in demand. Reinagle's *A Selection of the Most Favorite Scots Tunes Variations for the Piano Forte or Harpsichord* appeared in 1787. In Boston, Peter van Hagen began his *Musical Magazine* containing songs and keyboard music in 1797.[37]

The serious keyboard genre in Europe was the sonata, usually in three or more contrasting movements. Beginning with Frederick Rausch in 1794–1795, American composers and publishers also provided the more proficient keyboard amateurs among their clientele with keyboard sonatas. Composers in Philadelphia included Carr and Taylor. Reinagle also wrote sonatas; however, they were not published during his lifetime, possibly because their length and difficulty made them unmarketable even to the better amateur players in the city.[38]

Programmatic piano pieces, usually imitating the sounds of battle, also enjoyed a measure of popularity. In general they were divided into several brief movements, beginning with a march and ending with either another march or a dance. A printed narrative usually accompanied the music. Probably the best known of these pieces is Benjamin Hewitt's *Battle of Trenton*, subtitled "a Favorite Military Sonata Dedicated to General Washington," published in 1797. The piece is made up of a number of short sections, each with a descriptive title, representing the army in motion, trumpets signaling the start of the battle, guns, cannon, and so on. The sorrow of the continentals for their fallen comrades (of whom there were few at the real Battle of Trenton) is signified with the Scottish air "Roslyn Castle," associated at the time with mourning. Their victory celebration is symbolized, as might be expected, with a rollicking rendition of "Yankee Doodle."[39]

Some patriotic lyrics that were specially written for a particular event or occasion to be sung to a familiar tune were still printed in periodicals or on individual broadsides; however, from the 1750s, first in New England and then elsewhere, patriotic and political ballads, children's poems, theatrical lyrics, and especially Masonic texts began appearing more and more in collections called "songsters." Like the broadsides, these songsters contained only the words, and were intended for wide distribution.[40]

CONCLUSION

At century's end, the new American nation had only just emerged from its war for independence; it would shortly fight the British yet again to assert that independence, once and for all. Americans, in short, were busily engaged in building an economic and political base. In a real sense then, Adams was correct. Cultivated music, like the other fine arts, could flower fully only through generations of patronage by a wealthy and leisured aristocracy, and that was precisely the class Adams had in mind as exemplifying decadent European culture.

Yet music as an amateur pastime, music for social dancing, music as a component of popular theatre—*useful* music, in other words—suited the young republic. Lacking aristocratic patronage as it did, music was forced to compete in the American marketplace. Lacking aristocratic patronage as they did, musicians were forced to become entrepreneurs. Men like James Hewitt, no longer secure in his musical post at the Court in London, now had to stitch together a living in New York, performing, conducting, composing, publishing, merchandising, promoting concerts, playing the organ in churches, and so on.

Perhaps the most penetrating critique of American musical culture would be delivered well into the next century by Alexis de Tocqueville, though in the instance he was commenting on painting rather than music. Tocqueville had heard a good bit of singing and playing during his visit in 1831 and 1832, little of which he cared for, and he ventured no real musical insights. But of painting he observed, "Aristocracies produce a few great pictures, democracies a multitude of little ones." Tocqueville might well have made the same observation about music in a democracy. For all his enterprises and industry, Hewitt's only similarity to Beethoven was his life span covering the same years, birth to death. America in the 1780s and 1790s had no Beethoven; but America had Hewitt, Carr, Reinagle, and Taylor. They did not compose a few great pieces of music; indeed, they composed no great works of music. Men who were at best modestly gifted, they produced, among them, a multitude of little pieces, music of no real consequence. But in a real sense they set the course for an American musical culture that would remain flexible and vibrant enough to accommodate a constantly expanding diversity of different vernacular styles: a musical culture that would remain distinctively populist and entrepreneurial in the years to come.[41]

An A–Z of Early American Musical Figures

Adgate, Andrew (1762–1793)

A native of Connecticut, Adgate moved to Philadelphia in 1783 and founded the Institute for the Encouragement of Church Music, later reorganized as the Uranian Society. Under his direction, the Society's chorus and orchestra presented several concerts of sacred music. Adgate also compiled collections of music and wrote and published two textbooks. His life and work were cut short by the yellow fever epidemic that struck Philadelphia in 1793.

Antes, John (1740–1811)

Antes was a Moravian minister and leading composer. He was born in Pennsylvania and built string instruments there as a young man. After study in Europe, he became a missionary in Egypt. Imprisoned and tortured there, he returned to Europe and spent his last years among the Moravians of Bristol, England. Antes composed a number of excellent anthems and instrumental pieces for Moravian musicians.

Beissel, Conrad (1690/91–1768)

Beissel emigrated from Germany to Pennsylvania in 1720 and in 1732 established his own religious commune at Ephrata. A religious mystic and self-taught composer, Beissel wrote a large number of hymns set to his own distinctive melodies and harmonies and trained the choir of the Ephrata Cloister to sing them with the peculiar vocal quality he demanded.

Belcher, Supply (1752–1836)

Belcher spent his early years as a merchant, tavern keeper, and farmer in the Boston area. From 1735 on, he lived in Maine, working as a teacher, public official, and musician. His performances and compositions moved a local newspaper to characterize him as "the Handel of Maine."

Billings, William (1746–1800)

A tanner by trade and self-taught musician, Billings is the best known of the Revolutionary-era American singing masters and the foremost composer of the time. He lived and worked in Boston, teaching singing schools as far away as Maine. Billings composed some 350 pieces for voices, issuing them in six collections. Many were widely reprinted by later editors and compilers.

Bremner, James (d. 1780)

Bremner arrived in Philadelphia from England in 1763. He served as organist of St. Peter's Church until 1767, when he took up the same duties at Christ Church. He also taught several instruments, numbering among his pupils the patriot, composer, and signer of the Declaration of Independence, Francis Hopkinson.

Carr, Benjamin (1768–1831)

Carr, son of a London music merchant, was active as a performer and composer prior to his settling in Philadelphia in 1793. He promptly started his own music and publishing business. In 1794, his father and brother immigrated and set up a branch of the store in Baltimore. Carr opened yet another branch in New York which was taken over by James Hewitt in 1797. Carr became a central figure in Philadelphia's music. In addition to his business success, he taught, performed, conducted, composed, and authored instruction books.

Clemm (Klemm), John (Johann Gottlob) (1690–1762)

Clemm apprenticed as an organ builder in Germany. He immigrated to Philadelphia in 1733 and made a number of keyboard instruments, including a large organ for Trinity Church in New York, built in 1741. In 1757, he moved to the Moravian colony at Bethlehem, Pennsylvania, where he worked with David Tannenberg in his last years.

Crehore, Benjamin (1765–1831)

Crehore lived and worked in the Boston area all his life, making string and keyboard instruments. He is especially remembered for the pianos he built after 1797.

Durán, Narciso (1776–1846)

A Franciscan missionary, Durán established a renowned school for training Native musicians at Mission San José, California, in 1806. He developed a distinctive and effective curriculum and compiled a collection of church music including some of his own pieces.

Eckhard, Jacob (1757–1833)

Ekhard came to America with a Hessian regimental band during the Revolution. After the war he spent a brief time in Richmond, then settled in Charleston in 1786. He served as organist of St. John's Church and then of St. Michael's, and compiled an important body of church music.

Feyring, Philip (1730–1767)

Feyring emigrated from Germany to Philadelphia around 1750. He quickly gained recognition as a maker of keyboard instruments, including organs for three prominent churches in Philadelphia. His work was cut short by his premature death from tuberculosis.

Flagg, Josiah (1737–1795)

Flagg was both a singing master and band conductor in Boston during the ten years preceding the Revolution. His two compilations contain tunes by other composers but no music of his own. During the Revolution he became an officer in the Continental Army and seems to have done little if anything with music after the war.

Franco, Hernando (1532–1585)

Trained as a choirboy at Segovia, Franco may have come to Spanish America as early as 1554. He is first seen in 1573 as music director at Guatemala Cathedral. In 1575, he was appointed music director at Mexico City Cathedral, where he spent the remainder of his life, highly respected as both a singer and a composer.

Gante, Pedro de (1480–1572)

One of the original group of Franciscan missionaries who landed in Mexico in 1524, Gante taught music to the natives and trained boys for choirs in the Mexico City area.

Gardner, Newport (1746–1826)

As a slave in Newport, he was apprenticed by his master to the singing master Andrew Law. He subsequently bought his freedom and that of his family, and became a highly regarded performer, teacher, and composer.

Geib, John (1744–1818)

An immigrant from his native Germany, Geib established a successful piano factory in London. In 1797, he relocated with his family to New York, where he built fine pianos, as well as church and chamber organs. His sons and descendents carried on the family business up to the eve of the Civil War.

Graupner, Gottlieb (1767–1835)

Graupner served as an oboist in a German regimental band, then moved to London. In 1796, he arrived in Charleston; however, a year later he married a singer from Boston and relocated there. He established himself as a publisher and dealer, organized concerts, performed, and conducted. In 1809, he helped organize the Philharmonic Society, and in 1815 he played a prominent role in the formation of the Handel and Haydn Society.

Herbst, Johannes (1735–1812)

A Moravian clergyman, Herbst worked in his native Germany and England before settling in Lititz, Pennsylvania, in 1786. Shortly before his death he became a bishop and moved to Salem, North Carolina. In addition to the approximately 400 pieces of music Herbst composed, he also collected a large number of pieces by other composers. Herbst's music library is preserved in the Moravian Music Archives in Winston-Salem, North Carolina.

Hewitt, James (1770–1827)

Hewitt arrived in New York from London in 1792 and took over conducting the band at the Park Street Theatre. He also taught and composed. In 1797, Hewitt bought out Benjamin Carr's New York music store and publishing concern. Between 1805 and 1812 he was in Boston, as organist of Trinity Church and music director at the Federal Street Theatre. During his last years he maintained his residence in Boston while traveling to New York and Charleston.

Holden, Oliver (1765–1844)

A singing master, composer, and compiler, Holden was born in rural Shirley, Massachusetts. He worked as a farmer and carpenter, fought in the Revolution, then settled in Charlestown, near Boston, where he became a town official and eventually a representative in the state legislature. Holden also taught singing schools and published a number of highly popular compilations of church music, including over 250 of his own compositions.

Holyoke, Samuel (1762–1820)

Holyoke was a Massachusetts singing master who knew and collaborated with Holden. Unlike Holden, however, he was a Harvard graduate and for a time taught school. Most of Holyoke's efforts were given over to composing over 600 pieces, performing, and teaching singing schools in eastern Massachusetts and nearby states.

Hopkinson, Francis (1737–1791)

Hopkinson was a prominent Philadelphia patriot, statesman, and signer of the Declaration of Independence. A graduate of the College of Philadelphia (now the University of Pennsylvania), he was a talented writer and draftsman, and a fine musician. Hopkinson studied with James Bremner and for a period substituted for him as organist of Christ Church and trained boys for the church's choir. Hopkinson compiled collections of church music and composed solo songs in the fashionable, refined style of his time.

Kelpius, Jonas (1673–1708)

Kelpius arrived from Germany in 1694 along with a group of forty religious "hermits" who established their community near Philadelphia. The hermits brought musical instruments with them and provided occasional special music for German churches in the area. Kelpius also compiled a small collection of hymns.

Law, Andrew (1749–1821)

A native of Connecticut and graduate of Rhode Island College (now Brown University), Law was a prominent singing master who taught singing schools as far away as Philadelphia and Charleston, compiled collections, and authored instruction texts. He developed a notation system using note heads of different shapes in place of staff lines and spaces.

Lyon, James (1735–1794)

Lyon graduated from the College of New Jersey (now Princeton University). For the next three years, he taught in Philadelphia, composed, and compiled the first large collection of church music published in America, entitled *Urania*. In 1762, Lyon entered the ministry and for his remaining years served churches in Nova Scotia and Maine.

Moller, John Christopher (1755–1803)

Moller left his native Germany for London in 1775, and moved to Philadelphia in 1790. For five years he was organist of Zion Church in Philadelphia, where he collaborated in managing a concert series, performed, composed and carried on a publishing business. When Zion burned in December of 1795, Moller moved to New York, where he was organist of Trinity Church and managed another concert series.

Pachelbel, Charles Theodore (1690–1750)

Son of the great German master Johann Pachelbel, young Charles immigrated to Boston in 1732. After a year in Newport and a brief period in New York, he moved in 1737 to Charleston, where he spent the rest of his life as organist of St. Philip's church and a successful teacher.

Padilla, Juan de (1500–1542)

Padilla, a Franciscan missionary, arrived in Mexico from Spain in 1528 or 1529. In 1540, he followed Coronado to New Mexico, where he taught music to Native children in the mission schools. Padilla was killed in 1542 on a mission in what is now Kansas.

Pelham, Peter, Jr. (1721–1805)

Pelham arrived in Boston from London as a child in 1726. In 1732, his father, an engraver and artist, apprenticed him to the organist Charles Theodore Pachelbel. Pelham followed Pachelbel to Newport and Charleston. After seven years as organist of Trinity Church in Boston, Pelham moved to Virginia in 1750. From 1755 to 1802 he was organist of Bruton Parish Church in Williamsburg. He also composed, taught, performed, and ran a music store, supplementing his income with such nonmusical enterprises as overseeing the printing of currency and superintending the town's jail.

Pelissier, Victor (1740?–1820?)

Pelissier was one of a number of French musicians who fled the revolution in their country and the Caribbean unrest, and settled in America in 1792. From 1793 to 1811, Pelissier played the French horn in New York orchestras, composed and arranged music for the theatre, and taught. In 1811, he moved to Philadelphia and devoted much of his time to preparing and publishing twelve volumes of piano music, entitled *Pelissier's Columbian Melodies*.

Peter, Johann Friederich (1746–1813)

> Born in the Netherlands and educated in Germany, Peter arrived in America in 1770 to work in the Moravian communities of Pennsylvania and North Carolina. He composed especially fine vocal and chamber music.

Read, Daniel (1757–1836)

> Read was born in Attleboro, Massachusetts, not far from Providence, Rhode Island. He may have been a pupil of Andrew Law and of William Billings. In 1782 he moved to New Haven, Connecticut, where he spent the rest of his life. Read fought with the Connecticut militia during the Revolution. After the war's end, he ran a general store in New Haven while he compiled a number of collections and composed a considerable amount of music. Unlike such singing masters as Law and Billings, Read seldom ran singing schools.

Reinagle, Alexander (1756–1809)

> Reinagle built a solid musical reputation in England and Scotland before his immigration to America in 1786. He settled in Philadelphia, gaining quick recognition as a conductor, performer, composer, and teacher. In 1791, he collaborated in forming a theatre company. Reinagle conducted the music from the piano, and composed and arranged music for the productions. He moved to Baltimore in 1803 and spent his last years there.

Selby, William (1738/39–1798)

> Selby was highly regarded as an organist and composer in London when his brother and fellow musician John Selby (1741–1804) immigrated to Boston as organist of King's Chapel. William followed in 1773, becoming organist of Trinity Church in Newport. A year later, he joined his brother in Boston, as organist of Trinity Church. John left for Halifax with the British army in March of 1776; however, William remained, and after the war took over his brother's old post at King's Chapel in 1782. He remained there for the rest of his life, composing, performing, teaching, and organizing concerts.

Tannenberg, David (1728–1804)

> Tannenberg was the finest eighteenth-century organ builder in America. Trained as a cabinet maker in Germany, Tannenberg and a community of fellow Moravians settled in Pennsylvania in 1749. From 1757 to 1762, Tannenberg worked with the older organ builder, John Clemm, and carried on the business after Clemm's death in 1762.

Taylor, Rayner (1747–1825)

Taylor was a highly successful teacher, performer, and theatre composer in London. One of the most gifted musicians of his era, he moved to America in 1792 and after a brief period in Maryland, settled in Philadelphia. He became organist of St. Peter's Church and enjoyed high regard as a composer, performer, and teacher.

Tuckey, William (1708–1781)

Tuckey was a choir singer in Bristol, England, prior to his immigration in 1753. He settled in New York as clerk of Trinity Church. There he trained choir boys, organized concerts of sacred music, taught, and performed until 1773. Sometime after 1773, Tuckey moved to Philadelphia where, in 1778, he became clerk of St. Peter's.

Van Hagen, Peter (1755–1803)

Van Hagen and his wife arrived in Charleston from Amsterdam in 1774. In 1789, the couple and their eight-year-old son, already a proficient violinist, relocated in New York and organized a successful concert series. In 1796 the family moved again, this time to Boston, where van Hagen conducted, performed, and established a successful publishing firm.

Xuárez, Juan (d. 1555)

A priest and musician, Xuárez arrived from Spain in 1530 to become the first director of music at Mexico City Cathedral.

Appendix 1: Timeline

1492	Columbus lands in Central America
1494	First recorded instance of European music in America
1506	Columbus dies in Spain
1512	Ponce de León explores Florida Santo Domingo Cathedral and choir founded
1517	Luther begins the Reformation in Germany
1521	Cortés conquers Tenochtitlàn (Mexico City)
1523	Gante arrives in Mexico
1525/26	Palestrina born in Italy
1526	Alonzo Ortiz teaches dancing in Mexico City
1528	Mexico City Cathedral and choir established
1530	Mexico City installs its first organ; Xuárez appointed first choirmaster
1532	Gante writes Emperor Charles V praising his native choir Calvin begins his reformation, leading to the Puritans
1535	First printing press in the hemisphere set up in Mexico City

1539	Puebla Cathedral completed, Mexico
1540	Bishop of Mexico City asks Charles V for choir funds Santo Domingo Cathedral completed
1545	Council of Trent begins
1556	Charles V abdicates; Philip II King of Spain First printing of music in America, in Mexico City Mexico church council reduces the number of Native choirs
1558	Elizabeth I Queen of England
1562	Day's Psalter (Old Version) published in London Fighting between Catholics and Huguenots in France
1567	Monteverdi born in Italy
1575	Franco appointed choirmaster of Mexico City Cathedral
1586	Drake sails to West Indies
1588	Spanish Armada defeated by England
1594	Palestrina dies in Italy
1598	Quiñones begins teaching music to New Mexico Indians
1603	James I King of England
1604	Hampton Court Conference; James I denounces Puritans First American-composed music printed, Mexico City
1607	English colony established at Jamestown, Virginia
1611	King James Bible printed
1618	Thirty Years' War begins in Europe
1619	First recorded sale of slaves in the British colonies, at Jamestown
1620	John Utie, first professional musician, arrives in Jamestown Benevides reports to Philip IV of Spain on New Mexico choirs Plymouth Colony established in Massachusetts
1621	Dutch West Indies Company established in Amsterdam
1622	Padilla appointed choirmaster of Pueblo Cathedral

1624	Dutch establish Fort Orange (Albany) in New Netherlands
1626	Dutch purchase Manhattan Island, establish New Amsterdam
1630	Massachusetts Bay Colony (Boston) founded
1636	Harvard College founded, Massachusetts
1640	Bay Psalm Book published
1642	English Civil War begins
1643	Monteverdi dies in Italy
1647	Cotton publishes *Singing of Psalms a Gospel Ordinance* in Boston
1649	Charles I of England beheaded
1658	Oliver Cromwell dies
1660	Monarchy restored in England; Charles II
1664	Dutch surrender New Netherlands to the English; renamed New York
1670	Charles-Town (Charleston), South Carolina established
1675/76	King Philip's War in New England
1678	Vivaldi born, Italy
1682	Philadelphia established
1683	German immigrants establish Germantown, near Philadelphia
1685	James II King of England Handel born, Germany Bach born, Germany Protestantism outlawed in France
1688	Glorious Revolution in England, William and Mary crowned
1692	Salem witch panic in Massachusetts
1693	College of William & Mary established, Virginia
1694	Kelpius and his Hermits arrive in Philadelphia

1696	Tate and Brady's Psalter (New Version) published, London
1698	First Bay Psalm Book with tunes published in Boston
1702	Anne Queen of England
1703	Falckner ordained, Philadelphia; music by Kelpius's Hermits
1708	Watts's *Hymns and Spiritual Songs* published, London
1710	First mention of a concert in New York
1713	First church organ in colonies in King's Chapel, Boston
1714	First recorded singing school, Boston George I King of England
1716	First theatre in the colonies opens, Williamsburg
1719	Watts's *Psalms of David Imitated* published in London
1720	Burnet arrives in New York as Royal Governor Symmes publishes *The Reasonableness of Regular Singing*, Boston
1721	Mather publishes *The Accomplished Singer*, Boston Walter publishes *The Grounds and Rules of Musick Explained*, Boston Tufts publishes *Introduction to the Singing of Psalm-Tunes*, Boston Robert Walpole first British Prime Minister
1727	Burnet gives Dutch Reformed Church in New York his chamber organ Burnet leaves New York for Boston George II King of England
1728	*The Beggar's Opera* first performed in London Christ Church, Philadelphia and St. Philip's Charleston, install organs
1731	First recorded public concert in Boston
1732	First recorded public concert in Charleston Beissell and his followers establish Ephrata, Pennsylvania Haydn born, Austria
1733	Pachelbel arrives in Newport Clemm, instrument maker, arrives in Pennsylvania

1735	First American ballad opera, *Flora or Hob in the Wall*, Charleston
1736	Pachelbel presents two concerts in New York First recorded fiddling contest, rural Virginia
1737	Pachelbel settles in Charleston
1739	Trinity Church, New York, establishes a choir of charity school boys
1740	Moravians settle in Pennsylvania and North Carolina Great Awakening religious revivals
1741	Clemm completes an organ in Trinity Church, New York Vivaldi dies, Italy
1744	Musick Club of amateurs founded, Philadelphia Moravians form *Collegium Musicum* in Pennsylvania
1745	Hamilton and others form the Tuesday Club, Baltimore
1747	Beissel completes Ephrata hymn collection, *Turteltaube*
1750	Peter Pelham settles in Williamsburg Bach dies, Germany
1752	Hallam's London Company performs *The Beggar's Opera*, Williamsburg
1753	Tuckey becomes music director at Trinity Church, New York
1754	Deblois opens a concert hall in Boston
1755	Tuckey presents his first concert in New York First known printing of the "Yankee Doodle" tune, London Bruton Parish Church, Williamsburg, installs an organ Peter Pelham appointed organist of Bruton Parish Church Seven Years' (French and Indian) War begins
1756	Mozart born, Austria
1757	First recorded concert in Philadelphia, given by John Palma Washington attends second Palma concert, Philadelphia
1759	Hopkinson composes the first known piece of American music St. Anne's, Annapolis, installs an organ Handel dies, London

| 1760 | Hulett organizes a concert series at Ranlegh Gardens in New York |
| | George III King of England |

1761	Lyon's *Urania* published, Philadelphia
	Benjamin Franklin invents the glass harmonica
	Hopkinson performs his *Ode in Memory of George II*

| 1762 | St. Cecilia Society founded, Charleston |

1763	Treaty ending Seven Years' War signed in Paris
	Bremner arrives in Philadelphia
	Hopkinson publishes *Collection of Psalm Tunes*, Philadelphia

1764	Bremner concert for the Christ Church, Philadelphia organ fund
	Flagg publishes *A Collection of the Best Psalm Tunes*, Boston
	Trinity Church, New York, installs an organ by Snetzler of London

1765	Stamp Act passed in Parliament
	Bremner organizes a concert for the Philadelphia Charity School
	Patrick Henry delivers "Give me liberty or give me death" speech
	Christ Church, Savannah, installs an organ
	Psalmodia Evangelica, first German Lutheran hymnal, New York
	Stamp-Act Congress, Philadelphia

1766	Stamp Act repealed in Parliament
	Flagg publishes *Sixteen Anthems*, Boston
	Feyring completes an organ for Christ Church, Philadelphia

1767	John Street Theatre opens, New York
	Vauxhall Gardens opens, New York
	Townshend Acts passed in Parliament
	Dickinson publishes first *Letters from a Farmer*

1768	Snetzler organ in St. Michael's, Charleston
	Dickinson publishes "Liberty Song" broadside
	British army units land in Boston

| 1769 | Tuckey sings lead in *The Beggar's Opera*, New York |

Serra establishes San Diego mission, California
Napoleon born, Corsica

1770   Tuckey presents parts of Handel's *Messiah*, New York
Boston Massacre
Lord North British Prime Minister
Repeal of Townshend Acts
Amateur Harmonic Society formed, New York
Rivington opens a music store, New York
Billings publishes *The New England Psalm Singer*
Beethoven born, Germany

1771   John Selby arrives in Boston as organist of King's Chapel
Flagg presents concerts in Boston with a British military band
Flagg presents another concert in Boston with the British military band

1772   John Selby presents a benefit concert for Boston's poor
British vessel *Gaspeé* grounded and burned, Rhode Island

1773   Parliament passes tax on tea
John Selby presents a concert of Handel's music in Boston
William Selby arrives in Newport
Boston "Tea Party"

1774   "Intolerable Acts" passed in Parliament
Congress convenes in Philadelphia
Congress publishes a resolution against entertainments
Peter van Hagen arrives and presents a concert in Charleston

1775   Battles of Lexington, Concord, Bunker (Breed's) Hill, Fort Ticonderoga
Washington appointed commander of the Continental Army

1776   Thomas Paine publishes *Common Sense*
John Selby leaves Boston with the British army evacuation
Declaration of Independence drafted
British army occupies New York
Much of New York burns, including Trinity Church
William Selby arrives in Boston from Newport
Washington's victory at Trenton

1777	Congress drafts Articles of Confederation
	British occupy Philadelphia
	Burgoyne surrenders at Saratoga
	Washington encamps at Valley Forge
1778	France allies with America against British
	British evacuate Philadelphia, Congress returns
	Congress renews resolution against entertainment, Philadelphia
	Billings publishes *The Singing Master's Assistant*, Boston
	Tuckey appointed clerk at St. Peter's, Philadelphia
	British occupy Savannah
1779	Billings publishes *Music in Miniature*, Boston
	Spain allies with France and America
1780	British occupy Charleston
	French land at Newport
	Charleston suspends the St. Cecilia concerts
	Benedict Arnold deserts to British
1781	Billings publishes *The Psalm-Singer's Amusement*, Boston
	Cornwallis surrenders, Yorktown
	French and American thanksgiving concert in Zion, Philadelphia
1782	Peace negotiations, Paris
	British band musicians present a concert, New York
	Peace terms agreed on
1783	War officially ends; Treaty of Paris signed
	Continental Army disbands
	Oliver Holden publishes *The Union Harmony* in Boston
	St. Cecilia concerts resume in Charleston
1784	Adgate forms Music Institute, Philadelphia
1785	Bentley organizes a subscription concert series in Philadelphia
	Brown begins a subscription concert series in New York
1786	Adgate organizes a "Grand Concert," Philadelphia
	William Selby forms the Musical Society in Boston
	Reinagle arrives in New York
1787	Aitken publishes *A Compilation of Litanies*, Philadelphia

1788	Hopkinson's *Seven Songs* published, Philadelphia
	Draft completed by Constitutional Convention, Philadelphia
1789	Pennsylvania repeals the law against theatres
	Congress convenes, New York
	Washington inaugurated president
	Bastille stormed, beginning of French revolution
1790	Tannenberg completes organ for Zion Church, Philadelphia
	Benefit concert for Billings by William Selby at King's Chapel, Boston
	Moller arrives in New York
1791	Mozart dies, Austria
	Bill of Rights adopted
	Toussaint l'Ouverture leads a slave revolt, Haiti
1792	Van Hagen and Capron organize a concert series, New York
	Pelissier arrives in Philadelphia
	Hewitt arrives in New York
	Taylor arrives in New York
1793	France abolishes slavery in its colonies
	Taylor settles in Philadelphia
	Reinagle and Wignell open theatre, Philadelphia
	Carr opens Music Repository, Philadelphia
	Pelissier performs in New York
	Boston repeals its ordinance against theatres
	Read publishes *The Columbia Harmonist*, Boston
1793/94	Reign of Terror, Paris; Louis XVI beheaded
1794	Paisiello's *Barber of Seville* in English by a touring company
	Federal Street Theatre opens, Boston
	Hewitt and Capron begin City Concerts in New York
	William Billings publishes *The Continental Harmony* in Boston
1796	Carr's *The Archers* performed in New York
	Van Hagen and his family relocate to Boston
	Napoleon invades Italy
1797	Hewitt buys Carr's New York publishing house and store
	Graupner arrives in Boston
	Geib arrives in New York

1798   Park Street Theatre opens in Boston
                Geib builds his first pianos and organs, New York
                Napoleon invades Egypt

1799   Washington dies

Appendix 2:
Selected Concert Programs

I. Presented October 16, 1765, in the Orange Garden Theatre, Queen Street, Charleston, South Carolina, organized by Thomas Pike, music and dancing instructor, "performed by gentlemen of the place, for the entertainment of all lovers of music. Concerto on the French Horn and Bassoon by Mr. Pike" (*South Carolina Gazette*, September 7–14, 1765).

Act I

French Horn Concerto

2d Concerto of [John] Stanley

Solo on the Violoncello

5th Concerto of Stanley

Bassoon Concerto

Song

Ouverture [*sic*] in Scipio [an opera by George Frideric Handel]

Act II

French Horn Concerto

Concerto on the Harpsichord

Trio

Note: Page numbers refer to Oscar G. T. Sonneck, *Early Concert-Life in America, 1731–1800* (Leipzig: Breitkopf & Härtel, 1907; reprint, New York: Musurgia, 1949).

Bassoon Concerto

Song

French Horn Concerto of [Johann Adolf] Hasse (15)

    II. A "Mr. Stotherd" presented a concert at "Mr. Burn's room" in New York, February 9, 1770, along with "Several gentlemen who [were] pleased to patronize the concert." (*New York Journal*, February 1, 1770).

Act 1st

1st Overture of [J. C.] Bach, Opera prima

3rd Concerto of [Charles] Avison, Opera quarta

A Hunting Song—Black Sloven [?]

A French Horn Concerto, by Mr. Stotherd

4th Concerto of Stanley

Duet on the French Horn

8th Periodical Overture

Act 2d

Overture of [Handel's] Saul

Select pieces for four French Horns

2d Concerto of Humphries [?]

A Hunting Song

A French Horn Concerto, by Mr. Stotherd

3d Concerto of [Archangelo] Corelli

Overture of [Handel's] Atalanta

After the concert there will be a ball (170–171)

    III. "*To the Public.* By particular desire, on Friday, (being the 12th October [1770]) a concert of music will be directed by Mr. [Giovanni] Gualdo, in which the following pieces will be performed in two acts." The concert took place in Philadelphia at "Mr. Davenport's in Third Street" (*Pennsylvania Chronicle*, October 1–8, 1770).

Act I

Overture with Violins, German Flutes, French Horns, etc.—

Concerto with Solos for two German Flutes—Quartetto—

Trio—Solo upon the Clarinet—Symphony—

Solo upon the Violin.

Act II

Overture—Concerto upon the German Flute—Solo upon the Harpsichord—Quartetto—

Solo upon the Mandolin—Symphony (74)

IV. On May 17, 1771, Josiah Flagg offered Boston music lovers a program of "vocal and instrumental musick accompanied by French horns, hautboys, etc. by the band of the 64th [British] Regiment" (*Boston Evening Post*, May 13, 1771).

Act I

Overture Ptolomy[*sic*]. . . . . Handel
Song "From the East breaks the morn"
Concerto 1st. . . . . Stanley
Symphony 3d. . . . . [J. C.] Bach

Act II

Overture 1st. . . . . [Friedrich] Schwindl
Duet to "Turn fair Clora"
Organ concerto
Periodical Symphony . . . . . [Johann] Stamitz

Act III

Overture 1st . . . . [Carl Friedrich] Abel
Duetto "When Phoebus the tops of the hills"
Solo Violin
A new Hunting Song, set to music by. . . Mr. Morgan [organist of Trinity Church Newport]
Periodical Symphony . . . . Pasquale Ricci (262)

V. John Selby, organist of King's Chapel in Boston, organized a concert to commemorate the twelfth anniversary of George III's accession, October 26, 1772, at Deblois Concert Hall (*Boston Evening Post*, October 5 and 12, 1772).

Act First

1st. Periodical sinphonia [*sic*] . . . . . [J. C.] Bach
Song
2d. Corelli's [*sic*] Concerto
Song
4th Periodical Sinphonia . . . . [?] Filitz

2d. Act [*sic*]

1st. Abel's 7th opera [?]
Song
Harpsichord
20th Periodical Sinphonia. . . . . [Niccolò] Piccini
Handel's Grand Coronation Anthem in 22 parts [probably "Zadok the Priest"] (273)

VI. "MUSIC. On Tuesday Evening the 17th instant will be performed at Mr. Hull's Tavern, for the use of Mr. Caze, an extraordinary instrumental and vocal *Concert* in two acts, consisting of different solos, upon various instruments, unknown in this country, to be executed by the gentlemen of the Harmonic Society, who have been pleased to promise their assistance" (*New York Mercury*, May 16, 1774).

1st Act.

A grand Orchestry's [*sic*] Symphony

A French Ariette will be sung accompanied with the guitar and violin

Mr. Caze will play his own composed music, on the violin with Mr. Zedtwitz

A Concert on the Flute

A Sonada [*sic*] on the Spanish Guitar

The first Act to end with a March

IId Act.

A Grand Orchestry's Symphonie [*sic*]

A French Ariette accompany'd with the Mandolin and Violin

A Solo on the Violin

A Duo on the Mandoline and Violin

A Sonada of the Saltario [?]; and d'Exaudet's [?] Minuet with echos [*sic*].

The Concert to finish with a March of the grand Orchestry

After the Concert, there will be a ball (174–175)

VII. A concert was presented at the German Reformed Church, Race Street in Philadelphia, April 12, 1787, under the direction of Andrew Adgate (*Pennsylvania Packet*, April 9, 1787).

Syllabus

I. [Giovanni Battista] Martini's celebrated Overture

II. Jehovah reigns: an anthem from the 97th Psalm . . . . [William] Tuckey

III. Te Deum Laudamus . . . . [Samuel] Arnold

IV. Violin Concerto. . . . . By Mr. [Philip] Phile of New York

V. I heard a great Voice: an Anthem from Rev. XIV . . . . [William] Billings

VI. Vital Spark: an Anthem on Mr. Pope's ode

    The dying Christian to his soul . . . . Billings

VII. Overture in Ataxerxes . . . . [Thomas Augustin] Arne

VIII. Friendship thou charmer of the Mind: From Watts's

    Lyric Poems . . . . [James] Lyon

IX. The Rose of Sharon: an Anthem from 2d of Canticles . . . . . Billings
X. Flute Concerto. . . . . By the Chevalier Du Ponceau
XI. Sundry Scriptures: an Anthem on the Nativity of Christ. . . . [?] Williams
XII. The Hallelujah chorus: on the extent and duration of Christ's
 Government (from the Messiah) . . . . Handel (114)

VIII. On October 15, 1792, Peter van Hagen and his family presented the first of three concerts at Corrie's Hotel in New York (*Daily Advertiser,* October 1, 1792).

Act I

Grand Overture of . . . . [Ignaz] Pleyel
Song . . . . Mrs. Mechtler
Forte Piano Concerto . . . . . Mrs. Van Hagen
Flute Concerto . . . . Mr. Saliment

Act II

Violin Concerto . . . . Mr. Van Hagen
Song . . . . Mrs. Mechtler
Forte Piano Concerto . . . . . Mrs. Van Hagen
Sinfonia Finale of . . . . Pleyel

Several gentlemen, amateurs, of the St. Cecilia Society in this city, have obligingly consented to honor the performers with their assistance. (190)

IX. On March 6, 1794, the St. Cecilia Society of Charleston sponsored a concert at West and Bignall's Theatre "for the benefit of the distressed inhabitants of St. Domingo now in this city" (*City Gazette,* March 6, 1794).

Act 1st.

Sinfonie . . . . Pleyel
Song, Mr. Chambers
Quartett Violin . . . . Pleyel
Song, Mr. Clifford
Overture . . . . [André] Gretrie [*sic*]

Act 2d.

Grand Overture (la Chasse) . . . . [François-Joseph] Gossec
Song, Mr. West
Sonata Pianoforte, Rondo by Mrs. Sully
Duett, Mr. Chambers & Mrs. Chambers

Act 3d.

Grand Overture. . . . . Haydn
Song, Mr. Chambers

Concerto Violin, by Mr. Petit . . . . . [Giovanni Batista] Viotti
Glee, Mr. Chambers, Mrs. Chambers, and Mr. West

AFTER THE CONCERT

A Double Allemande and Reel, by Mr. M. Sully, Mrs. Chambers and Miss Sully.

A Grand Ballet, by Mons. Francesquy, Mons. Dainville, Mons. Val and Madame Val.

The whole to conclude with Manly Feats of Activity [?] by Mr. M. Sully.

Boxes to be taken as usual. Tickets at 5 s[hillings] each . . . None but the managers admitted on stage. (29–30)

   X. On March 9, 1797, several gentlemen as "instrumental principal performers" and two singers presented a concert in Williams's Long Room in Charleston for the benefit of the widow of a deceased musician, Joseph Lafar (*City Gazette*, March 6 and 8, 1797).

PLAN OF THE CONCERT

Act 1st.

Overture in Iphigenie . . . . Gluck
Song, Mrs. Placide
Concerto, Mr. Devillers . . . [Jean Baptiste] Krumpholtz
Duet, Mr. West and Mrs. Placide
Rondo . . . . Pleyel

Act 2d.

Grand Simfonie [*sic*] . . . . Mozart
Song, Mr. West
Concerto Violin, Mr. Petit. . . . Jarnovick [?]
Song, Mr. West
Simfonie . . . . [Louis] Massonneau (36–37)

Appendix 3:
Selected Discography

America Sings: 1. The Founding Years. Gregg Smith Singers. Vox CDX5080.

This is a relatively old recording, remastered on compact disc from earlier Vox albums. The two compact discs offer a variety of seventeenth- and eighteenth-century American music, from Puritan psalms to Revolutionary-era singing masters, Moravian music, and Hopkinson's songs.

An American Journey: Bound for the Promised Land. Waverly Consort, directed by
  Michael Jaffee. Angel Records.

The music spans the years from 1750 to 1855; however, a good portion of it is from the Colonial and Revolutionary periods, including pieces from Playford's *Dancing Master's Assistant*, and vocal music by late-eighteenth-century singing masters.

Ballads by the Waters of Colonial America. The D-Major Singers. Privately issued.

A quartet of singers presents a program of twenty-eight folk ballads from the Colonial era, accompanied by guitar, violin, and harpsichord.

The Birth of Liberty: Music of the American Revolution. New World Records 80276-2.

A variety of ensembles perform vocal and instrumental music, including marches, popular pieces, political songs, and other music of the Revolutionary era.

A Choir of Angels I. I Cantori, directed by Edward Cansino. Civic Records [no number].

Although the program on this disc spans several centuries, it includes pieces by seventeenth-century Spanish colonial composers.

A Choir of Angels II: Mission Music. Zephyr—Voices Unbound. Civic Records [no number].

A program of seldom heard, never recorded pieces, both Native and Spanish, from California's missions, along with a *Magnificat* by Francisco Capillas, seventeenth-century choirmaster of Mexico City Cathedral.

Christmas in Early America. The Columbus Consort. Channel Classics 5693.

The program includes music by late-eighteenth-century Moravian composers, as well as William Billings and Benjamin Carr. Of particular interest is Carr's "Anthem for Christmas," a medley of melodies from Handel's *Messiah* and Haydn's *Creation.*

Come and Trip It: Instrumental Dance Music, 1780s to 1920s. Federal Music Society et al. New World Records 80293-2.

Though the span of years is large, there is a selection of early pieces including fiddle tunes and a minuet by Reinagle.

Early American Choral Music. His Majestie's Clerkes, directed by Paul Hillier. Classical Express 3957048 and 3957128.

These two compact discs, available separately, are inexpensive reissues of earlier recordings, one of them *Goostly Psalms* (see below), but without the extensive booklet notes that accompanied the original release. Together, they provide a broad sampling of music by American "tunesmiths" of the eighteenth century and the English tunebook composers who influenced them.

The Flowering of Vocal Music in America, 1767–1823. New World Records 806467-2

The two compact discs contain Moravian and Anglo-American music for voices and instruments, including Benjamin Carr's song cycle "The Lady of the Lake."

Goostly Psalms: Anglo-American Psalmody, 1550–1800. His Majestie's Clerkes, directed by Paul Hillier. Harmonia Mundi 907128.

This compact disc contains a variety of psalmody from England and America, accompanied by an especially comprehensive booklet of notes.

The Gospel Ship: Baptist Hymns and White Spirituals from the Southern Mountains. New World Records 80294-2.

This recording, made on location, contains nineteenth-century hymns, rather than colonial psalmody; however, this conservative congregation has retained the "Old Style" of singing, including lining out by a leader, such as would have been heard in a seventeenth-century New England church.

Liberty Tree: Early American Music, 1776–1861. Boston Camerata, directed by Joel Cohen. Erato 3984-21668-2.

The program includes songs, marches, and popular music of the late eighteenth century, accompanied by a careful and complete set of booklet notes.

Lost Music of Early America: Music of the Moravians. The Boston Baroque, directed by Martin Pearlman. Telarc 80482.

The music, for voices and instruments, is by no means lost, notwithstanding this compact disc's title. On the other hand, much of it is recorded here for the first time. The performances, using instruments of the era, are especially fine.

Make a Joyful Noise: Mainstreams and Backwaters of American Psalmody. Oregon State University Choir, directed by Ron Jeffers. New World Records 80255-2.

This CD includes not only pieces by well known "tunesmiths" like Billings, Read, and Holden, but also lesser known figures such as Timothy Swan and Supply Belcher.

Marching Out of Time. The Fifers and Drums of Colonial Williamsburg. Colonial Williamsburg Digital Series [no number].

A generous selection of marches, dances, and song medleys, along with an illustrated booklet.

El Milagro de Guadalupe. San Antonio Vocal Arts Ensemble. Iago CD214.

Sixteenth-century Mexican sacred music in both Spanish and the Aztec language, Nahuatl. Some of the pieces utilize Aztec instruments to excellent effect.

Music of the Federal Era. Federal Music Society, directed by John Baldon. New World Records 80299-2.

A selection of instrumental music by Holyoke, Taylor, Carr, Pelissier, and others not available elsewhere.

New Britain: The Roots of American Folksong. Boston Camerata, directed by Joel Cohen. Erato Records 2292-45474-2.

A fine recording by a leading ensemble, this record traces the evolution of the modern American folk song back to its origins in Britain and on the European continent.

Nueva España: Close Encounters in the New World, 1590–1690. Boston Camerata, directed by Joel Cohen. Erato 2292-45977-2.

The varied program is accompanied by a booklet with full program notes.

Rivers of Delight: American Folk Hymns from the Sacred Harp Tradition. Word of Mouth Chorus. Nonesuch 971360-2.

Although the *Sacred Harp* first appeared in the nineteenth century, it is a direct descendent of the eighteenth-century singing school tradition, and many of its hymns were reprinted from the works of New England singing masters like Billings, Read, and Holden. The chorus's vocal production is open and nasal, in the late-eighteenth-century style.

La Siècle d'or à la Cathédrale de Mexico. La Capella Cervantina, directed by Horacio Franco. Association Française d'Action K617 M7 865.

Music of Mexico City Cathedral from the sixteenth to the eighteenth centuries.

Songs of the People of Colonial America. The D-major Singers. Privately issued.

Twenty-five seventeenth- and early-eighteenth-century folk ballads, performed by a quartet of singers, some of them accompanied by guitar, fiddle, or harpsichord.

Spain in the New World: Renaissance, Baroque and Native American Music from New Spain. Hesperus, directed by Scott Reiss and Tina Chancey. Koch International 3-7451-2H1.

This program opens with a selection of sixteenth-century Spanish music, but the larger part consists of pieces from seventeenth- and eighteenth-century Latin America.

Trav'ling Home: American Spirituals (1770–1870). The Boston Camerata, directed by Joel Cohen. Erato 0630-12711-2.

Although it covers a century, the content of this disc includes Revolutionary- and Federal-period pieces composed or compiled by lesser known singing masters like Timothy Swann, Moses Kimball, and Jeremiah Ingalls.

White Spirituals from the Sacred Harp. Field recording of the 1959 Alabama Sacred Harp Convention. New World Records 80205-2.

The rural *Sacred Harp* tradition preserves the open, nasal vocal style and the format of the late-eighteenth-century singing school, both of which are documented on this disc.

William Billings: Wake Ev'ry Breath. William Appling Singers. New World Records
     80539-2.
This disc is devoted exclusively to Billings and offers a representative sampling of his music.

The World Turned Upside Down. Barry Phillips and Friends. Gourd GM110.
Not especially authentic, but nonetheless charming arrangements of folktunes and dances of the Colonial and Revolutionary eras.

Appendix 4:
Music Examples

1. Psalm 95 from Ainsworth's *The Booke of Psalmes* (1612). Ainsworth's psalter of 1612, used by the Plymouth colonists, gives this tune for Psalm 97, but indicates it is to be used also for Psalms 37, 45, and 95, each of them having a pattern of ten syllables for each line.

> Come, let us to the Lord showt joyfully;
> to the rock of our health showt triumphantly.
> Let us prevent his face with thanksgiving;
> let us with psalms to him triumphant sing.
>
> because the Lord is a great God mightie;
> a great king eke, above al Gods is hee.
> In whose hand are the earth's deep secrecies;
> the strong heights of the mountains eke are his. . . .

2. Psalm 95 from *The Whole Booke of Psalmes* (Bay Psalm Book), 9th edition (1698). The Puritan ministers of the Massachusetts Bay Colony published the

first edition of their own metrical psalm translations in 1640 without music. The ninth edition of the Bay Psalm Book, as it was popularly known, published in 1698, was the first to include tunes, taken unchanged from Playford's *An Introduction to the Skill of Musick* (1674, 1679). Playford's publication was intended for instruction and recreation, so the tunes contained an added bass part, although only the melody was sung in public worship. The tune and text, in rigid common meter, lack the flow and grace of Ainsworth's tune and text.

O come let us unto the Lord,
shout forth with joyful voice;
To th' Rock of our salvation
let's make triumphant noise.

Let us with giving thanks draw nigh
his holy presence to;
Let us with Psalms triumphantly
unto him sing also.

For god the Lord most mighty is,
great king o'er all gods he.
Th' earths deeps are in his hand & his
the strengths of mountains be. . . .

3. Sedauny, or Dargason, from Playford's *The English Dancing Master* (1651) is better known as "The Irish Washerwoman." A popular dance and ballad tune dating from the sixteenth century, it also appears in Ravenscroft's collection of part songs, *Pammelia* (1609), to the text,

Oft have I ridden upon my gray nag
and with his cut tail he played the wag,
and down he fell upon his cragge
fa la re la, la re dan dino.

4a. Chevy Chase (Child No. 162) was one of the most popular British folk songs of the eighteenth century, both in Britain and America. The lengthy ballad tells of a battle between bands of English and Scottish knights over hunting rights. It is in common meter and dates from the fifteenth century. The first two stanzas of the text:

God prosper long our noble king,
Our lives and safeties all.
A woeful hunting once there did
In Chevy Chase befall.

To drive the deer with hound and horn,
Lord Percy took the way;
The child may rue, that is unborne,
The hunting of that day . . .

4b. The popular Chevy Chase tune appeared in eighteenth-century ballad operas, either complete or in part. This fragment of the air is from Act III, Scene 13 of John Gay's *The Beggar's Opera*. Macheath is imprisoned and condemned to hang. "In a melancholy Posture," he drinks as he sings: "But now again my Spirits sink; I'll raise them high with Wine."

5. "Yankee Doodle," sung to political ballads by both sides, is perhaps the best known air from the American Revolution. This version of the tune, headed "Yankey Doodle," appears as a dance tune without any text in an American manuscript dating from about 1730.

6. William Billings's tune "Chester," along with the first stanza of its patriotic text, appeared first in *The New-England Psalm Singer* (1770), published in Boston the year of the so-called "Boston Massacre," when feeling was running high.

Let tyrants shake their iron rods,
And slav'ry clank her galling chains.
We fear them not, we trust in God.
New England's God forever reigns.

An ardent patriot, Billings reprinted it with four additional stanzas in *The Singing Master's Assistant* (1778), at the height of the war.

7. According to legend, though there is no substantial evidence, the defeated British marched out of Yorktown to "The World turned upside down." In fact, the tune was popular with the troops and well known to British regimental fifers, whether or not they played it on the occasion of Cornwallis's surrender. The air was associated with two popular texts dating from the seventeenth century, either one of which might have seemed appropriate to the demoralized British: "The World turned upside down," and "When the King enjoys his own again."

Listen to me and you shall hear
New hath not been this thousand year.
Since Herod, Caesar and many more,
You never heard the like before.
Holy days are despis'd, new fashions are devised,
Old Christmas is kicked out of Town.
Yet let's be content and the times lament,
You see the world turned upside down. . . .

Let rogues and cheats prognosticate
Concerning king's or kingdom's fate.
I think myself to be as wise
As he that gazeth on the skies.
My sight goes beyond the depth of a pond,
Or rivers in the greatest rain,
Whereby I can tell that all will be well
When the King enjoys his own again. . . .

8. "Windham," a solemn tune by the Connecticut tunesmith Daniel Read, appeared in his 1785 collection, *The American Singing Book*, set to an appropriately solemn text by Isaac Watts.

Broad is the road that leads to death,
And thousands walk together there.
But wisdom chose the narrow'r path
With here and there a traveler. . . .

9. "Washington's March," sometimes called "Washington's March at the Battle of Trenton," by an unknown composer, was quite popular at the end of the eigheenth century. This version for piano, published in New York around 1800, is typical of the large amount of undemanding music composed and printed during the period for those with limited skills. In 1798, a New York dealer, Gilbert's Musical Magazine, published and sold a vocal arrangement of the same piece, "The Ladies Patriotic Song, Sung by Mrs. Hodgkinson with Universal Applause At the Columbia Gardens." Doubtless the applause was for the sentiments rather than the awkward poetry.

Columbians arise, INDEPENDENCE proclaim;
'Tis Beauty now calls you in Liberty's Name,
'Tis Beauty now calls you in Liberty's Name . . .

10. Oliver Holden's "Coronation" is probably the best known eighteenth-century American hymn. It appears in virtually every twentieth-century hymnal of almost every denomination, with the original hymn text, written in 1779 by the English Methodist minister Edward Perronet (1726–1792).

Notes

CHAPTER 2

1. J. H. Elliot, *Imperial Spain, 1469–1716* (London: Penguin, 1970), 67, 61. See also David J. Weber, *The Spanish Frontier in North America* (New Haven, CT: Yale University Press, 1992); Alan Taylor, *American Colonies* (New York: Viking, 2001), 58; Elliot, *Imperial Spain, 1469–1716*, 57.

2. Bartolomé de las Casas, *History of the Indies*, trans. and ed. Andrée Collard (New York: Harper & Row, 1971), 78–81; Jacob Maurice Coopersmith, "Music and Musicians of the Dominican Republic: A Survey," Pt. 1, *Musical Quarterly* 31:1 (January 1945), 76–81. The estimate of 90 percent is from de las Casas's *History of the Indies*, 115.

3. Bernal Díaz de Castillo, *The True Story of the Conquest of Mexico*, trans. and ed. Albert Idell as *The Bernal Díaz Chronicles* (Garden City, NY: Doubleday, 1957), 160, 368.

4. Robert M. Stevenson, *Music in Aztec and Inca Territory* (Berkeley: University of California Press, 1973), 8, 104.

5. Hugh Thomas, *Conquest: Montezuma, Cortés, and the Fall of Old Mexico* (New York: Simon and Schuster, 1993), 292, 388, 418.

6. Stevenson, *Music in Aztec and Inca Territory*, 41, 63. Stevenson lists and describes the Aztec instruments in some details, 30–85. Robert M. Stevenson, *Music in Mexico* (New York: Thomas Y. Crowell, 1952), 17–31.

7. In modern Latin America, the term *villancico* has come to mean a type of Christmas song, much as *carol*, originally a group dance, has come to mean a Christmas song in English-speaking countries.

8. Daniel Mendoza de Arce, *Music in Ibero-America to 1850* (Lanham, MD: Scarecrow Press, 2001), 4–5; Stevenson, *Music in Aztec and Indian Territory*, 155–156.

9. Stevenson, *Music in Mexico*, 54; Thomas, *Conquest*, 589.

10. Gilbert Chase, *The Music of Spain* (New York: W. W. Norton, 1941; reprint, New York: Dover Publications, 1959), 258.

11. Stevenson, *Music in Mexico*, xi–xii, 53–54, 58–59. See also Lota M. Spell, "Music in the Cathedral of Mexico in the Sixteenth Century," *The Hispanic-American Historical Review* 26:3 (August 1946), 293–319.

12. Stevenson, *Music in Mexico*, 138–139.

13. Mendoza de Arce, *Music in Ibero-America*, 113–114. See also Steven Barwick, "Mexico," in *The Early Baroque Era*, ed. Curtis Price (Englewood Cliffs, NJ: Prentice Hall, 1994), 349–360.

14. Leonard Ellinwood, *The History of American Church Music* (New York: E. P. Gorham, 1953; reprint, New York: Da Capo Press, 1970), 4; Mendoza de Arce, *Music in Ibero-America*, 114–117; Robert M. Stevenson, "Mexico City Cathedral Music," *Inter-American Music Review* 9:1 (Winter 1987), 81.

15. Mendoza de Arce, *Music in Ibero-America*, 285–286.

16. Robert M. Stevenson, "Puebla Chapelmasters and Organists: Sixteenth and Seventeenth Century," *Inter-American Music Review* 5:2 (Spring–Summer 1983), 21.

17. Ibid., 22; Stevenson, *Music in Mexico*, 122.

18. Stevenson, *Music in Mexico*, 119, 122.

19. Mendoza de Arce, *Music in Ibero-America*, 39, 43–44, 65; Stevenson, *Music in Aztec and Inca Territory*, 163, 171.

20. Stevenson, *Music in Aztec and Inca Territory*, 164; Stevenson, *Music in Mexico*, 60–64; Chase, *The Music of Spain*, 261.

21. Stevenson, *Music in Aztec and Inca Territory*, 167; Stevenson, *Music in Mexico*, 64; Orpha Ochse, *The History of the Organ in the United States* (Bloomington: Indiana University Press, 1975), 3.

22. Stevenson, *Music in Aztec and Indian Territory*, 169–170.

23. Stevenson, *Music in Mexico*, 68.

24. John Fesperman, *Organs in Mexico* (Raleigh, NC: Sunbury Press, 1979), 15; Ochse, *History of the Organ in the United States*, 3.

25. Stevenson, *Music in Mexico*, 63, 68; Mendoza de Arce, *Music in Ibero-America*, 45.

26. Stevenson, *Music in Mexico*, 33, 68; Fesperman, *Organs in Mexico*, 3; Chase, *The Music of Spain*, 259. An enlightened Spanish priest and missionary who had founded the School of Santa Cruz in 1536 for children of the Indian aristocracy, Sahagún (1499?–1590) was also the author of a twelve-volume history of the Aztecs from Native sources and traditions, including a narrative of the Mexican conquest based on Aztec accounts.

27. Stevenson, *Music in Mexico*, 160–164; Mendoza de Arce, *Music in Ibero-America*, 6–7, 161, 163, 207.

28. Wiley L. Housewright, *A History of Music and Dance in Florida* (Tuscaloosa: University of Alabama Press, 1991), 26–28.

29. Ibid., 34–39.

30. Robert M. Stevenson, *Protestant Church Music in America* (New York: W. W. Norton, 1966), 1.

31. Housewright, *Music and Dance in Florida*, 17–20.

32. Ellinwood, *History of American Church Music*, 5; Fesperman, *Organs in Mexico*, 4.

33. Lincoln Bunce Speiss, "Benevides and Church Music in New Mexico in the Early Seventeenth Century," *Journal of the American Musicological Society* 17:2 (Summer 1964), 147–150.

34. Robert Stevenson, "Music in California: A Tale of Two Cities," *Inter-American Music Review* 5:1 (Fall/Winter 1988), 41; Norman A. Benson, "Music in the California Missions, 1602–1848," *Student Musicologists at Minnesota* 3 (1968–1969), 134–135.

35. Francis Fletcher, *The World Encompassed by Sir Francis Drake* (London, 1652), 72.

36. Benson, "Music in the California Missions," 154–156.

37. Ardis O. Higgins, "The Revival of Early Mission Music," *Music/AGO* 10:1 (January 1976), 28; James Boeringer, "Early American Church Music in California," *Journal of Church Music* 18:5 (May 1976), 3; William Summers, "California Mission Music," in *The New Grove Dictionary of American Music,* ed. H. Wiley Hitchcock and Stanley Sadie (New York: Macmillan, 1986), 1:345–347. See Owen da Silva, *Mission Music of California* (Los Angeles: W. F. Lewis, 1941, 1954).

38. Summers, "The Organs of Hispanic California," *Music/AGO* 10:11 (November 1976), 50–51; Ochse, *History of the Organ in the United States*, 8; Benson, "Music in the California Missions," 158.

39. Benson, "Music in the California Missions," 138.

CHAPTER 3

1. Bruce C. Daniels, *Puritans at Play: Leisure and Recreation in Colonial New England* (New York: St. Martin's Press, 1995), 52. The primary study is still Percy Scholes, *The Puritans and Music in England and New England* (London: Oxford University Press, 1934; reprint, 1969).

2. Nicholas Temperley, *The Music of the English Parish Church* (Cambridge: Cambridge University Press, 1979), 59–60, 68.

3. Edmund S. Morgan, *Visible Saints* (Ithaca, NY: Cornell University Press, 1975), 54–56. The separatists among the Puritans held that the English church could not be purified from within and therefore separated themselves from it.

4. Lorraine Inserra and H. Wiley Hitchcock, *The Music of Henry Ainsworth's Psalter*

(Amsterdam, 1612) (Brooklyn, NY: I.S.A.M. Monographs, 1981), 3; Edward Winslow, *Hypocrasie Unmasked* (London: Richard Cotes for John Bellamy, 1646), 91.

5. Cotton Mather, *Magnalia Christi Americana*, ed. Raymond J. Cunningham (New York: Unger, 1970), 21: "[T]hey did, as the light of nature itself directed them, immediately in the harbor sign an instrument, as a foundation of their future and needful government"; Sidney Ahlstrom, *A Religious History of the American People* (New Haven, CT: Yale University Press, 1972), 136–137.

6. David Hackett Fischer, *Albion's Seed: Four British Folkways in America* (New York: Oxford University Press, 1989), 13–39.

7. Cotton Mather, *Ratio Disciplinae Nov-Anglorum* (Boston: S. Gerrish, 1726), 5; emphasis in original.

8. Larzer Ziff, *Puritanism in America* (New York: Viking, 1973), 53; Darret B. Rutman, *American Puritanism* (New York: W. W. Norton, 1977), 12–13.

9. Temperley, *The Music of the English Parish Church*, 41.

10. Thomas Symmes, *The Reasonableness of Regular Singing, or, Singing by Note* (Boston: B. Green for Samuel Gerrish, 1721), 18.

11. Scholes, *The Puritans and Music*, 260–261.

12. A relatively accessible source for the text is Elwyn A. Weinandt, *Opinions on Church Music* (Waco, TX: Baylor University Press, 1974), 28–35; Henry Wilder Foote, *Three Centuries of American Hymnody* (Cambridge, MA: Harvard University Press, 1940; reprint, Hamden, CT: Shoe String Press, 1961).

13. *The Psalms, Hymns and Spiritual Songs of the Old & New Testament: Faithfully Translated into English Metre* (Boston: B. Green and J. Allen, 1698). The tunes also had letters, representing singing syllables: F[a] S[ol] L[a] and M[i]. For a list of tunes, facsimiles, and discussion, see Richard G. Appel, *The Music of the Bay Psalm Book* (Brooklyn, NY: I.S.A.M. Monographs, 1975); and Zoltan Haraszti, *The Enigma of the Bay Psalm Book* (Chicago: University of Chicago Press, 1956). On Playford's tunes, see also Charles Edward Lindley, "Scoring and Placement of the 'Air' in Early American Tunebooks," *Musical Quarterly* 58:3 (July 1972), 365–382; Irving Lowens, "The Bay Psalm Book in 17th Century New England," in Lowens, *Music and Musicians in Early America* (New York: W. W. Norton, 1964), 36–38, suggested that an earlier edition, possibly an unknown sixth or seventh edition published in London by Chiswell, also contained tunes.

14. There is evidence that as early as 1594 most congregations were singing all the psalms to only four tunes. See Temperley, *The Music of the English Parish Church*, 68; Foote, *Three Centuries of American Hymnody*, 370–382. The practice appeared about the same time in England, and for the same reasons; see also Nicholas Temperley, "John Playford and the Metrical Psalms," *Journal of the American Musicological Society* 25:3 (Fall 1972), 331–378. In the service, the psalm was usually read in prose and expounded on by the minister before the congregation sang it. Ainsworth's psalter printed the prose and metrical versions side by side, as well as a comment below on the page. Temperley, *The Music of the English Parish Church*, 82, suggests that lining

out would also have helped in the learning of a new psalm translation, for instance, the Bay Psalm Book.

15. M. Halsey Thomas, ed., *The Diary of Samuel Sewall, 1674–1729* (New York: Farrar, Strauss and Giroux, 1973), 1: 283 and *passim*; David McKay and Richard Crawford, *William Billings of Boston* (Princeton: Princeton University Press, 1975), 13; Foote, *Three Centuries of American Hymnody*, 374–386; Scholes, *The Puritans and Music*, 262–265; David W. Music, "The Diary of Samuel Sewall and Congregational Singing in Early New England," *The Hymn* 41:1 (January 1990), 7–15.

16. The conservative Puritan ministers of Boston regarded Brattle Street Church as dangerously close to Anglicanism. Their suspicions can only have been confirmed by that congregation's refusal to adopt the practice of lining out and the choice of Tate and Brady's New Version rather than the Bay Psalm Book.

17. Robert Stevenson, *Protestant Church Music in America* (New York: W. W. Norton, 1966), 13–14.

18. See W. Thomas Marocco and Harold Gleason, *Music in America* (New York: W. W. Norton, 1964), 21–22; Richard Crawford, *The Core Repertory of Early American Psalmody* (Madison, WI: A-R Editions, 1984), 11–12.

19. Thomas Symmes, *The Reasonableness of Regular Singing*, 10.

20. Thomas Symmes, *Utile Dulci, or, a Joco Serious Dialogue Concerning Regular Singing* (Boston: B. Green for S. Gerrish, 1723), 17; Thomas Walter, *The Grounds and Rules of Musick Explained: Or, an Introduction to the Art of Singing by Note Fitted to the Meanest Capacities* (Boston: J. Franklin for S. Gerrish, 1721), 3.

21. Walter, *The Grounds and Rules*, 3.

22. Thomas Symmes, *The Reasonableness of Regular Singing, or Singing by Note* (Boston: B. Green for Samuel Gerrish, 1720), under the pseudonym, "Philomusicus." The text may be found in George Hood, *A History of Music in New England* (Boston: Wilkins, Carter & Co., 1846; reprint, New York: Johnson Reprints, 1970, 91–104. See also Allen P. Britton, "Theoretical Introductions in American Tune-Books to 1800" (Ph.D. dissertation, University of Michigan, 1949), 96–100.

23. Kenneth Silverman, *The Life and Times of Cotton Mather* (New York: Columbia University Press, 1985), 303–305; Cotton Mather, *The Diary of Cotton Mather 1709–1724* (Boston: Massachusetts Historical Society, 1912), 560, 660; Cotton Mather, *The Accomplished Singer . . . How the Melody of Regular Singing, and the Skill of doing it, according to the Rules of it, may be easily arrived unto* (Boston: B. Green for S. Gerrish, 1721). An excerpt is in Perry Miller and Thomas H. Johnson, eds., *The Puritans* (New York: Harper, 1963), 452–453.

24. Nicholas Tawa, *From Psalm to Symphony: A History of Music in New England* (Boston: Northeastern University Press, 2001), 28–29.

25. Daniels, *Puritans at Play*, 54–56; Foote, *Three Centuries of American Hymnody*, 383. The letter is dated March 20, 1722, and signed by one Ephraim Rotewell.

26. Mather, *Diary*, 8:796–797. See also Foote, *Three Centuries of American*

Hymnody, 383–386; Stevenson, *Protestant Church Music in America*, 23; Ellinwood, *The History of American Church Music*, 21; Irving Lowens, "Music in the American Wilderness," in Lowens, *Music and Musicians in Early America*, 19.

27. Irving Lowens, "The First American Music Textbook," in Lowens, *Music and Musicians in Early America*, 39–57; Allen P. Britton, Irving Lowens, and Richard Crawford, *American Sacred Music Imprints, 1698–1810* (Worcester, MA: American Antiquarian Society, 1990), 584–586.

28. Lowens, "The First American Music Textbook," 51.

29. Hood, *A History of Music in New England*, 138–139. Two consistent complaints against the revivals were that there was too much singing at the meetings, and that the singing was "hymns of human composure," rather than psalms.

30. Joanne Grayeski Weiss, "The Relationship Between the 'Great Awakening' and the Transition from Psalmody to Hymnody in the New England Colonies" (D.A. dissertation, Ball State University, 1988), argues that the rapid adoption of Watts's texts in America, even in anti-revivalist congregations, was an integral part of the Great Awakening.

31. Hood, *A History of Music in New England*, 155; Silverman, *The Life and Times of Cotton Mather*, 304; Foote, *Three Centuries of American Hymnody*, 50–68.

32. Weiss, "The Relationship," 145, 162–164.

33. Carleton Sprague Smith, "Broadsides and Their Music in Colonial America," in *Music in Colonial Massachusetts, 1630–1820* (Boston: Colonial Society of Massachusetts, 1985), 157–163; Cynthia Hoover, "Epilogue to Secular Music in Early Massachusetts," in *Music in Colonial Massachusetts*, 766–768.

34. The most accessible book is Claude M. Simpson, *The British Broadside Ballad and Its Music* (New Brunswick, NJ: Rutgers University Press, 1966).

35. Joy van Cleef and Kate van Winkle Keller, "Selected American Country Dances and Their English Sources," in *Music in Colonial Massachusetts*, 6–11.

36. Scholes, *The Puritans and Music*, 58; [Increase Mather?], *An Arrow against Profane and Promiscuous Dancing. Drawn out of a Quiver of the Scriptures By the Ministers of Christ at Boston in New-England* (Boston: Printed by Samuel Green to be Sold by Joseph Brunning, 1684), 30; Hoover, "Epilogue," 734–735; Barbara Lambert, "Music Masters in Colonial Boston" (Appendix C), *Music in Colonial Massachusetts*, 946–954; Kate van Winkle Keller and Charles Cyril Hendrickson, *George Washington: A Biography in Social Dance* (Sandy Hook, CT: The Hendrickson Group, 1998), 20–21.

37. Van Cleef and Keller, "Selected American Country Dances," 8–11.

38. Thomas, ed., *The Diary of Samuel Sewall*, 1: 195, 198, 418; The Covent Garden Theatre opened in 1732, so the "Consort Musick" took place in a private home or concert rooms. Scholes, *The Puritans and Music*, 46.

39. Barbara Lambert, "Social Music, Musicians and Their Musical Instruments in and Around Colonial Boston," in *Music in Colonial Massachusetts* 453, 467. Lambert found thirty-eight owners of instruments among the original Bay settlers. Her complete inventory of musical instruments and their owners appears on pp. 422–441.

40. Thomas, ed., *The Diary of Samuel Sewall*, 1:602; Samuel P. Fowler, ed., *Diary of Rev. Joseph Green, of Salem Village* (Salem, MA: Essex Institute Historical Editions 10:1, 1869), 90.

41. Barbara Owen, *The Organs and Music of King's Chapel*, 2nd ed. (Boston: King's Chapel, 1993), 2–7, 32–33. See also Owen, *The Organ in New England* (Raleigh, NC: Sunbury Press, 1979), 1–20. Trinity Church, Newport, Rhode Island, received an English organ in 1733, the gift of the philosopher and bishop George Berkeley.

42. Lambert, "Social Music," 409; a facsimile is given on 410.

43. Lambert, "Social Music," 497. The list appears on 499 and in facsimile on 500.

44. Barbara Owen, "Eighteenth Century Organs and Organ Building in New England," in *Music in Colonial Massachusetts*, 670–671.

CHAPTER 4

1. Giles Milton, *Big Chief Elizabeth* (New York: Picador, 2000), 6–15. Milton provides an accessible account of early British adventures in America.

2. "Sir Richard Greenville for Sir Walter Ralegh to Virginia, in the Yeere 1585," in *Virginia 1584–1607*, ed. Alan Smith (London: Theodore Brun, 1957), 18–27; Richard Beale Davis, *Intellectual Life in the Colonial South, 1585–1763* (Knoxville: University of Tennessee Press, 1978), 149, 1254–1256.

3. Victor Yellin, "Musical Activity in Virginia Before 1620," *Journal of the American Musicological Society* 22 (Fall 1969), 284–289; Albert Stoutamire, *Music of the Old South: Colony to Confederacy* (Rutherford, NJ: Fairleigh Dickinson University Press, 1972), 16–17; Davis, *Intellectual Life in the Colonial South*, 152, 1254–1255.

4. Eileen Southern, *The Music of Black Americans*, 3rd ed. (New York: W. W. Norton, 1997), 3; Peter Kolchin, *American Slavery, 1619–1877* (New York: Hill and Wang, 1993), 42; Richard Jobson, *The Golden Trade* (London, 1623), quoted in Southern, *The Music of Black Americans*, 5; Robert J. Allison, ed., *The Interesting Narrative of the Life of Olaudah Equiano [or Gustavus Vassa, the African] Written By Himself* ([London, 1789; New York, 1791] New York: St. Martin's Press, 1995), 36.

5. Maurer Maurer, "The 'Professor of Musicke' in Colonial America," *Musical Quarterly* 36:4 (October 1950), 511.

6. Ronald L. Davis, *A History of Music in American* Life (Malabar: FL: Robert Krieger, 1982), 55; R. B. Davis, *Intellectual Life*, 1255–1256, 1259; Maurer Maurer, "A Musical Family in Colonial Virginia," *Musical Quarterly* 34:3 (July 1948), 361.

7. Maurer, "A Musical Family," 359–361.

8. John Barry Talley, *Secular Music in Colonial Annapolis: The Tuesday Club, 1745–1756* (Urbana: University of Illinois Press, 1988), 30; R. B. Davis, *Intellectual Life*, 1259; Maurer, "A Musical Family," 363.

9. Louis B. Wright, *Life in Colonial America* (New York: Capricorn Books, 1971),

192–195; Edmund S. Morgan, *Virginians at Home: Family Life in the Eighteenth Century* (Williamsburg, VA: Colonial Williamsburg, 1952), 75.

10. The only popular abridgement, Louis B. Wright and Marion Tinling, eds., *The Great American Gentleman: The Secret Diary of William Byrd of Westover in Virginia* (New York: Capricorn Books, 1963), is no longer in print as of this writing.

11. Southern, *The Music of Black Americans*, 27, 44–51; Stoutamire, *Music of the Old South*, 27.

12. Maurer, "A Musical Family," 358; Orpha Ochse, *The History of the Organ in the United States* (Bloomington: Indiana University Press, 1975), 33–34.

13. Wright and Tinling, eds., *The Great American Gentleman*, 118–119.

14. John W. Molnar, "A Collection of Music in Colonial Virginia: The Ogle Inventory," *Musical Quarterly* 49:2 (April 1963), 150–162.

15. R. B. Davis, *Intellectual Life*, 1268; Helen Cripe, *Thomas Jefferson and Music* (Charlottesville: University of Virginia Press, 1974), 6.

16. Talley, *Secular Music in Colonial Annapolis*, 26, 24.

17. Ibid., 24.

18. Ibid., 36–39, 45–54; Carl Bridenbaugh, ed., *Gentleman's Progress: The Itinerarium of Dr. Alexander Hamilton, 1744* (Pittsburgh: University of Pittsburgh Press, 1948), xii–xvi. Hamilton's "The History of the Ancient and Honorable Tuesday Club" exists in three parts, one each in the Maryland Historical Society, the Library of Congress, and the library of The Johns Hopkins University. Robert J. Micklus's three-volume *History of the Ancient and Honorable Tuesday Club* (Chapel Hill: University of North Carolina Press, 1990), a revised version of his 1980 University of Delaware dissertation, is both costly and hard to find; however, a shortened version (Baltimore, MD: Johns Hopkins University Press, 1995) is available at this writing.

19. Talley, *Secular Music in Colonial Annapolis*, 25, 36, 54–57, 110–111, 116–118; R. B. Davis, *Intellectual Life*, 1266–1267.

20. Talley, *Secular Music in Colonial Annapolis*, 50, 57–58; Bridenbaugh, *Gentleman's Progress*, 118–122.

21. Talley, *Secular Music in Colonial Annapolis*, 16.

22. R. B. Davis, *Intellectual Life*, 1266.

23. Talley, *Secular Music in Colonial Annapolis*, 11, 27.

24. *The Churches of Charleston and the Low Country* (Charleston: Preservation Society of Charleston), v.

25. Richard Hofstadter, *America at 1750* (New York: Random House Vintage, 1973), 166.

26. Thomas J. Wertenbaker, *The Golden Age of Colonial Culture* (Ithaca, NY: Cornell University Press), 9–10.

27. Maurer, "The 'Professor' of Music," 518.

28. Elise Pinckney, ed., *The Letterbook of Eliza Lucas Pinckney 1739–1762* (Chapel Hill: University of North Carolina Press, 1972), 25–26, 48–49.

29. Oscar G. T. Sonneck, *Early Concert-Life in America 1731–1800* (Leipzig: Breitkopf & Härtel, 1907), 11–12.

30. Ronald L. Davis, *Music in American Life*, 48; R. B. Davis, *Intellectual Life*, 1264; Henry Charles Lahee, *Annals of Music in America* (1922; reprint, Freeport, NY: Books for Libraries, 1970), 4.

31. Sonneck, *Early Concert-Life*, 14.

32. Ronald L. Davis, *Music in American Life*, 49; Sonneck, *Early Concert-Life*, 16–17; Maurer, "The 'Professor' of Music," 518.

33. R. B. Davis, *Intellectual Life*, 1270.

34. Ochse, *The History of the Organ in the United States*, 33; Talmadge W. Dean, "The Organ in Eighteenth Century Colonial America" (Ph.D. dissertation, University of Southern California, 1960), 42–43.

35. Sonneck, *Early Concert-Life*, 13; Virginia Larkin Redway, "Charles Theodore Pachelbell [sic], Musical Emigrant," *Journal of the American Musicological Society* 5:1 (Spring 1952), 30–36.

36. Elizabeth A. Fenn and Peter H. Wood, *Natives and Newcomers: How We Lived in North Carolina before 1770* (Chapel Hill: University of North Carolina Press, 1983), 24–35; Marvin L. Michael Kay and Lorin Lee Cary, *Slavery in North Carolina, 1748–1775* (Chapel Hill: University of North Carolina Press, 1995), 11, 15–16.

37. Ron Byrnside, *Music in Eighteenth-Century Georgia* (Athens: University of Georgia Press, 1997), 62–71.

38. Ibid., x, 8–15.

39. Hofstadter, *America at 1750*, 171; Byrnside, *Music in Eighteenth-Century Georgia*, 24–25.

40. Byrnside, *Music in Eighteenth-Century Georgia*, 26, 30–31, 33.

41. William B. Clarke Jr. and Jacquelyn A. Royal, *Organs of Savannah* (Savannah, GA: Savannah Blue Print Co., 2000), Chapter 2 [unpaginated typescript]; Byrnside, *Music in Eighteenth-Century Georgia*, 55.

42. Byrnside, *Music in Eighteenth-Century Georgia*, 33, 35; Ochse, *History of the Organ in the United States*, 92; Dean, "The Organ in Eighteenth-Century Colonial America," 42–44; Byron K. Wolverton, "Keyboard Music and Musicians in the Colonies and United States of America before 1830" (Ph.D. dissertation, Indiana University, 1966), 164.

43. James G. Leyburn, *The Scotch-Irish: A Social History* (Chapel Hill: University of North Carolina Press, 1962), 157–158, 176–178, 185; Patrick Griffin, *The People with No Name: Ireland's Ulster Scots, America's Scots Irish, and the Creation of a British Atlantic World, 1689–1764* (Princeton, NJ: Princeton University Press, 2001), 100–103.

44. Stoutamire, *Music of the Old South*, 24; Morgan, *Virginians at Home*, 81; Chris Goertzen, "Balancing Local and National Approaches at American Fiddle Contests," *American Music* 14:3 (Fall 1996), 353–354; Thomas Jefferson Wertenbaker, *The Southern Colonies* (New York: Charles Scribner's Sons, 1942), 205.

CHAPTER 5

1. Martin Medforth, "The Low Countries," in *The Early Baroque Era*, ed. Curtis Pierce (Englewood Cliffs, NJ: Prentice Hall, 1994), 206–217; E. S. De Beer, ed., *The Diary of John Evelyn* (New York: Oxford University Press, 1959), 29.

2. Charles H. Kaufman, *Music in New Jersey, 1655–1860* (Teaneck, NJ: Fairleigh Dickinson University Press, 1981), 24; Jon Butler, *Becoming America: The Revolution Before 1776* (Cambridge, MA: Harvard University Press, 2000), 185.

3. Kate van Winkle Keller, "Secular Music to 1800," in *Cambridge History of American Music*, ed. David Nicholls (London: Cambridge University Press, 1998), 53.

4. Barbara Lambert, "Social Music, Musicians and their Musical Instruments in and around Colonial Boston," in *Music in Colonial Massachusetts, 1630–1820* (Boston: Colonial Society of Massachusetts, 1985), 2:497–502.

5. *Travels through the Middle Settlements in North-America in the years 1759 and 1760 with observations upon the state of the Colonies, By the Rev. Andrew Burnaby, A.M.* (London: T. Payne, 1755; reprint, Ithaca, NY: Cornell University Press, 1960), 80–81; Keller, "Secular Music to 1800," 54.

6. Sonneck, *Early Concert-Life*, 158–162.

7. Amy Aaron, "William Tuckey: A Choirmaster in Colonial New York," *Musical Quarterly* 44:1 (January 1978), 79–97; Arthur Messiter, *A History of the Choir and Music of Trinity Church, New York* (New York: E. P. Graham, 1906; reprint, New York: AMS Press, 1970), 19–31.

8. *New York Mercury*, March 11, 1754.

9. A complete example of Tuckey's work, his tune "Knighton," to the text of Tate & Brady's Psalm 100, from Simeon Jocelin's *The Chorister's Companion* (New Haven, 1782), is reprinted in W. Thomas Marrocco and Harold Gleason, *Music in America* (New York: W. W. Norton, 1964), 181–182.

10. Keller, "Secular Music to 1800," 54; Sonneck, *Early Concert-Life*, 163–171; Kenneth Silverman, *A Cultural History of the American Revolution* (New York: Thomas Y. Crowell, 1976), 37–38.

11. John Ogasapian, *Organ Building in New York City, 1700–1900* (Braintree, MA: Organ Literature Foundation, 1977), 1–2. The first church, it will be recalled, was Boston's King's Chapel, which in 1713 had received a small organ from the estate of Thomas Brattle.

12. Messiter, *A History of the Choir and Music of Trinity Church, New York*, 290; William H. Armstrong, *Organs for America* (Philadelphia: University of Pennsylvania, 1967), 13–14, 19; Ogasapian, *Organ Building in New York City*, 3–6.

13. Carl Bridenbaugh, ed., *Gentleman's Progress: The Itinerarium of Dr. Alexander Hamilton, 1744* (Pittsburgh: University of Pittsburgh Press, 1948), 45; Messiter, *A History of the Choir and Music of Trinity Church*, 9–31; Carl Bridenbaugh, *Cities in Revolt: Urban Life in America, 1743–1776* (New York: Oxford University Press, 1955), 194.

14. Edward C. Wolf, "Lutheran Church Music in America During the Eighteenth and Early Nineteenth Centuries" (Ph.D. dissertation, University of Illinois, 1960), 37–46.

15. Percy Scholes, *The Puritans and Music in England and New England* (Oxford: Clarenden Press, 1934), 52–53.

16. Keller, "Secular Music to 1800," 54. Nicholas Tawa, "Philadelphia: A City in the New World," in *The Classical Era*, ed. Neal Zaslaw (Englewood Cliffs, NJ: Prentice Hall, 1989), 368–369; Oscar G. T. Sonneck, *Francis Hopkinson, the First American Poet-Composer (1737–1791), and James Lyon, Patriot, Preacher, Psalmodist (1735–1794): Two Studies in Early American Music* (Washington, DC: McQueen, 1905; reprint, New York: Da Capo Press, 1967), 11–13.

17. Bridenbaugh, *Gentleman's Progress*, 191, 22–23.

18. Sonneck, *Early Concert-Life*, 64; Silverman, *A Cultural History of the American Revolution*, 31.

19. *Church Music and Musical Life in Pennsylvania in the Eighteenth Century*, 4 vols. [CMML] (Philadelphia: Publications of the Pennsylvania Society of the Colonial Dames of America, 1926–1947; reprint, New York: AMS Press, 1972), III(1):240–241; Sonneck, *Francis Hopkinson and James Lyon*, 29; Silverman, *A Cultural History*, 33–34.

20. Sonneck, *Early Concert-Life*, 66–68, 73.

21. [Burnaby], *Travels*, 54.

22. Sonneck, *Francis Hopkinson and James Lyon*, 122–128.

23. Esmond Wright, *Franklin of Philadelphia* (Cambridge, MA: Harvard University Press, 1986), 127–128; H. W. Brands, *The First American* (New York: Doubleday Anchor, 2000), 325.

24. Sonneck, *Francis Hopkinson and James Lyon*, 29–34, 128.

25. Francis Hopkinson, *A Collection of Psalm Tunes, with a few Anthems and hymns, some of them entirely new, for the use of the United Churches of Christ Church and St. Peter's Church in Philadelphia* [Philadelphia: Henry Dawkins?], 1763; CMML III(1): 240–241; Sonneck, *Francis Hopkinson and James Lyon*, 29.

26. Dedication of Hopkinson's *Seven* [actually, eight] *Songs For Harpsichord* (Philadelphia: J. Aitken, 1788).

27. CMML III(1):261.

28. The resulting barform, AAB, is typical of the German art song of the time.

29. CMML I:12–17, 21–165; Robert Stevenson, *Protestant Church Music in America* (New York: W. W. Norton, 1966), 32–33.

30. CMML I:166–176, 197, 211. The Swedish churches ministered to the Lutherans among the early German immigrants, even though the Church of Sweden was orthodox and ceremonial, while most of the Germans were pietists. Kelpius and his Hermits had supplied music for the consecration of Gloria Dei on July 2, 1700. Talmadge W. Dean, "The Organ in Eighteenth Century English Colonial America" (Ph.D. dissertation, University of Southern California, 1960), 80–88; Julius Sachse, *Justus*

Falckner (Philadelphia, 1903), 45–46, 64; Raymond J. Brunner, *That Ingenious Business: Pennsylvania Organ Builders* (Birdsboro, PA: The Pennsylvania German Society, 1990), 46–48, 60.

31. E. G. Altderfer, *The Ephrata Commune: An Early American Counterculture* (Pittsburgh: University of Pittsburgh Press, 1975), 54.

32. Stevenson, *Protestant Church Music in America*, 34.

33. The major study is Betty Jean Martin, "The Ephrata Cloister and Its Music, 1732–1785: The Cultural, Religious and Bibliographical Background" (Ph.D. dissertation, University of Maryland, 1974); CMML III(1):242–246; CMML II:44; Stevenson, *Protestant Church Music in America*, 34–38; Julius Friederich Sachse, *The Music of the Ephrata Cloister* (Lancaster, PA, 1903; reprint, New York: AMS Press, 1971), 46, 57.

34. CMML II:39–40. According to *Chronicon Ephratense* (Ephrata, 1786), the tune manuscripts were "reverently presented" to Beissel by members of the order. See CMML III(1):242.

35. Sachse, *The Music of the Ephrata Cloister*, 49–51.

36. The first collections of Moravian congregational hymn texts were published in 1501 and 1505, more than a decade before Luther nailed his ninety-five theses to the Castle Church door in Wittenberg.

37. CMML II:209–219; Leonard Ellinwood, *The History of American Church Music* (New York: E. P. Graham, 1953; reprint, New York: Da Capo Press, 1971), 36; Russell N. Squire, *Church Music* (St. Louis, MO: Bethany, 1962), 228–229, citing Rufus A. Grider, *Historical Notes on Music in Bethlehem, Pennsylvania* (Philadelphia: Pile, 1873).

38. Brunner, *That Ingenious Business*, 39; Edward C. Wolf, "Music in Old Zion, Philadelphia, 1750–1850," *Musical Quarterly* 58:4 (October 1972), 623.

39. Wolf, "Lutheran Church Music in America," 117; Brunner, *That Ingenious Business*, 42–54.

40. Dean, "The Organ in Eighteenth Century English Colonial America," 89–92; CMML I:234.

41. CMML III(1):268, 271; Wolf, "Lutheran Church Music in America," 143–148.

42. E. Clifford Nelson, ed., *The Lutherans in North America* (Philadelphia: Fortress Press, 1980), 66–67; CMML III(1):298–299.

CHAPTER 6

1. The use of the words "cultivated" and "vernacular" to denote European-style "classical" art music on one hand, and indigenous "popular" music on the other, was first suggested in the 1970s by H. Wiley Hitchcock. It has since become standard terminology and the usual means for making the distinction.

2. H. Wiley Hitchcock, *Music in the United states, A Historical Introduction*, 4th ed. (Englewood Cliffs, NJ: Prentice Hall, 1999), 28–29; Francis James Child, *English and*

Scottish Popular Ballads, 5 vols. (Boston: Houghton Mifflin, 1882–1898; reprint, New York: Dover, 1965).

3. Charles Hamm, *Music in the New World* (New York: W. W. Norton, 1982), 48–49.

4. Ronald L. Davis, *A History of Music in American Life*, vol. 1 (Malabar, FL: Robert Krieger, 1982), 233–234; Bruno Nettl, *Folk Music in the United States*, 3rd ed., rev. by Helen Myers (Detroit: Wayne State University Press, 1976), 18; Helen Myers, *Ethnomusicology: Historical and Regional Studies* (New York: W. W. Norton, 1993), 136; Michael Broyles, "Immigrant, Folk and Regional Music in the Nineteenth Century," in *The Cambridge History of American Music*, ed. David Nicholls (London: Cambridge University Press, 1998), 145; Hamm, *Music in the New World*, 54–55.

5. Roger D. Abrahams and George Foss, *Anglo-American Folksong Style* (Englewood Cliffs, NJ: Prentice Hall, 1968), 37. Leslie Shepard, *The Broadside Ballad: A Study in Origins and Meaning* (Hatboro, PA: Legacy Books, 1962), 33–34; Kip Lornell, *Introducing American Folk Music* (New York: McGraw-Hill, 1993), 53. The main reference is Bertrand Harris Bronson, *The Singing Tradition of Child's Popular Ballads* (Princeton, NJ: Princeton University Press, 1976).

6. Richard Crawford, *America's Musical Life: A History* (New York: W. W. Norton, 2001), 57–60; Hamm, *Music in the New World*, 50; Nettl, *Folk Music*, 67; Bertrand Harris Bronson, *The Ballad as Song* (Berkeley: University of California Press, 1969), 96.

7. Bronson, *The Ballad as Song*, 18–36.

8. Bertrand Harris Bronson, *The Traditional Tunes of the Child Ballads: With Their Texts, According to the Extant Records of Great Britain and America*, 4 vols. (Princeton, NJ: Princeton University Press, 1959–1972), contains the airs associated with Child's ballad texts; Bronson, *The Ballad as Song*, 79–91.

9. Claude M. Simpson, *The British Broadside Ballad and Its Music* (New Brunswick, NJ: Rutgers University Press, 1966), xii–xiii.

10. Simpson, *The British Broadside Ballad*, x–xi.

11. Simpson, *The British Broadside Ballad*, 299–300; Vera Brodsky Lawrence, *Music for Patriots, Politicians and Presidents* (New York: Macmillan, 1975), 26.

12. Percy Scholes, *The Puritans and Music in England and New England* (Oxford: Clarendon, 1934), 58; [Increase Mather?], *An Arrow against Profane and Promiscuous Dancing, Drawn out of a Quiver of the Scriptures By the Ministers of Christ at Boston in New England* (Boston: Samuel Green, 1684), 30.

13. Hugh Mellor and Leslie Bridgewater, eds., *The English Dancing Master: Or Plaine and easie Rules for the Dancing of Country dances, with the Tune to each Dance* (London: Thomas Harper for John Playford, 1651; reprint, London: Dance Books, Ltd., 1984), page unnumbered.

14. Kate van Winkle Keller and Charles Cyril Hendrickson, *George Washington: A Biography in Social Dance* (Sandy Hook, CT: The Hendrickson Group, 1998), 20.

15. Keller and Hendrickson, *George Washington*, 21–23; Joy van Cleef and Kate van

Winkle Keller, "Selected American Country Dances and Their English Sources," in *Music in Colonial Massachusetts, 1630–1820* (Boston: Colonial Society of Massachusetts, 1985), 12.

16. Crawford, *America's Musical Life*, 72; Hamm, *Music in the New World*, 67; Keller and Hendrickson, *George Washington*, 13–16; Hunter Dickinson Farrish, ed., *Journal and Letters of Philip Vickers Fithian, 1773–1774: A Plantation Tutor of the Old Dominion* (Williamsburg, VA: Colonial Williamsburg, 1943), 76.

17. Crawford, *America's Musical Life*, 74–75; Simpson, *The British Broadside Ballad*, 129, 165–166, 730.

CHAPTER 7

1. Robert M. Stevenson, "Written Sources for Indian Music Until 1882," *Ethnomusicology* 17:1 (1973), 15–21; Victor Fell Yellin, "Music in Early Virginia," *American Music* 20:4 (Winter 2002), 367–368.

2. Yellin, "Music in Early Virginia," 365; Richard Crawford, *America's Musical Life: A History* (New York: W. W. Norton, 2001), 8; Robert M. Stevenson, "English Sources for Indian Music Until 1882," *Ethnomusicology* 17:3 (1973), 405–406; Stevenson, "Written Sources," 15–21.

3. A facsimile of Smith's map may be found in Alan Smith, ed., *Virginia 1584–1607, The First English Settlement in North America* (London: Theodore Brun, 1957), 96; Yellin, "Music in Early Virginia," 366–368; Stevenson, "English Sources," 400–401.

4. Stevenson, "Written Sources," 3–5; Yellin, "Music in Early Virginia," 366–367.

5. Stevenson, "English Sources," 404.

6. Marcia Herndon, *Native American Music* (Darby, PA: Norwood Editions, 1982), 11–18, 31; Bruno Nettl, "Native American Music," in Bruno Nettl, ed., *Excursions in World Music*, 2nd ed. (Upper Saddle River, NJ: Prentice Hall, 1997), 258–262.

7. Herndon, *Native American Music*, 19–28; Nettl, "Native American Music," 260–263.

8. Francis Fletcher, *The World Encompassed by Sir Francis Drake* (London: Nicholas Bourne, 1652), 72; Stevenson, "Written Sources," 16–17.

9. Stevenson, "English Sources," 409–410.

10. The most accessible study of African music is J. H. Kwabena Nketia, *The Music of Africa* (New York: W. W. Norton, 1974).

11. Ibid., 3–20.

12. Ibid., 140–176.

13. Ibid., 67–107.

14. For contemporary descriptions, see Eileen Southern, *The Music of Black Americans*, 3rd ed. (New York: W. W. Norton, 1997), 91–96.

15. Dena Epstein, "African Music in British and French America," *Musical Quarterly* 69:1 (January 1973), 64–79; Southern, *The Music of Black Americans*, 47.

16. Rhys Isaac, *The Transformation of Virginia, 1740–1790* (Chapel Hill: University of North Carolina Press, 1982), 84–85; Crawford, *America's Musical Life*, 111.

17. Southern, *The Music of Black Americans*, 2–5; Robert J. Allison, ed., *The Interesting Narrative of the Life of Olaudah Equiano [or Gustavus Vassa, the African] Written by Himself* ([London, 1789; New York, 1791] New York: St. Martin's Press, 1995), 36; Epstein, "African Music," 66–68.

18. Helen Cripe, *Thomas Jefferson and Music* (Charlottesville: University Press of Virginia, 1974), 92–93; Southern, *The Music of Black Americans*, 25–27.

19. Eugene D. Genovese, *Roll Jordan Roll: The World the Slaves Made* (New York: Random House, 1972), 185.

20. Eileen Southern, *Readings in Black American Music* (New York: W. W. Norton, 1971), 62–64; Peter Kolchin, *American Slavery, 1619–1877* (New York: Hill and Wang, 1993), 42; William Francis Allen, Charles Pickard Ware, and Lucy McKim Garrison, *Slave Songs of the United States* (N.p., 1867; reprint, Bedford, MA: Applewood Books, n.d.), xii–xv.

21. Crawford, *America's Musical Life*, 108, 113–114.

22. Robert M. Stevenson, *Protestant Church Music in America* (New York: W. W. Norton, 1966), 93; Lawrence W. Levine, *Black Culture and Black Consciousness* (New York: Oxford University Press, 1977), 5; Epstein, "African Music," 82; Southern, *The Music of Black Americans*, 68–69; Southern, *Readings in Black American Music*, 36–39.

CHAPTER 8

1. Kenneth Silverman, *A Cultural History of the American Revolution* (New York: Thomas Y. Crowell, 1976), 30.

2. Charles Burney, *A General History of Music* (4 vols., London, 1776–1789; reprinted, 2 vols., New York: Dover, 1957), 1:xiii.

3. Albert Stoutamire, *Music of the Old South: Colony to Confederacy* (Rutherford, NJ: Fairleigh Dickinson University Press, 1972), 28.

4. Silverman, *A Cultural History*, 36.

5. Ibid., 31–33, 184.

6. Carl Bridenbaugh, *Cities in Revolt: Urban Life in America, 1743–1776* (New York: Oxford University Press, 1955), 400; Silverman, *A Cultural History*, 33, 185.

7. Cynthia Hoover, "Secular Music in Massachusetts," in *Music in Colonial Massachusetts, 1630–1820* (Boston: Colonial Society of Massachusetts, 1985), 752, 763, 765–766; Kate van Winkle Keller and Charles Cyril Hendrickson, *George Washington: A Biography in Social Dance* (Sandy Hook, CT: The Hendrickson Group, 1998), 15–16.

8. Hunter Dickinson Farrish, ed., *Journal and Letters of Philip Vickers Fithian, 1773–1774, A Plantation Tutor of the Old Dominion* (Williamsburg, VA: Colonial Williamsburg, 1943), 158, 167, 208; Silverman, *A Cultural History*, 33.

9. George Hood, *A History of Music in New England* (Boston: Wilkins, Carter, & Co., 1846), 138–139; Joanne Grayeski Weiss, "The Relationship Between the 'Great Awakening' and the Transition from Psalmody to Hymnody in the New England Colonies" (D.A. dissertation, Ball State University, 1988).

10. Irving Lowens, "The Origins of the American Fuging-Tune," in Irving Lowens, *Music and Musicians in Early America* (New York: W. W. Norton, 1964), 243–244; David McKay and Richard Crawford, *William Billings of Boston* (Princeton, NJ: Princeton University Press, 1975), 22; Richard A. Crawford, ed., *The Core Repertory of Early American Psalmody* (Madison, SWI: A-R Editions, 1984), x.

11. Farrish, *Journal and Letters*, 256.

12. Ralph T. Daniel, *The Anthem in New England before 1800* (Evanston, IL: Northwestern University Press, 1966; reprint, New York: Da Capo Press, 1979), 16–17. By 1775 only the Scottish and Scotch-Irish who emigrated from about 1720 and settled away from the cosmopolitan urban centers along the seaboard clung to the custom of the deacon lining out with a clerk to "raise the tune."

13. Letter from Ezra Barker to Moses Stebbins, 1780, quoted in Kenneth Logan, "Living Issues in Early American Psalmody," *Reformed Liturgy and Music* 13:1 (Winter 1989), 10. Logan's source for the letter is Vinson Bushnell, "Daniel Read of New Haven (1757–1836): The Man and His Musical Activities" (Ph.D. dissertation, Harvard University, 1978), 36–37.

14. Ibid., 10.

15. "F. B." to the *Boston News Letter*, quoted in Logan, "Living Issues," 11, from Bushnell, "Daniel Read," 34–35.

16. Daniel, *The Anthem in New England*, 39, 97; "Francis Hopkinson His Book. Philadelphia 1759" (Library of Congress), 180.

17. *Urania, or A Choice Collection of Psalm-Tunes, Anthems and Hymns, from the Most Approv'd Authors, with some entirely new; in two, three, and four parts . . . adapted to the use of churches, and private families* (Philadelphia: Henry Dawkins, 1761; reprint, New York: Da Capo Press, 1971). See Allen P. Britton, Irving Lowens, and Richard Crawford, *American Sacred Music Imprints, 1698–1810* (Worcester, MA: American Antiquarian Society, 1990), 444–448. On Lyons, see Frank J. Metcalf, *American Writers and Compilers of Sacred Music* (N.p., 1925; reprint, New York: Russell & Russell, 1967), 32–42.

18. Robert M. Stevenson, *Protestant Church Music in America* (New York: W. W. Norton, 1966), 47; Elwyn A. Weinandt and Robert H. Young, *The Anthem in England and America* (New York: Free Press, 1970), 176.

19. Daniel, *The Anthem in New England*, 39–40; David W. Music, "Josiah Flagg," *American Music* 7:2 (Summer 1989), 140–145.

20. Nathaniel Gould, *Church Music in America* (Boston: A. N. Johnson, 1853;

reprint, New York: AMS Press, 1972), 46. The standard biography is David McKay and Richard Crawford, *William Billings of Boston* (Princeton, NJ: Princeton University Press, 1975).

21. Nym Cooke, "William Billings in the District of Maine, 1780," *American Music* 9:3 (Fall 1991), 243–259; Karl Kroeger, *Catalogue of the Musical Works of William Billings* (Westport, CT: Greenwood, 1991); Karl Kroeger and Hans Nathan, *The Complete Works of William Billings (1746–1800)* (Charlottesville: University of Virginia Press, 1977–1990); Richard Crawford, "William Billings (1746–1800) and American Psalmody: A Study of Musical Dissemination," in Richard Crawford, *The American Musical Landscape* (Berkeley: University of California Press, 1993), 111–150; Daniel, *The Anthem in New England*, 102–119.

22. William Billings, *The New-England Psalm-Singer* (Boston: Edies and Gill, 1770), 19.

23. Metcalf, *American Writers and Compilers of Sacred Music*, 57–64; Daniel, *The Anthem in New England*, 199–207.

24. Allen P. Britton, "Theoretical Introductions in American Tune-Books to 1800" (Ph.D. dissertation, University of Michigan, 1949), 348–349.

25. Vera Brodsky Lawrence, *Music for Patriots, Politicians and Presidents* (New York: Macmillan, 1975), 45–46; McKay and Crawford, *William Billings*, 64, 97–98.

26. Silverman, *A Cultural History*, 188–189; Barbara Owen, "Colonial Organs: Being an Account of Some Early English Instruments Exported to the Eastern United States," *Journal of the British Institute of Organ Studies* 3 (1979), 92–107; Barbara Owen, *The Organ in New England* (Raleigh, NC: Sunbury Press, 1979), 1–26; Orpha Ochse, *The History of the Organ in the United States* (Bloomington: Indiana University Press, 1975), 9–35; John Ogasapian, *Organ Building in New York City, 1700–1900* (Braintree, MA: Organ Literature Foundation, 1977), 1–20; Raymond J. Brunner, *That Ingenious Business* (Birdsboro, PA: Pennsylvania German Society, 1990), 2.

27. Gardner M. Day, *The Biography of a Church* (Cambridge: Riverside Press, 1951), 24, 30; Henry Melchior Muhlenberg, *Notebook of a Colonial Clergyman [Journals]*, trans. and ed. Theodore C. Tappert and John W. Doberstein (Philadelphia: Fortress Press, 1959), 183; Owen, *The Organ in New England*, 699.

28. Keller and Hindrickson, *George Washington*, 7.

29. Lawrence, *Music for Patriots*, 45–46, 74–77.

30. William Arms Fisher, ed., *The Music that Washington Knew* (Boston: Oliver Ditson, 1931), v; Lawrence, *Music for Patriots*, 26–31; Arthur F. Schrader, "Songs to Cultivate the Sensations of Freedom," in *Music in Colonial Massachusetts* (Boston: Colonial Society of Massachusetts, 1980), 105–107.

31. Carlton Sprague Smith, "Broadsides and Their Music in Colonial America," *Music in Colonial Massachusetts*, 268–271; Keller and Hindrickson, *George Washington*, 9; Lawrence, *Music for Patriots*, 36–37.

32. Smith, "Broadsides and Their Music," 226; Lawrence, *Music for Patriots*, 32–33, 53; Oscar G. T. Sonneck, *Report on the Star-Spangled Banner, Hail Columbia, America,*

and Yankee Doodle (Washington, DC: Library of Congress, 1909; reprint, New York: Dover Publications, 1972), 79–156.

33. Lawrence, *Music for Patriots*, 57, 71, 91–93; Fisher, *Music that Washington Knew*, vi; Sonneck, *Report*, 193.

34. Julian Mates, *The American Musical Stage before 1800* (New Brunswick, NJ: Rutgers University Press, 1962), 72–73.

35. Ibid., 89, 98–99.

36. Susan L. Porter, *With an Air Debonair: Musical Theatre in America, 1785–1815* (Washington, DC: Smithsonian Institution Press, 1991), 2–4; John Dizikes, *Opera in America* (New Haven, CT: Yale University Press, 1993), 18–23; Richard Crawford, *America's Musical Life: A History* (New York: W. W. Norton, 2001), 92.

37. Mates, *The American Musical Stage*, 144, 150–151, 156.

38. Ibid., 29, 44.

39. Dizikes, *Opera in America*, 23; Porter, *With an Air Debonair*, 4–5; Oscar G. T. Sonneck, *Early Concert-Life in America* (Leipzig: Breitkopf & Härtel, 1907), 77; *Church Music and Musical Life in Pennsylvania in the Eighteenth Century*, 4 vols. [CMML] (Philadelphia: Publications of the Pennsylvania Society of the Colonial Dames of America, 1926–1947; reprint, New York: AMS Press, 1972), III(2):389, 391.

40. Raoul F. Camus, *Military Music of the American Revolution* (Chapel Hill: University of North Carolina Press, 1975), 46–47.

41. Sonneck, *Early Concert-Life*, 182–183; Robert M. Ketchum, *Divided Loyalties: How the American Revolution Came to New York* (New York: Henry Holt, 2002), 8–9.

42. Sonneck, *Early Concert-Life*, 184.

43. Ibid., 78.

44. Robert R. Grimes, "John Aitkin and Catholic Church Music in Philadelphia," *American Music* 16:3 (Fall 1998), 290.

45. Edward C. Wolf, "Lutheran Church Music in America During the Eighteenth and Early Nineteenth Centuries" (Ph.D. dissertation, University of Illinois, 1960), vi–vii, 166–167.

46. Sonneck, *Early Concert-Life*, 22–24; Oscar Sonneck, "A Contemporary Account of Music in Charleston, S.C. of the Year 1783," *New Music Review and Church Music Review* 11:129 (August 1912), 373–376; reprinted in *Oscar Sonneck and American Music*, ed. William Lichtenwanger (Urbana: University of Illinois Press, 1983), 94–99.

47. Raoul Camus, *Military Music of the American Revolution* (Chapel Hill: University of North Caroline Press, 1975), 46; Camus, "Military Music of Colonial Boston," in *Music in Colonial Massachusetts* (Boston: Colonial Society of Massachusetts, 1985), 84–87.

48. Silverman, *A Cultural History*, 355, 357; Camus, "Military Music of Colonial Boston," 85–88; Camus, *Military Music of the American Revolution*, 8–18, 179–184; 188–190 lists published collections of marches and band music.

49. Camus, *Military Music of the American Revolution*, 51–53; Silverman, *A Cultural History*, 357.

50. Camus, *Military Music of the American Revolution*, 48–49; Camus, "Military Music of Colonial Boston," 88–91; Silverman, *A Cultural History*, 354–356; Sonneck, *Early Concert-Life*, 262–263; Music, "Josiah Flagg," 146–150.

51. Silverman, *A Cultural History*, 52, 358.

52. Camus, *Military Music of the American Revolution*, 57; Camus, "Military Music in Colonial Boston," 100; Silverman, *A Cultural History*, 356; Christopher Hibbert, *Redcoats and Rebels* (New York: W. W. Norton, 1990), 329.

53. Arthur Shrader, "The World Turned Upside Down: A Yorktown March, or Music to Surrender By," *American Music* 16:2 (Summer 1998), 180–215.

CHAPTER 9

1. David P. McKay and Richard Crawford, *William Billings of Boston* (Princeton, NJ: Princeton University Press, 1975), 166–176; Henry M. Brooks, *Olden-Time Music* (Boston: Ticknor, 1888; reprint, New York: AMS Press, 1973), 263–265.

2. The definitive study of Law is Richard Crawford, *Andrew Law, American Psalmodist* (Evanston, IL: Northwestern University Press, 1968; reprint, New York: Da Capo Press, 1981). See also Kenneth Silverman, *A Cultural History of the American Revolution* (New York: Thomas Y. Crowell, 1976), 477; Frank J. Metcalf, *American Writers and Compilers of Sacred Music* (Privately printed, 1925; reprint, New York: Russell & Russell, 1967), 68–79.

3. Irving Lowens, "Daniel Read's World: The Letters of an Early American Composer," in Lowens, *Music and Musicians in Early America* (New York: W. W. Norton, 1964), 159–177; Metcalf, *American Writers and Compilers*, 94–103; Ralph T. Daniel, *The Anthem in New England before 1800* (Evanston, IL: Northwestern University Press, 1966; reprint, New York: Da Capo Press, 1979), 124–126.

4. Quoted in Allen P. Britton, Irving Lowens, and Richard Crawford, *American Sacred Music Imprints, 1698–1810* [ASMI] (Worcester, MA: American Antiquarian Society, 1990), 292–293.

5. Oscar G. T. Sonneck, *Early Concert-Life in America, 1731–1800* (Leipzig: Breitkopf & Härtel, 1906; reprint, New York: Musurgia, 1949), 103–104; Brooks, *Olden-Time Music*, 228–229.

6. Carol Pemberton, *Lowell Mason: His Life and Work* (Ann Arbor, MI: UMI Research Press, 1985), 7; Nathaniel Gould, *Church Music in America* (Boston: A. N. Johnson, 1853; reprint, New York: AMS Press, 1972), 168–183.

7. Franklin Bowditch Dexter, ed., *The Literary Diary of Ezra Stiles, D.D. LL.D*, 3 vols. (New York: Charles Scribner's Sons, 1901), 1:57–58.

8. In the end, the instrument was set up in the church and gave the congregation reliable service until it was finally replaced in 1872, by this time without controversy.

9. Brattle's organ went to St. Paul's Church in Newburyport. It now stands in a side gallery in St. John's Church, Portsmouth, New Hampshire.

10. Orpha Ochse, *The History of the Organ in the United States* (Bloomington: Indiana University Press, 1975), 89.

11. Brooks, *Olden-Time Music*, 267–269; Barbara Owen, *The Organ in New England* (Raleigh, NC: Sunbury Press, 1979), 28–34.

12. John Ogasapian, *Organ Building in New York City, 1700–1900* (Braintree, MA: Organ Literature Foundation, 1977), 20–36.

13. Ochse, *The History of the Organ in the United States*, 15–19.

14. Raymond J. Brunner, *That Ingenious Business: Pennsylvania German Organ Builders* (Birdsboro, PA: Pennsylvania German Society, 1990), 55. Feyring's first organ of record, built in 1762 for St. Paul's Church in Philadelphia, earned a word of praise from Benjamin Franklin in his *Pennsylvania Gazette* of December 23, 1762. The main sources on Tannenberg are William H. Armstrong, *Organs for America: The Life and Works of David Tannenberg* (Philadelphia: University of Pennsylvania Press, 1967), and Carol A. Traupman-Carr, ed., *Pleasing for Our Use: David Tannenberg and the Organs of the Moravians* (Bethlehem, PA: Lehigh University Press, 2000).

15. Brunner, *That Ingenious Business*, 70. The York instrument is extant and playable in the York Historical Society.

16. Brunner, *That Ingenious Business*, 9, 85–87; Armstong, *Organs for America*, 44–47, 100–101.

17. Barbara Owen, "The Other Mr. Selby," *American Music* 8:4 (Winter 1990), 477–482.

18. Barbara Owen, *The Organs and Music of King's Chapel*, 2nd ed. (Boston: King's Chapel, 1993), 41–42; Nicholas Temperley, *Bound for America: Three British Composers* (Urbana: University of Illinois Press, 2003), 20–23.

19. Brooks, *Olden-Time Music*, 90–91; Sonneck, *Early Concert-Life*, 278.

20. Brooks, *Olden-Time Music*, 96–98; Sonneck, *Early Concert-Life*, 282–283.

21. Brooks, *Olden-Time Music*, 225.

22. Daniel, *The Anthem in New England*, 85; Temperley, *Bound for America*, 30–51.

23. Sonneck, *Early Concert-Life*, 288–289; Silverman, *A Cultural History*, 473–474; McKay and Crawford, *William Billings*, 152, 163–164.

24. Edward C. Wolf, "Lutheran Church Music in America During the Eighteenth and Early Nineteenth Centuries" (Ph.D. dissertation, University of Illinois, 1960), vi–vii.

25. Edward C. Wolf, "Justus Henry Christian Helmuth—Hymnodist," *German-American Studies* 5 (1972), 117–147.

26. *Church Music and Musical Life in Pennsylvania in the Eighteenth Century*, 4 vols.

[CMML] (Philadelphia: Publications of the Pennsylvania Society of the Colonial Dames of America, 1926–1947; reprint, New York: AMS Press, 1972), III(1):245–247.

27. Francis Hopkinson, *A Collection of Psalm Tunes...* (Philadelphia: Henry Dawkins[?], 1763). Leonard Ellinwood, *The History of American Church Music* (New York: E. P. Gorham, 1953), 48.

28. CMML III(1):243.

29. Quoted in Ruth Mack Wilson, *Anglican Chant and Chanting in England and America, 1660–1820* (Oxford: Clarendon Press, 1996), 223.

30. Francis Hopkinson, "A Letter to the Rev. Doctor White, Rector of Christ Church and St. Peter's, on the Conduct of Church Organs," in *The Miscellaneous Essays and Occasional Writings of Francis Hopkinson, Esq.* (Philadelphia: T. Dobson, 1792), II: 119–126. The full text is given in Orpha Ochse, *The History of the Organ in the United States* (Bloomington: Indiana University Press, 1975), 427–430.

31. Wolf, "Lutheran Church Music in America," 30.

32. CMML III(1):304, 326–329.

33. ASMI, 215–218; Metcalf, *American Writers and Compilers of Sacred Music,* 139–140; Elwyn A. Weinandt and Robert H. Young, *The Anthem in England and America* (New York: Free Press, 1970), 224–225; Ronnie L. Smith, "The Church Music of Benjamin Carr" (D.M.A. dissertation, Southwestern Baptist Theological Seminary, 1969); Ellinwood, *The History of American Church Music,* 106–107.

34. John Rowe Parker, *Musical Biography* (Boston: Stone and Fovill, 1825), 179–182. The article on Taylor was probably written by Benjamin Carr. John A. Cuthbert, "Rayner Taylor and Anglo-American Musical Life" (Ph.D. dissertation, West Virginia University, 1980); Victor Fell Yellin, "Rayner Taylor," *American Music* 1:3 (Fall 1983), 48–71; Temperley, *Bound for America,* 52–122.

35. Henry Wansey, *Journal of an Excursion to the United States of America in the Summer of 1794,* published as *Henry Wansey and His American Journal,* ed. D. J. Jeremy (Philadelphia: American Philosophical Society, 1970), 84.

36. K. Roberts and A. M. Roberts, trans. and eds., *Moreau de St. Méry's American Journey, 1793–1794* (Garden City, NY: Doubleday, 1947), 149–150.

37. Edward C. Wolf, "Music in Old Zion, Philadelphia, 1750–1850," *Musical Quarterly* 48:4 (October 1972), 622–652; Arthur H. Messiter, *A History of the Choir and Music of Trinity Church, New York* (New York: E. P. Gorham, 1906; reprint, New York: AMS Press, 1970), 33. Messiter passes quickly over Moller, whom he refers to as "William Müller, of Philadelphia." The main study is still R. D. Stetzel, "John Christopher Moller (1755–1803) and His Role in Early American Music" (Ph.D. dissertation, University of Iowa, 1955).

38. Harry J. Kreider, *History of the United Lutheran Synod of New York and New England* (Philadelphia: Muhlenberg Press, 1954), 30–41.

39. Wolf, "Lutheran Church Music in America," 53–57, includes a list of the tunes.

40. Stevenson, *Protestant Church Music in America*, 55–56; George W. Williams, *St. Michael's, Charleston, 1751–1951* (Columbia: University of South Carolina Press, 1951), 205–206; George W. Williams, "Charleston Church Music, 1562–1833," *Journal of the American Musicological Society* 7:1 (Spring 1954), 38.

41. Wolverton, "Keyboard Music and Musicians," 146–160; Williams, *St. Michael's, Charleston*, 207. The practice of loaning out choirboys to theatres had been relatively common in London for some time, especially charity children for whom such engagements were seen as a means of their contributing to the cost of their own support.

42. Williams, *St. Michael's, Charleston*, 208.

43. George W. Williams, "Jacob Eckhard and His Choirmaster's Book," *Journal of the American Musicological Society* 7:1 (Spring 1954), 41–47.

CHAPTER 10

1. Robert E. Shalhope, *The Roots of Democracy: American Thought and Culture, 1760–1800* (Boston: Twayne, 1990), 55, 64.

2. Kenneth Silverman, *A Cultural History of the American Revolution* (New York: Thomas Y. Crowell, 1976), 470.

3. Irving Lowens, "James Hewitt, Professional Musician," in Lowens, *Music and Musicians in Early America* (New York: W. W. Norton, 1964), 196–197.

4. Anne McClenny Krauss, "Alexander Reinagle, His Family Background and Early Professional Career," *American Music* 4:4 (Winter 1986), 425–456; [John Rowe Parker], "Mr. Reinagle," *The Euterpeiad; or Musical Intelligencer* 2 (January 19, 1822), 170–171; Byron Wolverton, "Keyboard Music an Musicians in the Colonies and United States of America Before 1830" (Ph.D. dissertation, Indiana University, 1966), 326; Susan Porter, "English-American Interaction in American Musical Theatre at the Turn of the Nineteenth Century," *American Music* 4:1 (Spring 1986), 7.

5. Porter, "English-American Interaction," 7; Stephen Siek, "Benjamin Carr's Theatrical Career," *American Music* 11:2 (Summer 1993), 164.

6. John Rowe Parker, *A Musical Biography* (Boston: Stone and Fovill, 1825; reprint, Detroit: Information Coordinators, 1975), 179–182; the item was probably written by Benjamin Carr. Victor Fell Yellin, "Rayner Taylor," *American Music* 1:3 (Fall 1983), 48–71; Nicholas Temperley, *Bound for America: Three British Composers* (Urbana: University of Illinois Press, 2003), 52–122.

7. Siek, "Benjamin Carr's Theatrical Career," 159–165.

8. Ibid., 166.

9. Susan L. Porter, *With an Air Debonair: Musical Theatre in America, 1785–1815* (Washington, DC: Smithsonian Institution Press, 1991), 13–14. Hewitt's son, John Hill Hewitt, carried on the New York publishing business until the mid-nineteenth century.

10. Neil Butterworth, *The American Symphony* (Aldershott, UK: Ashgate, 1998), 5; Wolverton, "Keyboard Music and Musicians," 171.

11. Joseph J. Ellis, *After the Revolution* (New York: W. W. Norton, 1979), 129–133; Julian Mates, *The American Musical Stage before 1800* (New Brunswick, NJ: Rutgers University Press, 1962), 68–69, 73.

12. Mates, *The American Musical Stage*, 41–46.

13. Cynthia Adams Hoover, "Music in Eighteenth-Century American Theater," *American Music* 2:4 (Winter 1984), 7; Mates, *The American Musical Stage*, 93–94, 136; Porter, *With an Air Debonair*, 19, 71–78, 384–385.

14. Phile's "President's March" is better known today as the melody to which Francis Hopkinson's son Joseph (1770–1842) set his poem "Hail Columbia" in 1798.

15. Mates, *The American Musical Stage*, 71–73; Irving Lowens, "Benjamin Carr's *Federal Overture* (1794)," in Lowens, *Music and Musicians in Early America*, 99; David John Jeremy, ed., *Henry Wansey and His American Journal, 1794* (Philadelphia: American Philosophical Society, 1976), 58; Porter, *With an Air Debonair*, 365.

16. Susan L. Porter, "English-American Interaction," 5–7; *Church Music and Musical Life in Pennsylvania in the Eighteenth Century*, 4 vols. [CMML] (Philadelphia: Pennsylvania Society of the Colonial Dames of America, 1926–1947; reprint, New York: AMS Press, 1972), III(2):389–391; Henry Charles Lahee, *Annals of Music in America* (Boston, 1922; reprint, Freeport, NY: Books for Libraries, 1970), 12; Mates, *The American Musical Stage*, 147–150; David McKay, "Opera in Colonial Boston," *American Music* 3:2 (Summer 1985), 141.

17. Porter, *With an Air Debonair*, 23–30, 59–61.

18. Ibid., 38–40, 44; Mates, *The American Musical Stage*, 156–159; Anne Dhu Shapiro, "Action Music in American Pantomime and Melodrama, 1730–1913," *American Music* 2:4 (Winter 1984), 56.

19. Lahee, *Annals of Music in America*, 11.

20. Oscar G. T. Sonneck, *Early Concert-Life in America* (Leipzig: Breitkopf & Härtel, 1906; reprint, New York: Musurgia, 1949), 78–85.

21. Sonneck, *Early Concert-Life*, 82–86.

22. CMML III(2):400–403; Butterworth, *The American Symphony*, 5; Sonneck, *Early Concert-Life*, 93–94.

23. Sonneck, *Early Concert-Life*, 98–100.

24. Ibid., 186; Vera Brodsky Lawrence, *Music for Patriots, Politicians and Presidents* (New York: Macmillan, 1975), 115–119.

25. Sonneck, *Early Concert-Life*, 188–200; Lowens, "James Hewitt, Professional Musician," 199.

26. Wolverton, "Keyboard Music and Musicians," 210; Sonneck, *Early Concert-Life*, 200–201.

27. Sonneck, *Early Concert-Life*, 203, 207; Mates, *The American Musical Stage*, 28–30; Lahee, *Annals of Music in America*, 12.

28. Sonneck, *Early Concert-Life*, 208–212.

29. Ibid., 24–27.

30. Ibid., 28–39.

31. Wolverton, "Keyboard Music and Musicians," 171–172, 207; Mates, *The American Musical Theatre*, 9; Henry M. Brooks, *Olden-Time Music* (Boston: Ticknor and Company, 1888; reprint, New York: AMS Press, 1973), 99–100, 167–168.

32. Nicholas Tawa, "Secular Music in the Late-Eighteenth-Century American Home," *Musical Quarterly* 61:4 (October 1975), 512–515.

33. K. Roberts and A. M. Roberts, trans. and eds., *Moreau de St. Méry's American Journey, 1793–1798* (Garden City, NY: Doubleday, 1947), 290–291.

34. Tawa, "Secular Music," 521; Brooks, *Olden-Time Music*, 105, 101; emphasis in original.

35. Brooks, *Olden-Time Music*, 132; Wolverton, "Keyboard Music and Musicians," 173; Nancy Groce, *Musical Instrument Makers of New York* (Stuyvesant, NY: Pendragon Press, 1991), 31–32, 43–44.

36. Tawa, "Secular Music," 516–520; Porter, *With an Air Debonair*, 12.

37. Wolverton, "Keyboard Music and Musicians," 172; J. Bunker Clark, *The Dawning of American Keyboard Music* (Westport, CT: Greenwood Press, 1988), 84.

38. Clark, *The Dawning of American Keyboard Music*, 1, 4, 16; J. Bunker Clark, ed., *Anthology of Early American Keyboard Music, 1787–1830; Recent Researches in American Music*, vols. 1–2 (Madison, WI: A-R Editions, 1977); Robert Hopkins, ed., *Alexander Reinagle: The Philadelphia Sonatas; Recent Researches in American Music*, vol. 5 (Madison, WI: A-R Editions, 1978).

39. Clark, *The Dawning of American Keyboard Music*, 229–231, 236.

40. Irving Lowens, "Eighteenth-Century Massachusetts Songsters," in *Music in Colonial Massachusetts, 1630–1820* (Boston: Colonial Society of Massachusetts, 1985), 547–583.

41. Alexis de Tocqueville, *Democracy in America* [1835], trans. George Lawrence, ed. J. P. Mayer (New York: Harper & Row, 1966), 468.

Bibliography

Aaron, Amy. "William Tuckey: A Choirmaster in Colonial New York." *Musical Quarterly* 44:1 (January 1978), 79–97.

Abrahams, Roger D. and George Foss. *Anglo-American Folksong Style*. Englewood Cliffs, NJ: Prentice Hall, 1968.

Ahlstrom, Sidney. *A Religious History of the American People*. New Haven, CT: Yale University Press, 1972.

Alexander, J. Heywood. *To Stretch Our Ears: A Documentary History of American Music*. New York: W. W. Norton, 2002.

Allen, William Francis, Charles Pickford Ware, and Lucy McKim Garrison. *Slave Songs of the United States*. N.p., 1867; reprint, Bedford, MA: Applewood Books, n.d.

Allison, Robert J., ed. *The Interesting Narrative of the Life of Olaudah Equiano [or Gustavus Vassa, the African] Written by Himself.* [London, 1789; New York, 1791.] New York: St. Martin's Press, 1995.

Altderfer, E. G. *The Ephrata Commune: An Early American Counterculture*. Pittsburgh: University of Pittsburgh Press, 1975.

Appel, Richard G. *The Music of the Bay Psalm Book*. Brooklyn, NY: I.S.A.M. Monographs, 1975.

Appleby, Joyce. *Inheriting the Revolution*. Cambridge, MA: Harvard University Press, 2000.

Armstrong, William H. *Organs for America: The Life and Work of David Tannenberg*. Philadelphia: University of Pennsylvania Press, 1967.

Ayars, Christine Merrick. *Contributions to the Art of Music in America by the Music Industries of Boston, 1640–1936*. New York: H. W. Wilson, 1937; reprint, New York: Johnson Reprint Corp., 1969.

Bagdon, Robert J. "Musical Life in Charleston, South Carolina, from 1731 to 1776 as Recorded in Colonial Sources." Ph.D. dissertation, University of Miami, 1978.

Barwick, Stephen. "Mexico." In Curtis Price, ed., *The Early Baroque Era*. Englewood Cliffs, NJ: Prentice Hall, 1994.

Benson, Norman A. "Music in the California Missions, 1602–1848." *Student Musicologists in Minnesota* 3 (1968–1969), 128–167; 4 (1969–1970), 104–125.

Billings, William. *The New-England Psalm-Singer*. Boston: Edies and Gill, 1770.

Boeringer, James. "Early American Church Music in California." *Journal of Church Music* 18:5 (May 1976), 3–5.

Brands, H. W. *The First American*. New York: Doubleday Anchor, 2000.

Bridenbaugh, Carl. *Cities in Revolt: Urban Life in America, 1743–1776*. New York: Oxford University Press, 1955.

———. *Cities in the Wilderness: Urban Life in America, 1625–1742*. New York: Oxford University Press, 1954.

———, ed. *Gentleman's Progress: The Itinerarium of Dr. Alexander Hamilton, 1744*. Pittsburgh: University of Pittsburgh Press, 1948.

Britton, Allen P. "Theoretical Introductions in American Tune-Books to 1800." Ph.D. dissertation, University of Michigan, 1949.

Britton, Allen P., Irving Lowens, and Richard Crawford. *American Sacred Music Imprints, 1698–1810*. Worcester, MA: American Antiquarian Society, 1990.

Bronson, Bertrand Harris. *The Ballad as Song*. Berkeley: University of California Press, 1969.

———. *The Singing Tradition of Child's Popular Ballads*. Princeton, NJ: Princeton University Press, 1976.

———. *The Traditional Tunes of the Child Ballads: With Their Texts, According to the Extant Records of Great Britain and America*. 4 vols. Princeton, NJ: Princeton University Press, 1959–1972.

Brooks, Henry M. *Olden Time Music*. Boston: Ticknor & Co., 1888; reprint, New York: AMS Press, 1973.

Brunner, Raymond J. *That Ingenious Business: Pennsylvania German Organ Builders*. Birdsboro, PA: Pennsylvania German Society, 1990.

Buechner, Aalan Clark. *Yankee Singing Schools and the Golden Age of Choral Music in New England, 1760–1800*. Boston: Boston University and the Dublin Seminar for New England Folklife, 2003.

Burnaby, Andrew. *Travels through the Middle Settlements in North-America in the Years 1759 and 1760 with Observations upon the State of the Colonies, By the Rev. Andrew Burnaby, AM*. London: T. Payne, 1755; reprint, Ithaca, NY: Cornell University Press, 1960.

Bushnell, Vinson. "Daniel Read of New Haven (1757–1836): The Man and His Musical Activties." Ph.D. dissertation, Harvard University, 1978.

Butler, Jon. *Becoming America: The Revolution before 1776*. Cambridge, MA: Harvard University Press, 1998.

Butterworth, Neil. *The American Symphony*. Aldershott, UK: Ashgate, 1998.

Byrnside, Ron. *Music in Eighteenth-Century Georgia*. Athens: University of Georgia Press, 1997.

Camus, Raoul. *Military Music of the American Revolution*. Chapel Hill: University of North Carolina Press, 1975.

Casas, Bartholome de las. *History of the Indies*. Trans. and ed. Andreé Collard. New York: Harper & Row, 1971.

Chase, Gilbert. *America's Music From the Pilgrims to the Present*. 3rd ed. Urbana: University of Illinois Press, 1987.

———. *The Music of Spain*. New York: W. W. Norton, 1941; reprint, New York: Dover, 1959.

Child, Francis James. *English and Scottish Popular Ballads*. 5 vols. Boston: Houghton Mifflin, 1888–1898; reprint, New York: Dover Publications, 1965.

Church Music and Musical Life in Pennsylvania in the Eighteenth Century. 4 vols. Philadelphia: Publications of the Pennsylvania Society of the Colonial Dames of America, 1926–1947; reprint, New York: AMS Press, 1972.

Clark, J. Bunker. *Anthology of Early American Keyboard Music, 1787–1830; Recent Researches in American Music*. Vols. 1–2. Madison, WI: A-R Editions, 1978.

———. *The Dawning of American Keyboard Music*. Westport, CT: Greenwood Press, 1988.

Clarke, William B., Jr. and Jacquelyn A. Royal. *Organs of Savannah*. Savannah, GA: Savannah Blue Print Co., 2000.

Cooke, Nym. "William Billings in the District of Maine, 1780." *American Music* 9:3 (Fall 1991), 243–259.

Coopersmith, Jacob Maurice. "Music and Musicians of the Dominican Republic: A Survey." Pt. I. *Musical Quarterly* 31:1 (January 1945), 76–81.

Corry, Mary Janes, Kate van Winkle Keller, and Robert M. Keller. *The Performing Arts in Colonial American Newspapers, 1690–1783*. CD-ROM. New York: University Music Editions, 1997.

Crawford, Richard. *The American Musical Landscape*. Berkeley: University of California Press, 1993.

———. *America's Musical Life: A History*. New York: W. W. Norton, 2001.

———. *Andrew Law, American Psalmodist*. Evanston, IL: Northwestern University Press, 1968.

———. *The Core Repertory of Early American Psalmody*. Madison, WI: A-R Editions, 1984.

———. "A Historian's Introduction to Early American Music." *Proceedings of the American Antiquarian Society* 89:2 (October 1979), 261–298.

———. "William Billings (1746–1800) and American Psalmody: A Study of Musical Dissemination." In Richard Crawford, *The American Musical Landscape*. Berkeley: University of California Press, 1993, 111–150.

Cripe, Helen. *Thomas Jefferson and Music*. Charlottesville: University Press of Virginia, 1974.

Crow, John A. *The Epic of Latin America*. 4th ed. Berkeley: University of California Press, 1992.

Cuthbert, John A. "Rayner Taylor and Anglo-American Musical Life." Ph.D. dissertation, West Virginia University, 1980.

Da Silva, Owen. *Mission Music of California*. Los Angeles: W. F. Lewis, 1941, 1954.

Daniel, Ralph T. *The Anthem in New England before 1800*. Evanston, IL: Northwestern University Press, 1966; reprint, New York: Da Capo Press, 1979.

Daniels, Bruce C. *Puritans at Play: Leisure and Recreation in Colonial New England*. New York: St. Martin's Press, 1995.

Davis, Richard Beale. *Intellectual Life in the Colonial South 1585–1763*. 4 vols. Knoxville: University of Tennessee Press, 1978.

Davis, Ronald L. *A History of Music in American Life*. 3 vols. Malabar, FL: Robert Krieger, 1982.

Day, Gardner, M. *The Biography of a Church*. Cambridge: Riverside Press, 1951.

De Beer, E. S., ed. *The Diary of John Evelyn*. New York: Oxford University Press, 1959.

Dean, Talmadge W. "The Organ in Eighteenth Century English Colonial America." Ph.D. dissertation, University of Southern California, 1960.

Dexter, Franklin Bowditch, ed. *The Literary Diary of Ezra Styles, D.D., LL.D.* 3 vols. New York: Charles Scribner's Sons, 1901.

Diaz de Castillo, Bernal. *The True Story of the Conquest of Mexico.* Trans. and ed. Albert Idell as *The Bernal Diaz Chronicles.* Garden City, NY: Doubleday, 1957.

Dizikes, John. *Opera in America.* New Haven, CT: Yale University Press, 1993.

Ellinwood, Leonard. *The History of American Church Music.* New York: E. P. Gorham, 1953; reprint, New York: Da Capo Press, 1970.

Elliot, J. H. *Imperial Spain, 1469–1716.* London: Penguin Books, 1970.

Ellis, Joseph J. *After the Revolution.* New York: W. W. Norton, 1979.

Epstein, Dena. "African Music in British and French America." *Musical Quarterly* 69:1 (January 1973), 61–91.

Farrish, Hunter Dickinson, ed. *Journal and Letters of Philip Vickers Fithian, 1773–1774: A Plantation Tutor of the Old Dominion.* Williamsburg, VA: Colonial Williamsburg, 1943.

Fenn, Elizabeth A. and Peter H. Wood. *Natives and Newcomers: How We Lived in North Carolina before 1770.* Chapel Hill: University of North Carolina Press, 1983.

Fesperman, John. *Organs in Mexico.* Raleigh, NC: Sunbury Press, 1979.

Fischer, David Hackett. *Albion's Seed: Four British Folkways in America.* New York: Oxford University Press, 1989.

Fisher, William Arms. *The Music that Washington Knew.* Boston: Oliver Ditson, 1931.

Fletcher, Francis. *The World Encompassed by Sir Francis Drake.* London: Nicholas Bourne, 1652.

Foote, Henry Wilder. *Three Centuries of American Hymnody.* Cambridge, MA: Harvard University Press, 1940; reprint, Homden, CT: Shoe String Press, 1961.

Fowler, Samuel P., ed. *Diary of the Rev. Joseph Green of Salem Village.* Salem, MA: Essex Institute Historical Editions 10:1, 1869.

"Francis Hopkinson His Book. Philadelphia 1759." Manuscript, Library of Congress.

Genovese, Eugene D. *Roll Jordan Roll: The World the Slaves Made.* New York: Random House, 1972.

Goertzen, Chris. "Balancing Local and National Approaches at American Fiddle Contests." *American Music* 14:3 (Fall 1996), 353–354.

Gould, Nathaniel. *Church Music in America.* Boston: A. N. Johnson, 1853; reprint, New York: AMS Press, 1972.

Graf, Sharon Paulson. "Traditonalization at the National Old Time Fiddlers' Contest: Politics, Power and Authenticity." Ph.D. dissertation, Michigan State University, 1999.

Grider, Rufus A. *Historical Notes on Music in Bethlehem, Pennsylvania.* Philadelphia: Pile, 1873.

Griffin, Patrick. *The People with No Name: Ireland's Ulster Scots, America's Scots Irish, and the Creation of a British Atlantic World, 1689–1764.* Princeton, NJ: Princeton University Press, 2001.

Grimes, Robert R. "John Aitken and Catholic Church Music in Philadelphia." *American Music* 16:3 (Fall 1998), 289–310.

Groce, Nancy. *Musical Instrument Makers of New York: A Directory of Eighteenth- and Nineteenth-Century Urban Craftsmen.* Stuyvesant, NY: Pendragon Press, 1991.

Hamm, Charles. *Music in the New World.* New York: W. W. Norton, 1982.

Haraszti, Zoltan. *The Enigma of the Bay Psalm Book*. Chicago: University of Chicago Press, 1956.

Herndon, Marcia. *Native American Music*. Darby, PA: Norwood Editions, 1982.

Herskovits, Melville J. *The Myth of the Negro Past*. Boston: Beacon Press, 1951.

Hibbert, Christopher. *Redcoats and Rebels*. New York: W. W. Norton, 1990.

Higgins, Ardis O. "The Revival of Early Mission Music." *Music/AGO* 10:1 (January 1976), 28.

Hitchcock, H. Wiley. *Music in the United States: A Historical Introduction*. 4th ed. Englewood Cliffs, NJ: Prentice Hall, 1999.

Hitchcock, H. Wiley and Stanley Sadie, eds. *The New Grove Dictionary of American Music*. 4 vols. New York: Macmillan, 1986.

Hofstadter, Richard. *America at 1750*. New York: Random House Vintage, 1973.

Hood, George. *A History of Music in New England*. Boston: Wilkins, Carter, & Co., 1846; reprint, New York: Johnson Reprints, 1970.

Hoover, Cynthia Adams. "Music in Eighteenth-Century American Theater." *American Music* 2:4 (Winter 1984), 6–18.

Hopkins, Robert, ed. *Alexander Reinagle: The Philadelphia Sonatas: Recent Researches in American Music*. Vol. 5. Madison, WI: A-R Editions, 1978.

Hopkinson, Frances. *A Collection of Psalm Tunes, with a few Anthems and hymns, some of them entirely new, for the use of the United Churches of Christ Church and St. Peter's Church in Philadelphia*. [Philadelphia: Henry Dawkins?], 1763.

Housewright, Wiley L. *A History of Music and Dance in Florida*. Tuscaloosa: University of Alabama Press, 1991.

Howard, John Tasker. *Our American Music: A Comprehensive History from 1620 to the Present*. 4th ed. New York: Thomas Y. Crowell, 1965.

Inserra, Lorraine and H. Wiley Hitchcock. *The Music of Henry Ainsworth's Psalter (Amsterdam, 1612)*. Brooklyn, NY: I.S.A.M. Monographs, 1981.

Isaac, Rhys. *The Transformation of Virginia, 1740–1790*. Chapel Hill: University of North Carolina Press, 1982.

Jacoby, Mary Moore, ed. *The Churches of Charleston and the Low Country*. Charleston: Preservation Society of Charleston, 1994.

Jeremy, D. J. *Henry Wansey and His American Journal*. Philadelphia: American Philosophical Society, 1970.

Johnson, H. Earle. "The John Rowe Parker Letters." *Musical Quarterly* 62:1 (January 1976), 72–86.

Kamen, Henry. *Empire: How Spain Became a World Power, 1492–1763*. London: Penguin Books, 2002.

Kaufman, Charles H. *Music in New Jersey, 1655–1860*. Teaneck, NJ: Fairleigh Dickinson University Press, 1981.

Kay, Marvin L. Michael and Lorin Lee Cary. *Slavery in North Carolina, 1748–1775*. Chapel Hill: University of North Carolina Press, 1995.

Keller, Kate van Winkle and Charles Cyril Hendrickson. *George Washington: A Biography in Social Dance*. Sandy Hook, CT: The Hendrickson Group, 1998.

Ketchum, Robert M. *Divided Loyalties: How the American Revolution Came to New York*. New York: Henry Holt, 2002.

Kolchin, Peter. *American Slavery, 1619–1877*. New York: Hill and Wang, 1993.

Krauss, Anne McClenny. "Alexander Reinagle, His Family Background and Early Professional Career." *American Music* 4:4 (Winter 1986), 425–456.

Kreider, Harry J. *History of the United Lutheran Synod of New York and New England.* Philadelphia: Muhlenberg Press, 1954.

Kroeger, Karl. *American Fuging-Tunes, 1770–1820.* Westport, CT: Greenwood Press, 1994.

———. *Catalogue of the Musical Works of William Billings.* Westport, CT: Greenwood Press, 1991.

Lahee, Henry Charles. *Annals of Music in America.* N.p., 1922; reprint, Freeport, NY: Books for Libraries, 1970.

Lawrence, Vera Brodsky. *Music for Patriots, Politicians and Presidents.* New York: Macmillan, 1975.

Levine, Lawrence W. *Black Culture and Black Consciousness.* New York: Oxford University Press, 1977.

Leyburn, James G. *The Scotch-Irish: A Social History.* Chapel Hill: University of North Carolina Press, 1962.

Lindley, Charles Edward. "Scoring and Placement of the 'Air' in Early American Tunebooks." *Musical Quarterly* 58:3 (July 1972), 365–382.

Lornell, Kip. *Introducing American Folk Music.* New York: McGraw-Hill, 1993.

Lowens, Irving. *Music and Musicians in Early America.* New York: W. W. Norton, 1964.

Marrocco, W. Thomas and Harold Gleason. *Music in America.* New York: W. W. Norton, 1964.

Martin, Betty Jean. "The Ephrata Cloister and its Music, 1732–1785: The Cultural, Religious and Bibliographical Background." Ph.D. dissertation, University of Maryland, 1974.

Mates, Julian. *The American Musical Stage before 1800.* New Brunswick, NJ: Rutgers University Press, 1962.

Mather, Cotton. *The Diary of Cotton Mather, 1709–1724.* 4 vols. Boston: Massachusetts Historical Society, Collections, 1912.

———. *Magnalia Christi Americana*, ed. Raymond J. Cunningham. New York: Unger, 1970.

———. *Ratio Discipline Nov-Anglorum.* Boston: S. Gerrish, 1726.

Maurer, Maurer. "A Musical Family in Colonial Virginia." *Musical Quarterly* 34:3 (July 1948), 358–364.

———. "The 'Professor of Musicke' in Colonial America." *Musical Quarterly* 36:4 (October 1950), 511.

McCormick, David W. "Oliver Holden, Composer and Anthologist." D.S.M. dissertation, Union Seminary, 1965.

McKay, David. "Opera in Colonial Boston." *American Music* 3:2 (Summer 1985), 141.

———. "William Billings, Musical Émigré in Boston." *Musical Quarterly* 57:4 (October 1971), 609–627.

McKay, David and Richard Crawford. *William Billings of Boston.* Princeton, NJ: Princeton University Press, 1975.

Medforth, Martin. "The Low Countries." In Curtis Pierce, ed., *The Early Baroque Era.* Englewood Cliffs, NJ: Prentice Hall, 1994.

Mellor, Hugh and Leslie Bridgewater, eds. *The English Dancing Master: Or Plaine and easie Rules for the Dancing of Country dances, with the Tune to each Dance.* London: Thomas Harper for John Playford, 1651; reprint, London: Dance Books, Ltd., 1984.

Mendoza de Arce, Daniel. *Music in Ibero-America to 1850*. Lanham, MD: Scarecrow Press, 2001.

Messiter, Arthur. *A History of the Choir and Music of Trinity Church, New York*. New York: E. P. Gorham, 1906; reprint, New York: AMS Press, 1970.

Metcalf, Frank J. *American Writers and Compilers of Sacred Music*. N.p., 1925; reprint, New York: Russell & Russell, 1967.

Micklus, Robert J. *History of the Ancient and Honorable Tuesday Club*. 3 vols. Chapel Hill: University of North Carolina Press, 1990.

Miller, Perry and Thomas H. Johnson, eds. *The Puritans*. New York: Harper, 1963.

Milton, Giles. *Big Chief Elizabeth*. New York: Picador, 2000.

Molnar, John W. "A Collection of Music in Colonial Virginia: The Ogle Inventory." *Musical Quarterly* 49:2 (April 1963), 150–162.

Morgan, Edmund S. *Virginians at Home: Family Life in the Eighteenth Century*. Williamsburg, VA: Colonial Williamsburg, 1952.

———. *Visible Saints*. Ithaca, NY: Cornell University Press, 1975.

Muhlenberg, Henry M. *Notebook of a Colonial Clergyman*, trans. and ed. Theodre C. Tappert and John Doberstein. Philadelphia: Fortress Press, 1959.

Murray, Sterling E. "Music and Dance in Philadelphia's City Tavern, 1773–1790." In James R. Hentze, ed., *American Musical Life in Context and Practice to 1865*. New York: Garland Publishing, 1994, 3–48.

Music, David W. "The Diary of Samuel Sewall and Congregational Singing in Early New England." *The Hymn* 41:1 (January 1990), 7–15.

———. "Josiah Flagg." *American Music* 7:2 (Summer 1989), 140–145.

Music in Colonial Massachusetts, 1630–1820. 2 vols. Boston: Colonial Society of Massachusetts, 1985.

Myers, Helen. *Ethnomusicology: Historical and Regional Studies*. New York: W. W. Norton, 1993.

Nelson, E. Clifford, ed. *The Lutherans in North America*. Philadelphia: Fortress Press, 1980.

Nettl, Bruno. *Folk Music in the United States*. 3rd ed., rev. Helen Myers. Detroit: Wayne State University Press, 1976.

———. "Native American Music." In Bruno Nettl, ed., *Excursions in World Music*, 2nd ed. Upper Saddle River, NJ: Prentice Hall, 1997, 251–268.

New England Music: The Public Sphere, 1600–1900. Boston: Boston University and the Dublin seminar for New England Folklife, 1998.

Nicholls, David, ed. *Cambridge History of American Music*. London: Cambridge University Press, 1998.

Nketia, J. H. Kwabena. *The Music of Africa*. New York: W. W. Norton, 1974.

Ochse, Orpha. *The History of the Organ in the United States*. Bloomington: Indiana University Press, 1975.

Ogasapian, John. *Organ Building in New York City, 1700–1900*. Braintree, MA: Organ Literature Foundation, 1977.

Owen, Barbara. "Colonial Organs: Being an Account of Some Early English Instruments Exported to the Eastern United States." *Journal of the British Institute of Organ Studies* 3 (1979), 92–107.

———. *The Organ in New England*. Raleigh, NC: Sunbury Press, 1979.

———. *The Organs and Music of King's Chapel*. 2nd ed. Boston: King's Chapel, 1993.

———. "The Other Mr. Selby." *American Music* 8:4 (Winter 1990), 477–482.

Parker, John Rowe. *A Musical Biography*. Boston: Stone and Fovill, 1825; reprint, Detroit: Information Coordinators, 1975.

Pemberton, Carol. *Lowell Mason: His Life and Work*. Ann Arbor, MI: UMI Research Press, 1985.

Pinchieri, Louis. *Music in New Hampshire, 1623–1800*. New York: Columbia University Press, 1960.

Pinckney, Elise, ed. *The Letterbook of Eliza Lucas Pinckney, 1739–1762*. Chapel Hill: University of North Carolina Press, 1972.

Porter, Susan. "English-American Interaction in American Musical Theatre at the Turn of the Nineteenth Century." *American Music* 4:1 (Spring 1986), 7.

Porter, Susan L. *With an Air Debonair: Musical Theatre in America, 1785–1815*. Washington, DC: Smithsonian Institution Press, 1991.

The Psalms, Hymns and Spiritual Songs of the Old and New Testament: Faithfully Translated into English Metre. Boston: B. Green and J. Allen, 1698.

Redway, Virginia Larkin. "The Carrs, American Music Publishers." *Musical Quarterly* 18:1 (January 1932), 150–177.

———. "Charles Thedore Pachelbell [*sic*] Musical Emigrant." *Journal of the American Musicological Society* 5:1 (Spring 1952), 30–36.

Roberts, K. and A. M. Roberts. *Moreau de St. Méry's American Journey, 1793–1794*. Garden City, NY: Doubleday, 1947.

Rutman, Darret B. *American Puritanism*. New York: W. W. Norton, 1977.

Sachse, Julius Friederich. *Justus Falckner*. Philadelphia, 1903.

———. *The Music of the Ephrata Cloister*. Lancaster, PA, 1903; reprint, New York: AMS Press, 1971.

Schalk, Carl F. *God's Song in a New Land: Lutheran Hymnals in America*. St. Louis, MO: Concordia Publishing, 1995.

Scholes, Percy. *The Puritans and Music in England and New England*. Oxford: Clarendon Press, 1934; reprint, 1969.

Shalhope, Robert A. *The Roots of Democracy: American Thought and Culture, 1760–1800*. Boston: Twayne, 1990.

Shapiro, Anne Dhu. "Action Music in American Pantomime and Melodrama, 1730–1913." *American Music* 2:4 (Winter 1984), 49–72.

Shepard, Leslie. *The Broadside Ballad*. London: Herbert Jenkins, Ltd., 1962; reprint, Hartboro, PA: Legacy Books, 1978.

Shrader, Arthur F. "The World Turned Upside Down: A Yorktown March, or Music to Surrender By." *American Music* 16:2 (Summer 1998), 180–215.

Siek, Stephen. "Benjamin Carr's Theatrical Career." *American Music* 11:2 (Summer 1993), 158–184.

Silverman, Kenneth. *A Cultural History of the American Revolution*. New York: Thomas Y. Crowell, 1976.

———. *The Life and Times of Cotton Mather*. New York: Columbia University Press, 1985.

Simpson, Claude M. *The British Broadside Ballad and Its Music*. New Brunswick, NJ: Rutgers University Press, 1966.

Smith, Alan, ed. *Virginia 1584–1607, The First English Settlement in North America*. London: Theodore Brun, 1957.

Smith, Carleton Sprague. "Broadsides and Their Music in Colonial America." In *Music in Colonial Massachusetts, 1630–1820*. Boston: Colonial Society of Massachusetts, 1985.

Smith, Horace W. *Life and Correspondence of the Rev. William Smith, D.D., with Copious Extracts from his Writings.* Philadelphia: Ferguson Bros., 1880.

Smith, Ronnie L. "The Church Music of Benjamin Carr." D.M.A. dissertation, Southwestern Baptist Theological Seminary, 1969.

Sonneck, Oscar G. T. *A Bibliography of Early Secular American Music.* Revised and enlarged by William Treat Upton. Washington, DC: Library of Congress, 1902; reprint, New York: Da Capo Press, 1964.

———. "A Contemporary Account of Music in Charleston, S.C. of the year 1783." *New Music Review and Church Music Review* 11:129 (August 1912), 373–376; reprinted in William Lichtenwanger, ed., *Oscar Sonneck and American Music.* Urbana: University of Illinois Press, 1983.

———. *Early Concert-Life in America, 1731–1800.* Leipzig: Breitkopf & Härtel, 1907.

———. *Francis Hopkinson, the First American Poet-Composer (1737–1791), and James Lyon, Patriot, Preacher, Psalmodist (1735–1794): Two Studies in Early American Music.* Washington, DC: McQueen, 1905; reprint, New York: Da Capo Press, 1967.

———. *Report on the Star-Spangled Banner, Hail Columbia, America and Yankee Doodle.* Washington, DC: Library of Congress, 1909; reprint, New York: Dover, 1972.

Southern, Eileen. *The Music of Black Americans.* 3rd ed. New York: W. W. Norton, 1997.

———. *Readings in Black American Music.* New York: W. W. Norton, 1971.

Speiss, Lincoln Bruce. "Benevides and Church Music in New Mexico in the Early Seventeenth Century." *Journal of the American Musicological Society* 17:2 (Summer 1964), 147–150.

Spell, Lota M. "Music in the Cathedral of Mexico in the Sixteenth Century." *The Hispanic-American Historical Review* 26:3 (August 1946), 293–319.

Squire, Russell N. *Church Music.* St. Louis, MO: Bethany, 1962.

Stetzel, Ronald Delbert. "John Christpher Moller (1755–1803) and His Role in Early American Music." Ph.D. dissertation, University of Iowa, 1955.

Stevenson, Robert. "Music in California: A Tale of Two Cities." *Inter-American Music Review* 5:1 (Fall/Winter), 41.

Stevenson, Robert M. "English Sources for Indian Music Until 1882." *Ethnomusicology* 17:3 (1973), 399–442.

———. "Mexico City Cathedral Music." *Inter-American Music Review* 9:1 (Winter 1987), 75–114.

———. *Music in Aztec and Inca Territory.* Berkeley: University of California Press, 1973.

———. *Music in Mexico.* New York: Thomas Y. Crowell, 1952.

———. *Protestant Church Music in America.* New York: W. W. Norton, 1966.

———. "Written Sources for Indian Music Until 1882." *Ethnomusicology* 17:1 (1973), 1–40.

Stoutamire, Albert. *Music of the Old South: Colony to Confederacy.* Rutherford, NJ: Fairleigh Dickinson University Press, 1972.

Summers, William. "California Mission Music." In H. Wiley Hitchcock and Stanley Sadie, eds., *The New Grove Dictionary of American Music.* 4 vols. New York: Macmillan, 1986.

———. "The Organs of Hispanic California." *Music/AGO* 10:11 (November 1976), 50–51.

Symmes, Thomas. *The Reasonableness of Regular Singing, or Singing by Note*. Boston: B. Green for Samuel Gerrish, 1720.

———. *Utile Dulci, or a Joco Serious Dialogue Concerning Regular Singing*. Boston: B. Green for S. Gerrish, 1723.

Talley, John Barry. *Secular Music in Colonial Annapolis: The Tuesday Club, 1745–1756*. Urbana: University of Illinois Press, 1988.

Tawa, Nicholas. *From Psalm to Symphony: A History of Music in New England*. Boston: Northeastern University Press, 2001.

———. "Philadelphia: A City in the New World." In Neal Zaslaw, ed., *The Classical Era*. Englewood Cliffs, NJ: Prentice Hall, 1989.

———. "Secular Music in the Late-Eighteenth-Century American Home." *Musical Quarterly* 61:4 (October 1975), 511–527.

Taylor, Alan. *American Colonies*. New York: Viking Penguin, 2001.

Temperley, Nicholas. *Bound for America: Three British Composers*. Urbana: University of Illinois Press, 2003.

———. "John Playford and the Metrical Psalms." *Journal of the American Musicological Society* 25:3 (Fall 1972), 331–378.

———. *The Music of the English Parish Church*. Cambridge: Cambridge University Press, 1979.

Thomas, Hugh. *Conquest: Montezuma, Cortés, and the Fall of Old Mexico*. New York: Simon and Schuster, 1993.

Thomas, M. Halsey, ed. *The Diary of Samuel Sewall, 1674–1729*. 2 vols. New York: Farrar, Strauss and Giroux, 1973.

Tocqueville, Alexis de. *Democracy in America* [1835], trans. George Lawrence, ed. J. P. Mayer. New York: Harper & Row, 1966.

Traupmann-Carr, Carol A., ed. *Pleasing for Our Use: David Tannenberg and the Organs of the Moravians*. Bethlehem, PA: Lehigh University Press, 2000.

Van Cleef, Joy and Kate van Winkle Keller. "Selected American Country Dances and Their English Sources." In *Music in Colonial Massachusetts, 1630–1820*. Boston: Colonial Society of Massachusetts, 1985.

Walter, Thomas. *The Grounds and Rules of Musick Explained: Or, an Introduction to the Art of Singing by Note Fitted to the Meanest Capacities*. Boston: J. Franklin for S. Gerrish, 1721.

Weber, David J. *The Spanish Frontier in North America*. New Haven, CT: Yale University Press, 1992.

Weinandt, Elwyn A. *Opinions on Church Music*. Waco, TX: Baylor University Press, 1974.

Weinandt, Elwyn A. and Robert H. Young. *The Anthem in England and America*. New York: Free Press, 1970.

Weiss, Joanne Grayeski. "The Relationship Between the 'Great Awakening' and the Transition from Psalmody to Hymnody in the New England Colonies." D.A. dissertation, Ball State University, 1988.

Wertenbaker, Thomas J. *The Golden Age of Colonial Culture*. Ithaca, NY: Cornell University Press, 1949.

Wertenbaker, Thomas Jefferson. *The Southern Colonies*. New York: Charles Scribner's Sons, 1942.

Williams, George W. "Charleston Church Music, 1562–1833." *Journal of the American Musicological Society* 7:1 (Spring 1954), 35–40.

———. "Jacob Eckhardt and His Choirmaster's Book." *Journal of the American Musi-cological Society* 7:1 (Spring 1954), 41–47.

———. *St. Michael's, Charleston. 1751–1951.* Columbia: University of South Carolina Press, 1951.

Wilson, Ruth Mack. *Anglican Chant and Chanting in England, Scotland and America, 1660 to 1820.* Oxford: Clarendon Press, 1996.

Winslow, Edward. *Hypocrasie Unmasked.* London: Richard Cotes for John Bellamy, 1646.

Winslow, Ola Elizabeth. *Meetinghouse Hill, 1630–1783.* New York: Macmillan, 1952; reprint, New York: W. W. Norton, 1971.

Wolf, Edward C. "Justus Henry Christian Helmuth—Hymnodist." *German-American Studies* 5 (1972), 117–147.

———. "Lutheran Church Music in America During the Eighteenth and Early Nine-teenth Centuries." Ph.D. dissertation, University of Illinois, 1960.

———. "Music in Old Zion, Philadelphia, 1750–1850." *Musical Quarterly* 58:4 (October 1972), 622–652.

Wolverton, Byron K. "Keyboard Music and Musicians in the Colonies and United States of America before 1830." Ph.D. dissertation, Indiana University, 1966.

Wright, Esmond. *Franklin of Philadelphia.* Cambridge, MA: Harvard University Press, 1986.

Wright, Louis B. *Life in Colonial America.* New York: Capricorn Books, 1971.

Wright, Louis B. and Marion Tinling, eds. *The Great American Gentleman: The Secret Diary of William Byrd of Westover in Virginia.* New York: Capricorn, 1963.

Yellin, Victor Fell. "Music in Early Virginia." *American Music* 20:4 (Winter 2002), 361–380.

———. "Musical Activity in Virginia before 1620." *Journal of the American Musicological Society* 22:3 (Fall 1969), 284–289.

———. "Rayner Taylor." *American Music* 1:3 (Fall 1983), 48–71.

Ziff, Larzer. *Puritanism in America.* New York: Viking, 1973.

Index

Hulett, William Charles, 79
Hungar's Church, Northampton, VA, 60

Instrument making, 120, 171. *See also under makers' names*
Instruments, 13–14, 19–20, 30, 48, 50, 55, 57–58, 62, 71, 77, 114, 169; native, 106–9; African, 111–13. *See also under specific instruments and instrument families*

Jackson, George K., 141
Jefferson, Thomas, 4, 5, 58, 114, 118–19
Jerusalem, Ignacio de, 18
Jobson, Richard, 58, 113
John Street Theatre, New York (Theatre Royal), 132, 162, 164
Johnston, Thomas, 143
Jordan, Thomas, 57

Kalm, Peter, 150–51
Kelpius, Jonas, 86, 90, 93, 179, 221 n.30
Kethe, Thomas, 33
Keyboard instruments, 48, 57–58, 64, 144–45, 171
King's Chapel, Boston, 39, 47, 50, 128, 143, 146–48
Klemm, Johann Gottlob. *See* Clemm, John
Koek, Hendrick, 80
Kunze, Johann Christopher, 153–54

Lammond, John, 64
Langford, John, 58
Law, Andrew, 115, 117, 140–41, 179
Leavitt, Josiah, 144
Lining out, 38–39, 122, 214 n.14, 226 n.12
Lopez, Francisco, 17–18
Love, Charles, 64
Lyon, James, 83, 121, 123–25, 179

Malcom, Alexander, 63–64
Marot, Clement, 31

Massachusetts Compiler, The, 141
Mather, Cotton, 35, 41–45, 49–50, 54
Mather, Increase, 43, 47, 52
Melodrama, 164
Mexico City Cathedral, 16–18, 20
Military music, 8–9, 118, 130–31, 135–38
Mittelberger, Gottlieb, 83
Moller, John Christopher, 153, 167, 180
Moravians, 62, 70–71, 87, 89–90, 93, 154, 222 n.36
Muhlenberg, Henry Melchior, 80–81, 91, 128
Music and painting, 117–18
Music publishing, 10, 20, 171–72
Music retailing, 8, 10, 71, 78, 119, 169–72
Music teachers ("professors"), 7, 58–59, 64–65, 71–73, 78, 119, 169

Native Americans, 11–27, 105–9, 115–16
New Brick Church, Boston, 42
New Version psalms (Tate and Brady), 39, 44, 54, 80
Niles, Samuel, 42
North Dutch Reformed Church, New York, 152

Occum, Samson, 109
Ogle, Cuthbert, 61
Old South Church, Boston, 45
Old Version psalms (Sternhold and Hopkins), 32–36, 38–39, 44
Oratorios, 5. *See also* Sacred music concerts
Orchestras, 7, 25, 60, 63–64, 68, 73, 89, 164–69
Organs, 5, 20, 25–26, 30, 48–51, 58, 61, 69, 72, 76, 80, 90–92, 133–34; vandalism during the Revolution, 128–29
Ormsby, John, 64
Ortíz, Alonzo, 21

Pachelbel, Charles Theodore, 51, 61, 69, 78, 180

About the Author

JOHN OGASAPIAN is Professor of Music History at the University of Massachusetts, Lowell.